WORDLY WISE

145

James McDonald

WORDLY WISE

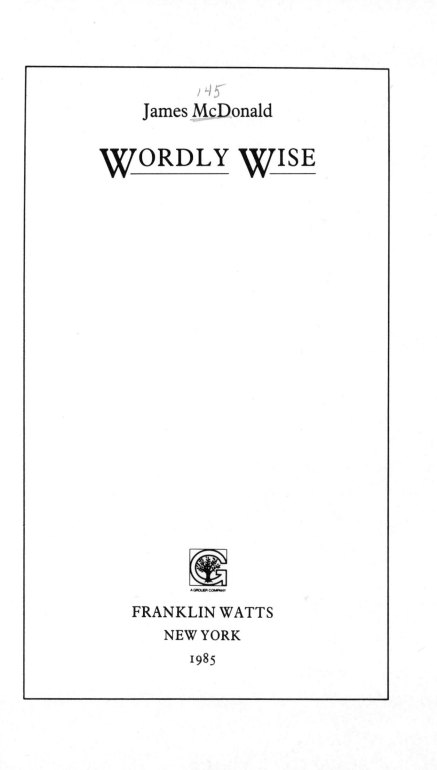

A GROLIER COMPANY

FRANKLIN WATTS

NEW YORK

1985

First published in the United Kingdom 1984 by
Constable and Company Ltd, 10 Orange Street, London WC2H 7EG

First United States publication 1985 by Franklin Watts, Inc.,
387 Park Avenue South, New York, New York 10016

ISBN 0-531-09772-2

Library of Congress Catalog Card Number: 84-51219

Printed in Great Britain

For my Mother

Acknowledgements

I would like to record my gratitude to Susannah Lewis who has cheerfully taken on the grim job of typing numerous drafts of this book. She has successfully deciphered my handwriting and corrected my spelling, tasks which had previously been thought impossible.

The illustration on p. 89 by W. Heath Robinson appears by kind permission of Gerald Duckworth & Co as publishers of *The Gentle Art of Advertising* and is copyright © 1979 Oliver Heath Robinson. The photograph of the print of 'The Bum Shop', 1785, is published by courtesy of The British Museum.

M.J.F.McD.
London 1984

Contents

Introduction

Hidden away within dictionaries are a vast number of unlikely, surprising and even incredible stories. The trouble is that dictionaries do not make easy reading, the plot being non-existent.

This book is intended for anyone who is interested in words and their origins. No expert knowledge of English, or of any other language, has been assumed. Background information has been filled in wherever it helps to explain why a word should have developed in the way that it has, but long involved stories, turgid minutiae and technical details have been avoided.

Terms such as Old English and Old French may be taken to mean simply that the word in question existed in English or French about a thousand years ago; and the description Anglo-Saxon may be taken to mean exactly the same as Old English. More precise explanations of these and other terms are contained in Appendix D.

Words and phrases are printed in small capitals where their origins are being discussed, and earlier forms, if given, are printed in italic. For example:

The word BEER has developed from the Anglo-Saxon *beor*.

To avoid going into detail, inverted commas have been used in the following way:

The word WINDOW can be rendered literally *'wind-eye'*.

This notation indicates that the word window is not really made up of the English words wind and eye, but rather that there exists another word meaning 'wind-eye' from which it is derived. In this example the Old Norse word *vindauga* and indeed any mention of the Old Norse language can thus be avoided. In fact the Vikings introduced Old Norse, a Scandinavian language, to the British Isles a little over a thousand years ago. Amongst the words that they brought across were *vind*, meaning 'wind' and *auga* meaning 'eye' which together formed the word *vindauga* and hence WINDOW, the name of a hole in the wall through which the wind blows and through which one can look. Similarly the DAISY is really a *'day's eye'*, a NOSTRIL is really a *'nose-thrill'* (a *'nose-drill'* or a nose-hole) and a HUSTING is, or was, a *'house-thing'*, a 'house assembly', since the word 'thing' originally denoted an assembly or council.

Entering into the spirit of it

Of all the inventions which supposedly distinguish mankind from the other animals there is one which signals the beginning of true civilisation. Harnessing fire and stumbling across the wheel are all very well, and developing a spoken language was undoubtedly a breakthrough; but surely the greatest single achievement was the discovery of alcohol. It is no accident that many alcoholic beverages are known as the water of life. In Gaelic the terms *uisge* and *beatha* mean 'water' and 'life' respectively, and *uisge beatha* means 'water of life'; changed into USQUEBAUGH, then into WHISKBAE, the expression acquired its more usual modern forms in the eighteenth century: now we make a nice distinction between Scotch WHISKY, without an 'e', and Irish WHISKEY with one. On the mainland of Europe many countries have words like *aquavita*, with exactly the same meaning, which are similarly used as the names of clear distilled spirits. These names are recognisable as variants of the Latin expression *aqua vitae* used by alchemists in the Middle Ages to describe pure alcohol. The French term *eau-de-vie*, also literally meaning 'water of life', is applied to what the English know as

Wordly wise

brandy. In each case the underlying idea is that of distilling the life-force or spirit, the very essence of life being condensed from the vapour of a heated, fermenting brew. The word BRANDY also reflects this for the word is a shortened form of BRANDY WINE, earlier BRANDEWINE, this word having been borrowed from the Dutch in whose language *brandewijn* means simply burned (i.e. distilled) wine.

The water of life is also 'little water' because its volume is small in comparison with the amount of liquid distilled; hardly surprising since the 'little water' contains only the vital essence. In Russian the word VODKA is a diminutive form of that for water, *voda*, but the Irish 'little-pot whiskey' or, more precisely, 'water little-pot', *uisge poitin*, generally known as POTEEN is 'little' for another reason: it is prepared in small movable stills because it is illegal to make it at all. SPIRITS are so-called because they embody the *spirit* or essence of the original liquid, but the word ALCOHOL leads back beyond European alchemy to the scientific sophistication of Arabia. Arabic *koh'l*, English KOHL, is a fine metallic powder used for eye make-up; 'the kohl' is a literal translation of the Arabic *al-koh'l* which has now become the familiar word ALCOHOL: first denoting a powder, then a powdered essence or spirit, then any liquid essence, the word finally came to denote a pure liquid spirit.

Some words continue down the centuries scarcely altered in form or meaning while others change continually. The words WATER, BEER and DRINK, for example, are almost identical to their ancient ancestors while others, like the term GROGGY, also associated with drinking, have relatively recent and varied histories. To be GROGGY was originally to be suffering from the effects of rum diluted with water, such a mixture being known as GROG. The word GROG is a contracted form of GROGRAM, the nickname of Admiral Vernon who, in 1740, was responsible for first watering down the naval rum ration, apparently because diluted rum will not keep as long as the pure spirit and the ratings could not, therefore, save up their daily allowances until they had accumulated enough to get drunk. Admiral Vernon had acquired his nickname as a result of his habitually wearing a grogram cloak, that is one made from a coarse material known as GROGRAM or earlier as *grograyn* from the French *gros grain*, literally meaning 'coarse grain' and so describing the rough fabric. The equivalent English words GROSS and GRAIN, of course, have their own stories, but the trail leads back only as far as the sixteenth century.

The word RUM is probably a contraction of the word RUMBULLION which itself has uncertain origins, but may be formed from *rome*, meaning 'fine' (like the city of Rome) and *bouillon*, a French word for a hot drink, so it seems that RUM should really be 'a fine hot drink' like a hot toddy. But TODDIES come from further away: earlier called TARRIES, their name derives from the Hindustani word *tari* which describes a drink made from parts of a *tar* or palm-tree. Another drink named from its contents is PUNCH, from the Hindustani *panch* meaning five: the five ingredients are alcohol, water, lemon, sugar and spice. Nearer to home the juniper berries which flavour GIN have given that drink its name, the Latin term *juniperus* having been corrupted on its journey to Holland where it became *genever* and then to England where it became *Hollands Geneva*, *Geneva* and finally GIN. GIN AND IT, however, is really gin and Italian vermouth.

Alcohol is also known as SPIRIT OF WINE since, like brandy, it can be prepared from wine. The word WINE has changed little from Anglo-Saxon times, the Saxons having acquired it from the Roman's *vinum* which also accounts for VINE and the name of sour wine, VINEGAR. One might be amused by its brutality. Wine which is neither red nor white may have a 'rosy' pink colour and thus be ROSÉ. Alternatively it might have a 'clear' yellowy hue and thus be known as CLARET. Now the term CLARET is applied, by the English, to red wines from Bordeaux while the original French term *vin claret* has fallen into disuse in its native country. Turning from clear yellow to light red, this wine has also produced the name of the colour CLARET. Many wines like CHAMPAGNE, CHIANTI and MADEIRA are named after their places of origin: MALMSEY wine came originally from *Malvasia* and SHERRY was *Sherris*, after the Spanish *vino de*

Xeres. The Spanish '*X*' has become 'Sh' in England although the city of Caesar, *Xeres* is now known as *Jeres*. Similarly PORT or PORT WINE comes from, or at least historically was shipped from, Oporto. *O Porto*, literally 'the port', has provided the name of the city as well as the country of which it is the capital, PORTUGAL.

Port is not to be confused with the dark beer known as PORTER, earlier called PORTER'S BEER because it was so popular amongst porters. Once the word PORTER had become established, the strong or *stout* variety came to be known as STOUT PORTER and later merely as STOUT. In German a similar sort of transfer process has taken place: the word *lager* in that language means a store and a beer made to be kept is thus a *lager bier*, hence the English LAGER. Like the word BEER, ALE has existed almost unchanged since Anglo-Saxon times, and as a tea is a tea-drinking session so an ale is one of ale drinking. Often held on Church property to celebrate or to raise money, ales were rowdy and enjoyable affairs known specifically, for example, as lamb-ales, clerk-ales, Midsummer-ales and Church-ales; because they were so enjoyable the authorities tried to stop them and puritan kill-joys eventually succeeded, but the ancient 'bride-ale' is still remembered in the word BRIDAL. More recently, in the nineteenth century, an inventor called Hiram Codd patented a new type of bottle with a glass marble in its neck. Mineral waters were sold in such bottles and, 'wallop' being a slang term for fizzy ale, the contents became known as *Codd's Wallop*. Now transferred in application to anything weak or generally disapproved of, the expression has become more familiar as CODSWALLOP.

Many names have been spread across the world in recent times from their places of origin; but there are also words which are so old that they have always been shared by a number of superficially different languages. Their original forms are lost to us since writing was unknown when such ancient words were first used. It is not difficult to imagine what sort of alcoholic drink our ancestors first invented, however, because so many languages have such similar words for honey and the sweet alcoholic brew made from it. Since the extensive development of writing, words almost identical to the Sanskrit *madhu* have been used throughout Europe and a large part of Asia. The Anglo-Saxon form *medu* has developed into the English word MEAD while the Greek one *methu*, again denoting an alcoholic drink, has an echo in the alcoholic, though poisonous, METH-YLATED SPIRITS, also known as METHS. The Greek word also features in the name of a magical stone, possession of which was supposed to protect against the inebriating effects of strong drink: now purely ornamental the stone is still called an AMETHYST.

Other well known types of alcoholic drink include liqueurs and cocktails. The word LIQUEUR is simply the modern French form of the English LIQUOR, both modern forms deriving from the Old French *licur*, ultimately from a Latin word which also gives us the word LIQUID. Liqueurs were great favourites in monasteries: the monks of the Order of *St Benedict* having produced BENEDICTINE while those of *La Grande Chartreuse* produced CHARTREUSE. Although more recent, the word COCK-TAIL has an unknown origin: there are many suggestions including the obvious 'cock-tail' but the most picturesque is provided by the name of an Aztec girl *Xochitl*. In any case the word was already being applied to mixed drinks by 1809. MARTINI is named after a firm, '*Martini and Rossi*', which became well-known for producing vermouth; but VERMOUTH itself is an old word with the same derivation as WORMWOOD. The German version *wermut* and the Anglo-Saxon *wormod* show how closely the words are connected, the original sentiment presumably being suggested by *wer*, man, and *mod*, mood, for WORMWOOD is a herb which was supposed to possess qualities as an aphro-disiac and thus aroused masculine feelings (amongst men at least). Mixed with white wine wormwood produces a basic vermouth. Some new cocktails appear at first sight to have much more blatant sexual implications although the names are really elaborate puns: A LONG SLOW COMFORTABLE SCREW, for example, is served in a *long* glass, contains *sloe* gin, 'Southern Comfort' and the elements of a '*Screw*driver', vodka and orange juice.

Cocoa drinkers have changed their collective image in recent times. The Mexicans, who were the original imbibers, enjoyed a rather more exotic diet than their modern counterparts: here, for example, is the Aztec god Tezcatlipoca enjoying a snack, the hand of a sacrificial victim. The god himself has lost one of his own feet, perhaps to another frenzied cocoa drinker with a taste for nether delicacies.

Sources of non-alcoholic drinks are often just as exotic as some alcoholic ones. COFFEE comes, via the Dutch *koffie*, from Turkish *kahveh* and ultimately from the Arabic *kahwa*. The Dutch have also provided TEA which to them was *thee*, derived from a Malay word and ultimately from a Chinese dialect word *t'e*. The Mandarin Chinese, however, called it *ch'a* which explains why it is also known as CHAR. From the Aztec *chocolatl* by way of the Spanish and French languages we have CHOCO-LATE which at some stage has been confused with the Aztec *cacava-atl*, the name of a drink made with seeds of the cacao-tree. From it we also have the word COCOA.

Drinking vessels tend to have more homely names and even the foreign ones usually come from no further than Italy. The word JUG is an unlikely variation of the name *Joan* once in common use; and the more prestigious Lady Jane, in French *Dame Jeanne*, has given us DEMIJOHN, the name of a type of bottle. A TOBY is entitled after the name *Tobias* but is now generally known as a TOBY-JUG since the old habit of using people's names for drinking vessels has fallen into disuse and the origin of the word JUG largely forgotten. From a common Latin source we have the terms BEAKER and PITCHER and from another Latin word meaning 'a drink' comes the word POT. The Latin verb meaning 'to drink' is *potare* from which we have a description of a good drink, POTABLE; the name of an alcoholic drink, POTATION; and of a toxic or medical one, POTION, along with the even less pleasant POISON. When asked to NAME YOUR POISON it is as well to remember that the medieval Latin verb meaning to poison was *intoxicare* from which we have the word INTOXICATE. Also from Italy comes the word FLASK as well as its original form FIASCO, for it seems that Venetian glass blowers held bad workmanship up to ridicule by sarcastically saying in effect, 'Look, a FIASCO'. The word FLAGON shares the same ultimate root and, like FLASK, originally denoted a container like a bottle but not necessarily made of glass. Indeed the word BOTTLE is derived from the Latin *bota* meaning thick skin or hide, for the first bottles were made of leather. Now bottles are usually made of glass, and BUTTS are made of wood, although the original material is still used for making BOOTS, the name of which derives from the same source. In recent times it has been necessary to invent words for different-sized bottles: a double-sized bottle is simply called a MAGNUM, after a Latin word for 'large', but even bigger ones are named after biblical characters. A JEROBOAM contains the equivalent of four ordinary bottles, a REHOBOAM six, a METHUSELAH eight, a SALMANAZAR twelve, a BALTHAZAR sixteen and a NEBUCHADNEZZAR twenty.

TUMBLERS are so-called for obvious reasons: having rounded

bases, the original ones would simply *tumble* over if put down. It has been the custom in many cultures to fashion drinking vessels with curved bottoms in order that they may not be set down until finished. Usually the draught had to be drunk in one, a tradition which survives in the practice of 'sconcing' at some Oxford Colleges. In Germany the word *garous!* meaning 'quite out!' was spoken as the freshly-emptied tankard was slammed down and those who follow similar modern practices are said to CAROUSE. Now taken over by Trades Unions, the English version was 'all out!' and one who *'tossed'* up or emptied a *pot* or tankard was a TOSSPOT. A similar practice was to sink a glass of alcohol as a toast. This use of the word TOAST derives from its application to bread which has been browned at the fire. The connection is provided by the practice of placing pieces of spiced TOAST into drinks and the supposed correspondence between the desirable flavour of the drink and the name of the person toasted. Making an informal toast it is usual to wish good health which is exactly what the Anglo-Saxons did when they said *wes hal*; now associated with Christmas festivities the expression has become WASSAIL but the two original parts have relations which survive in their own right. *Wes* meaning 'be' has gone but the past tense, WAS, remains, and *hal* has developed into the modern HALE. The related words HEALTH, WHOLE and HOLY reflect the association with well-being and completeness while the aspect of salutation is remembered in the word HAIL, as in the old form of greeting 'hail be thou', and also in the corresponding German word *Heil*.

Old words are extremely tenacious of life and, when threatened with extinction, often develop chameleon-like abilities to camouflage themselves within the jungle of the English language. Hiding in dark linguistic corners such words may easily disguise themselves by assuming the outward appearance of other still-thriving ones. The word *piggin*, for example, was once applied to a small pail such as might be used for serving beer. Like *wassail*, the term is little used now. But it may be that we remember them both in that well-known public house: the PIG AND WHISTLE.

2

A verbal diagnosis

In general, the common terms for external parts of the body and for the major internal organs have good, solid Anglo-Saxon ancestries. The word FINGER comes from *fangen*, to seize, as also does the word FANG; WRIST is derived from *wrest*, 'to turn', and ELBOW is just *el*, the length of an arm, and *bow*, to bend. BELLY is from Anglo-Saxon *belig*, a bag or bellows, and in a similar vein the word *blaeddre*, denoting a windbag, gives BLADDER and also the verb to BLITHER as in BLITHERING idiot. The word LIGHTS has changed little since the Anglo-Saxons wrote it *lihte* and applied it to the lungs because they are so lightweight. From the same prehistoric root as *lihte* comes the word LUNG. Nowadays the human being has lungs but the slaughtered animal has lights. The KIDNEY, literally a 'belly-egg', so-called from its position and shape, is another practical English word although its Anglo-Saxon components have otherwise disappeared. But the DUODENUM and PANCREAS are intruders from Greece and Rome respectively. The DUODENUM is really *duodenum digitorum* because it is the breadth of twelve fingers and the PANCREAS is *pan*, all, *krease*, flesh. GUTS, Anglo-

Saxon *guttas*, are older than BOWELS which are thus named as a result of butchers' practices. Intestines are used for sausage skins and the Latin for sausage is *botulus* which gave the French word *bouel*, a pudding, and thence the English BOWEL. Eating a sausage or *botulus* can, incidentally, cause BOTULISM.

It was once a widely-held belief that the organs of the body were responsible for various emotions and such beliefs are so well established in the English language that it is still easy to deduce some of the supposed associations. The bowels were thought to govern pity, hence the BOWELS OF COMPASSION; but passionate types would need to VENT THEIR SPLEEN – the spleen being the organ responsible for outbursts of anger. The HEART's association with affection and memory was usually prolific giving sweetheart, win the heart of, speak from the heart, heartache, heartbreak, heartless, cry one's heart out, eat one's heart out and the simple description HEARTY. A hearty reception is said to be CORDIAL, and is so-called from the Latin word *cor*, heart: thus also a hearty drink is called a CORDIAL and the very heart of an object is its CORE. The word RECORD contains a reference to the connection between the heart and memory for the idea behind it is similar to that implied by the phrase to LEARN BY HEART; now written records are kept to save the trouble of having to have inscriptions engraved upon metaphorical hearts. Hearts acting together result in CONCORD but those in conflict produce DISCORD. Also from the Latin word *cor*, by way of French, we have the word COURAGE since the heart is responsible for moral fibre; but physical courage is associated with the digestive system: those with sufficient 'guts' can 'stomach' anything.

Personality, temperament and general disposition were thought of as depending upon the mixture of four qualities or characteristics and four essential body fluids. Their combination determined the temperature and complexion although these two attributes originally had rather different meanings. Both words are derived from Latin: COMPLEXION and COMPLEX, like the word COMPLICATE, are derived from the verb *complicare* meaning literally 'to plait together', while the word TEMPERA-

TURE comes from *temperare*, meaning 'to mix'; in each case the implication is of a combination. The word COMPLEXION has come to mean natural colour, while TEMPERATURE has associated itself with the measurement of heat. TEMPER, TEMPERATE and TEMPERAMENT, however, have kept the suggestion of a mixture, especially a balanced one, and an unbalanced mixture might cause an affliction such as DISTEMPER. The four principal body fluids were called HUMOURS, from the Latin *humidus*, moist, which also provided the word HUMID. Like the words complexion and temperature, HUMOUR has changed its meaning; temper is now usually associated with bad temper while humour tends to be restricted to good humour, but it has also developed different senses in the adjective HUMOROUS and the verb to HUMOUR. As one of the cardinal humours, blood had an important effect upon man's characteristics. The description COLD BLOODED suggests a cool, composed disposition and the French equivalent SANG-FROID has been adopted by the English along with an implicit suggestion of praiseworthiness which is noticeably absent in the original French. On the other hand people are often said to be HOT BLOODED; when extremely angry they may find that their BLOOD BOILS. In the past those who were thought to be influenced by the blood more than by the other three humours were said to be SANGUINE. The word comes from the Latin *sanguinis*, bloody, and implies an amorous, courageous and hopeful disposition.

The other three important body fluids were yellow bile, black bile and phlegm. Yellow bile was responsible for irascibility and for angry outbursts; it was called CHOLER from the Greek *chole*, meaning bile. *Chole* itself is related to *cholera*, meaning diarrhoea, hence also the disease CHOLERA; COLIC, on the other hand, can be traced to a less unpleasant source, the part of the intestine known as the colon. As a name for a body fluid CHOLER has largely been replaced in everyday speech by the alternative names yellow bile and gall, although the adjective CHOLERIC is still frequently used to describe an irascible or angry temperament. Surprisingly perhaps the words YELLOW, GALL and CHOLER are all thought to have the same ultimate root which must have existed during the very infancy of the European languages. Derangement of the bile could cause BILIOUSNESS, a disorder to which, according to school sick notes, children seem to be particularly prone. Severe MELANCHOLY appears to affect them less, although its supposed cause is similar. Named from the Greek *melas*, black, and the familiar *chole*, bile, this affliction was thought to be caused by an excess of black bile produced by the liver. Such an excess caused a depression, sadness and a generally gloomy outlook. Even so, a surfeit of bile was preferable to a shortage of blood. Too little blood would result in a pale-coloured liver and thus cowardice. Phrases such as LILY-LIVERED, WHITE-LIVERED, YELLOW-LIVERED and simply YELLOW all reflect this ancient belief and, since pigeons were thought to possess no gall, PIGEON-LIVERED also came to mean cowardly. The liver, an important organ situated behind the rib cartilage, was held to be responsible for a wide range of ailments. As well as those already mentioned, hypochondria could result from its disorder. Indeed the very word HYPOCHONDRIA indicates the site of the organ supposedly responsible: *hypo* in Greek means 'under' and *chondros* means 'gristle': the liver lies under the cartilage or gristle of the ribs. Sluggishness and apathy were thought to be caused by an excess of the fourth humour, phlegm, so that slow and apathetic characters are described as PHLEGMATIC. They are also sometimes said to be cool, a paradoxical epithet since PHLEGM is derived from a Greek word meaning 'to burn', *phlegein*.

As long as the mix of the four humours was properly maintained then all was well. A small imbalance would account for the variations found throughout any normal population: sanguine, choleric, melancholy and phlegmatic dispositions are as common now as they presumably were in classical times or in the Middle Ages. With a little imagination many illnesses could be explained in terms of insufficient or excess production of the humours; a gradual dripping away of the humours was once thought to be the cause of gout. Indeed the word GOUT comes from the Latin *gutta*, a drop, although an alternative reason for this is another old belief – that the disease was caused by a drop of acrid fluid within the joints. Similarly an imbalance of *rheum* in the body was thought to cause RHEUMATISM.

Diseases are often named after their symptoms. Just as the word DISEASE itself is made up of the elements *dis* and *ease*, 'not at ease', so DYSENTERY comes from the Greek *dys*, bad, and *entera*, insides or entrails. 'Bad insides' is a prim but accurate description of the symptoms. DIPHTHERIA is derived from a Greek word for skin, *diphthera*, because one of its symptoms is a false skin formed in the throat. DIABETES, the Greek word for syphon, is applied to a disease one symptom of which is markedly increased urination. From the idea of clouding the mind, the Greek word *typhos*, smoke, gave names to two unrelated illnesses TYPHOID and TYPHUS. RABIES comes from *rabidus*, a Latin word meaning merely mad or furious, while the more prosaic QUINSY is ultimately named from a Greek word which meant 'dog-throttling'. Other complaints are named after their real or supposed causes. SYPHILIS, a word invented in the sixteenth century, was formed from the Greek *syn*, together, and *phileein*, to love; MALARIA, literally 'bad-air', was thought to be caused by marsh vapours while HYSTERIA, once thought to affect only women, was named from *hystera* the Greek word for a womb. Hence also the term HYSTERECTOMY denoting the surgical removal of the womb.

The words RECIPE and TREACLE have both escaped from the world of medicine and have found a new home in cookery. The word RECIPE is straightforward enough: it is derived from the Latin word *recipere* meaning to receive and used to appear at the head of medical prescriptions. It is now more familiar, in this context, as an abbreviation, ℞. The suggestion of a list of ingredients and procedures to be followed carried over to cookery quite naturally. The word TREACLE comes from the Greek *theriake* which is related to *therion*, a wild beast (as in the name of the PANTHER which, in Greek, is supposed to be *pan-ther*, 'all beast'). Originally treacle was an antidote for wild beast bites but, since it often contained a large proportion of molasses, the present meaning started to develop by the late seventeenth century.

The casual approach to brain surgery as demonstrated in a fourteenth century manuscript on anatomy. The patient is in a sense suffering from migraine, because the word MIGRAINE is formed from the middle section of the word HEMICRANIA; in Latin it means literally 'half skull'.

The word SURGEON is a corrupted form of CHIRURGEON which until recent times was the usual term; thus the degree of Master of Surgery is still abbreviated MCh. The word CHIRURGEON comes from the Greek *cheirourgos*, *cheir* meaning 'hand' and *ergon* meaning 'work': a surgeon is simply one who works with his hands.

The travelling medicine man could usually provide a sufficiently potent syrup for most ailments. He would stand on a bench, or '*mount-a-bank*', hence the title MOUNTEBANK; there he would chatter about his wares, a practice which provided an Italian word for him, *ciarlatano*, and therefore the English title CHARLATAN. To prattle was to *quack*, so one who prattled about ointments or *salves* was a QUACKSALVER or more simply a QUACK. As well as treacle the quack might sell his credulous customer a NOSTRUM. The name comes from Latin and means 'our', in this case 'our own patent medicine'. Sometimes the nostrum, salve or treacle was claimed to be able to cure all ills: to the Greeks a 'cure-all' had been a *panakeia*, and so in English it came to be called a PANACEA. Exaggerated claims were, of course, usually treated with a healthy scepticism so that demonstrations would be required. In order to show how efficient his treacle was, the quack's assistant would produce a supposedly poisonous toad, swallow it, drink the antidote, and miraculously would suffer no harm whatsoever – apart perhaps from slight indigestion. This practice confirmed the potency of the syrup and provided the language with the term *toad-eater* which has since been contracted to TOADY.

In the Middle Ages the boundary between magic and medicine was even less well defined than it is now and many of the techniques then in use now seem questionable. Modern science still cannot explain many physiological mechanisms so to that extent they are inexplicable, and cures which exploit them are in a sense supernatural. The expressions 'medicine man' and 'witch doctor' show how closely the known and unknown are interwoven in the mind of the healer and in the collective mind of the general population. Deliberate fraud, however, is soon detected by seasoned victims and a succession of medical titles have, therefore, followed one another down the dark path to critical use and eventual obscurity. Even the verb TO DOCTOR has taken on less than complimentary associations: doctored drinks, food, dice, cats and accounts are all less authentic than they might be. The term DOCTOR, from a Latin word meaning to lead or teach, was adopted by the medieval universities to describe the holders of certain degrees; although still used in this sense within universities, medical practitioners, most of whom do not possess doctoral degrees, seem to have adopted it for themselves. Such so-called doctors could be more accurately described as physicians, surgeons or even 'medics'.

The word MEDICINE is derived from *medicus*, the Latin for healer, but other medical terms tend to have more convoluted histories. The Latin word *hospitalis* denoted a place of rest and entertainment; from it the English language has contrived words such as HOST, HOSTEL, HOSTELRY, OSTLER, HOTEL, HOSPITALITY and, because of confusion with a similar French word, HOSTAGE. During the eleventh century the Knights of the Hospital of St John of Jerusalem provided refreshment for pilgrims; from them comes the present meaning of the word HOSPITAL. An AMBULANCE is so-called from the expression *hôpital ambulant*, the name of a 'walking' or field hospital, and an INFIRMARY is a place for the INFIRM: the *'un-firm'* or 'not solid'. The term CLINIC is ultimately derived from the Greek *kline*, bed. *Klinikos* meant 'confined to bed'; consequently a death-bed conversion became known as a 'CLINIC baptism' and later the term 'CLINIC teaching' was coined to describe medical instruction carried out by the bedside; it is from this latter use that the present meaning of the word CLINIC has developed.

Modern medicine has come a long way since ancient times, but hidden beneath the scientific façade is solid good sense and a little humour. The Romans, noticing how a muscle moves under the skin, called it a 'little mouse' or *musculus*, from which we have the English MUSCLE, and for that matter the name of a little sea mouse or MUSSEL. In many respects the ancients were more honest and descriptive than modern healers. They sought a panacea, an all-healing medicine, which they supposed to exist, but of course never found. Modern exponents call their more cynical equivalent a PLACEBO which in Latin means 'I shall be acceptable'. When there is no convenient pill to offer, the general practitioner can always prescribe a placebo in the certain knowledge that it will be of no physiological benefit whatsoever to the patient. It keeps the victim quiet and provides something tangible for the patient or the state to pay for. Perhaps the Greeks and Romans would have displayed the same healthy scepticism about modern medicine as we now display about ancient claims to have discovered a cure for all ills.

3

Moonshine

Medical practitioners of the Middle Ages had fairly rational explanations for most of the workings of the body and for many of the ways in which those workings might go wrong. Given the state of scientific knowledge at that time it is remarkable that they should have achieved as much as they did. Indeed some of their theories still find favour amongst modern researchers, even though they are neither proved nor disproved. The most contentious of these beliefs, still the subject of extensive research, is that there exists a correlation between the phases of the moon and the periodic occurrence of some types of madness. In fact we still use the term LUNATIC, derived from *luna*, the Latin word for the moon, to describe the insane, although in general usage the insanity referred to need not now be recurring. Also related is the slang word for a lunatic, LOONY, and other terms which reflect the same association are MOONSTRUCK, meaning mentally deranged; MOONSHINE, denoting foolish talk; and the verb to MOON, meaning to move about aimlessly as though moonstruck. But the moon's power was not limited to affecting mental states; it was also believed to be

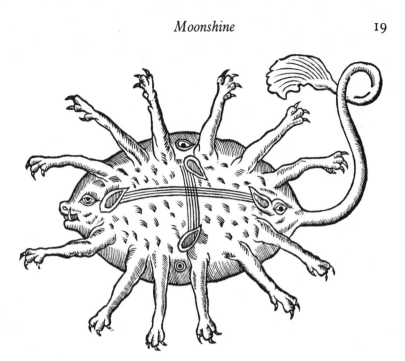

On land this would undoubtedly qualify as a moon-calf. Perhaps it was an aquatic equivalent; in any event no similar specimen has been reported since this one was sighted in the sea in 1562.

responsible for certain shapeless abortions known as MOON-CALVES. Later the term came to be applied to any malformed foetus and later to congenital idiots. Now anyone who moons around is liable to be called a MOON-CALF. Bear cubs, incidentally, were thought to be born without any form at all: only when they had been LICKED INTO SHAPE by their mothers did they even start to look like proper bears.

Anyone who was uncomplicated or ingenuous was liable to be thought of as foolish, and this cynical attitude has caused the words SIMPLE, DAFT and INNOCENT to acquire critical associations. The word SIMPLETON comes from SIMPLE, originally meaning only 'uncomplicated' and itself formed from the similar Latin word *simplus*. In Anglo-Saxon times the word *gedaefte* meant only gentle, meek or harmless but it has lost its prefix and become DAFT, although following another route it has also given the word DEFT. Similarly an INNOCENT should be quite harmless because the description is derived from the Latin elements *in* and *nocere* which together form a word meaning 'not to injure' or 'to do no harm'. The word INNOCENT is not necessarily uncomplimentary although its derivative NINNY is; furthermore, the word has affected the term NINCOMPOOP, the early forms of which suggest that it was really formed from the name *Nicodemus* and the obsolete word *poop*, meaning fool. In France, the name *Nicodème* still denotes a simpleton but in England 'Tomfool' has taken over that role. Another word which once also meant harmless is SILLY; but earlier still it had meant blissful or blessed. Other words relating to mental incapacity also reflect the connection with weakness or disability. For example, the word MAD, Anglo-Saxon *gemad*, comes ultimately from a word meaning 'crippled'; the term IMBECILE originally meant 'helpless', for its Latin components show that it means 'without a walking-stick'; and the word INSANE means merely 'not well' for the SANE part is derived from the Latin word *sanus* meaning 'healthy'.

A Greek word MORON was adopted early in this century as a title for people with retarded mental development but, as is so often the case with specialised technical terms, the word has passed into general use and its precise meaning lost. By contrast, the word IDIOT has long been used as a name for the insane: it was identical in Old French and comes from the Latin *idiota* which denoted an ignorant person. It is derived from a Greek word meaning a private person, that word being itself formed from *idios* meaning 'own' or 'peculiar' which has also provided the English words IDIOM and IDIOSYNCRASY. Both of these words refer to characteristics which are unique or at least particular to a restricted circle. Like the words idiot and moron, CRETIN has a precise technical meaning: originally it denoted one who suffered from a certain physical disability as well as idiocy, the combination being especially common at one time in Swiss Alpine valleys because of dietary deficiencies. Indeed the word CRETIN has been borrowed from the French who had fashioned it out of the Swiss patois *creitin* or *chrestin*, itself an adaptation of the Latin *christianus*; thus the words CHRISTIAN and CRETIN share the same origin. The less serious condition of stupidity, however, is more straightforward, for the word STUPID is derived from the Latin verb *stupere*, to stun or strike senseless.

In 1247 the Hospital of St Mary of Bethlehem was founded in London and in 1547 it was converted into a hospital specifically for the insane. Since patients were allowed out in order to beg, the hospital became well-known and its name was contracted by the populace to BETHLE'EM or BEDLEM and finally changed to BEDLAM. The word BEDLAM has survived to the present day but now it denotes any scene of frenzied activity befitting a mad-house.

The ancient Greeks, like their European counterparts of the Middle Ages, identified the heart as the seat of the mind. Their word *phren* meaning both 'heart' and 'mind' has provided a name for the nerve connecting the brain and the diaphragm (the PHRENIC nerve) along with the terms PHRENOLOGY, PHRENETIC and FRANTIC; and by way of Old French we also have FRENZY. Someone in a frenzy may be said to be 'beside themselves' as though some part of them, perhaps the mind or the spirit, were actually removed from the body. This idea is also inherent in the word ECSTASY which is taken, via the Old French and Latin, from the Greek word *ekstasis*, meaning both 'trance' and 'displacement'. Similarly the Romans created a word *delirium* from the elements *de*, from, and *lira*, furrow: to them madness was caused by the mind being dislodged from its rut, just as we now think of it being caused by having a 'screw loose'. We also say that delirious people are 'off their trolleys' or 'off their rockers': again the underlying idea is one of displacement.

The idea that the human body needs protection from the dangers of supernatural interference is extremely old and re-markably widespread. In English there are many terms which reflect this old belief in divine and demonic possession. Even this use of the word POSSESSION suggests a supernatural occu-pancy of the human faculties such as that experienced by the true 'enthusiast'. ENTHUSIASM, once a rather stronger word than it is now, was originally applied to people possessed by a God – as the word itself shows: the Greek components are *en*, in, and *theos*, god. In a similar way Norsemen went BERSERK when in the clutches of one of their gods and the Malaysians ran AMOK in similar circumstances. Divine possession was generally a dangerous business and those selected by the gods often went mad as a result of their experiences. The Greek word *mania* was once used to describe a divine frenzy but the medical profession has brought it down to earth where it joins the word fanatic. The Romans noticed that religious maniacs tended to manifest their symptoms at or near temples. From the Latin *fanum*, temple, comes the word FANATIC and thus also FAN (and those before and outside the temple were literally PROFANE). Back in England the Anglo-Saxons described a god-held man as *gydig*, a word which is now spelt GIDDY. The foolish were thought to be especially susceptible to divine possession and their Anglo-Saxon description *dysig* has similarly developed into the word DIZZY. When fighting against possession the victim may well appear to be fighting himself: thus the words FIT and FIGHT are both related to the Anglo-Saxon *fitt*, meaning 'conflict'.

Sometimes the belief was that a god's breath rather than the god himself would enter into the chosen one. Thus the Greek word *psyche*, which has provided numerous modern terms, such as PSYCHOLOGIST and PSYCHIATRIST, originally meant breath (of life). One who experienced the breath of a god was divinely inspired. From the Latin *in*, into, and *spirare*, to breathe, the word INSPIRE has many siblings in English: to CONSPIRE is to breathe together; to RESPIRE means to breathe again; to PERSPIRE is to breathe through (the skin); to ASPIRE means to breathe towards and to EXPIRE means to breathe out (possibly for the last time). To breathe across is, literally, to TRANSPIRE and the first part of this word also appears in the Latin word *transire*, to go across, which was applied to the crossing of a soul from life to death; from it is derived the word TRANCE which has lost much of the dread implicit in the earlier term. To be carried off to heaven would be marginally less traumatic; such a journey was called a RAPTURE from the Latin word *rapere*, to seize, but again the centuries have weakened its meaning, this time to little more than mere pleasure, although the word RAPE, which shares the same source, has retained its suggestion of forceful seizure. Also associated with *spirare* is the Latin word *spiritus*, breath of life, which has provided the English terms SPIRIT and SPRITE. Another word which connected the ideas of breathing and conscious life is the Latin *anima* from which we have words such as ANIMAL, ANIMATION and ANIMUS.

In its older sense, the word GHOST meant the same thing as SPIRIT, and it retains this association in the term HOLY GHOST (an alias of the deity who supposedly first breathed life into Adam's nostrils). The origin of the word GHOST is provided by the Anglo-Saxon *gaest* which has also given the adjective GHASTLY. The intrusive 'h' more properly belongs to the GHOUL whose title derives from the Arabic *ghul*, a word denoting an evil demon thought to seize and eat human beings. The star called ALGOL is really *al ghul*, the ghoul. The older form of the word GHOST, *gaest*, is clearly recognisable in another word distantly related and borrowed from modern German: in that language *poltern* means 'to be noisy' so a POLTERGEIST is simply a 'noisy spirit'. Nowadays a bugbear is any object of fear but originally the word denoted a '*bogy-bear*', a goblin in the form of a wild bear with which mothers frightened wayward children.

Phantoms belong to another world, that of sleep and dreams. The Greek word *phantasia*, nightmare, is the root of the word PHANTOM and is also closely related to PHANTASY (or FANTASY), FANCY and FANTASTIC. One who awakens from a nightmare sweating and breathing heavily is said to PANT: and again the source of the word is *phantasia*. A common theme of nightmares is a feeling of physical oppression for it often seems to the sleeper that something is lying upon his or her chest thus making breathing difficult. In Anglo-Saxon times the cause of this phenomenon was thought to be a mare which visited people in the night. In this sense the word MARE means not a horse but a demon, for it is connected to the Sanskrit *mara*, destroyer, and to the modern term MAR, to crush or to spoil. A MARE'S NEST is thus a demon's nest rather than a horse's nest, but a MARE'S TAIL (a cirrus cloud) is an equine, not a demonic possession. Sometimes the phantom visitors would make sexual advances. Men were especially troubled by these visitors and SUCCUBUS was the name given to such a phantom seducer. It is derived from the Latin *suc* (like *sub*), under, and *cubare*, to lie; these elements gave the Romans the word *succuba*, a strumpet, and also the modern English word SUCCUMB. The phantom male equivalent of the succubus who forced his attentions upon sleeping women was the INCUBUS; he also got his name from Latin, in which language *incubare* means 'to lie upon'. Thus also birds INCUBATE eggs by lying upon them, and duties which lie upon one are said to be INCUMBENT. Promiscuous supernatural beings performed a useful service because repressed sexuality could be given vent and the unfortunate victim could blame it all upon the concupiscent supernatural visitor. Of course the Church blamed witches for such ungodly doings; the accepted version was that witches directed the activities of incubi and succubi and occasionally assumed spectral forms themselves in order to join in the general naughtiness. Such witches were hags and their victims, humans or animals who were made to carry their tormentors over long distances, were literally HAG-RIDDEN. But the Anglo-Saxon form of the word HAG shows that originally hedges rather than people or animals were 'ridden': *haegtesse* meant literally 'hedge-rider'. So perhaps the original hags were merely people who looked as though they had been dragged through a hedge backwards.

From a Teutonic word *alp* meaning nightmare came the Anglo-Saxon word *aelf* and thence the modern ELF. The Dutch equivalent was *ouph* and this is noticeably similar to the word OAF. In fact an oaf was originally an elf's child whom the elves swapped for a human baby. Such children were likely to be stupid and also especially ugly. Indeed the very word UGLY comes from the Anglo-Saxon *oughlic*, *ough* meaning 'elf' and *lic* meaning 'like'. Also related was the Old Norse *uggr*, fear, which is not far removed from the modern echoic exclamation UGH!

4

Golden secrets

To the modern mind, medieval science seems rudimentary and often absurd. This image is largely undeserved since, in the past, research was severely restricted by a number of factors: equipment was difficult to obtain, expensive and of poor quality; original thought was discouraged by the Church; there was little advantage, and considerable danger, in communicating new ideas; existing theories had stood for up to two thousand years already and by their nature were difficult or impossible to disprove; and, perhaps most importantly, such theories provided plausible explanations for many phenomena which would otherwise be a complete mystery given only small scientific re-evaluations. Without the benefit of ancient or modern theories most people would find it difficult to account for such everyday things as tides, the phases of the moon, the saltiness of the sea, illness, dreams, gravity, fire, wind and even the colour of the sky. Equally difficult to explain are such phenomena as magnetism, static electricity, spontaneous combustion, rainbows, lightning and shooting stars. Without the influence of the Church, western civilisation might have produced better solutions to these problems much earlier. As it was, Greek theories were preserved without significant enhancement until the revival of learning and the Reformation. Searchers after truth were, until then, obliged to resort to ancient works in secret. Unravelling the ancient texts in Greek and Latin, Persian and Arabic, Hebrew and Aramaic, the medieval predecessor of the modern scientist had a difficult task indeed.

The popular conception of a chemist in a laboratory is little different from the medieval version of an alchemist in his. Equipped with stills, beakers and phials of mysterious coloured liquid, chemist and alchemist share the same objective: to discover something about matter by using chemical processes. They share more than this, however, for the word CHYMIST or CHEMIST is only a shortened form of ALCHEMIST, a word formed from the name of the art of ALCHEMY which in turn derives from the Arabic *al kimiya*, literally 'The Egyptian Art'. Arabic *al*, corresponding to English 'the', appears in a number of expressions which have been compressed and altered to give English words; amongst them are ALCOHOL, *al koh'l*, and ALKALI, *al qaliy*, both of which are also chemical words. Other disciplines which have drawn upon Arabic vocabulary are mathematics (with words like ZERO, CYPHER and ALGEBRA) and astronomy (with many star names beginning al- and the terms ZENITH and NADIR) but the English language has also benefited from the Arabian sweet tooth: as well as SUGAR, from *sukkar*, and CANDY, from *qandi*, we have SYRUP, *sharab*; SHERBET, *sharbat*; SORBET from the same source and SODA from *suda*, the name of a cure for headaches.

From *al 'iksir* comes the modern *elixir*. Now usually associated with a liquid preparation, it was originally used as a name for a powder and then later for the 'philosopher's stone'. The possession of this Elixir was the ultimate goal of the alchemists; with it the wonders of modern science could be achieved and even surpassed. Transmuting base metals into gold and conferring eternal life upon its possessor were only two of its many applications. One who had supposedly discovered the secret of the Elixir was described as ADEPT, from the Latin *adeptus* which means 'having attained', but now the world has found a wider meaning. Amongst the alchemists who were thought to have been adepts were a number who probably did not exist at all. For various reasons learned texts were often attributed to people other than the real writers, sometimes even to gods: amongst them were Moses, Cleopatra, Democritus, Hermes and Isis. The Greek deity Hermes or Hermes Trismegistus, Hermes the thrice great, was identified with the Egyptian god Thoth, the supposed founder of all occult science, and so alchemists were also known as HERMETICS. Since their experiments required equipment which was completely airtight the expression 'HERMETICALLY sealed' acquired its present meaning: 'perfectly closed'. Another writer to whom alchemical works were attributed was the Arab *Jabir* or *Geber*; because his writings were heavily coded, and therefore impossible for the uninitiated to understand, his name developed into the modern term GIBBERISH. The word OCCULT, incidentally, comes from the Latin *occultus* and means literally 'hidden'.

Many words have been used by alchemists and their meanings have sometimes been affected as a result. The words multiply and sublime might well have developed in the way that they did without the alchemists's influence, and doubtless the modern URINAL would have evolved as well. Derived from the Latin *urinare*, to wet or to pass water, a URINAL was once a sort of primitive test-tube used for inspecting various liquids, particularly urine. Also with a new function is the URINATOR: until the eighteenth century the word urinator was applied to those who dived into water (and so wet themselves), but as the new meaning developed it must have become apparent that undue confusion might arise and the older meaning fell into disuse. More directly influenced by the alchemist's art is the word 'spirit'. As the breath of life was thought to inhabit inanimate as well as animate objects, the word meaning 'essential quality' came to be applied to various substances which seemed to embody certain properties. For this reason a number of liquids became known as spirits and so we still have expressions like SPIRIT OF SALT (hydrochloric acid), SPIRIT OF WINE (alcohol), WHITE SPIRIT and METHYLATED SPIRITS.

A demon could be of service to the skilled alchemist. This is the Mercurial Demon as depicted in a medieval work on the transmutation of metals. He is supposed to embody the spirit of Mercury. The word TRANSMUTE means to change across or change into another form, which is exactly what the Latin word *transmutare* meant: *trans*, across, and *mutare*, to change. One of the alchemist's main objectives was to transmute base metals like lead into gold.

Four chief spirits recognised by the alchemists were quick-silver, also called HERMES after the Greek god and now called MERCURY after his Roman counterpart; sal ammoniac, salt of ammonia now called ammonium chloride; ORPIMENT, literally '*or-pigment*' or gold pigment, now known as arsenic trisulphide; and brimstone, the burning stone now more common in a powdered form and called sulphur. These spirits corresponded to the four bodily humours black bile, blood, yellow bile and phlegm; and to the four elements water, air, earth and fire; and to the four types of atmospheric phenomena known as METEORS from the Greek expression *ta meteora* meaning 'things on high'. Common meteors were: rain, corresponding to the element water; winds, corresponding to air; lightning and shooting stars, corresponding to earth; and rainbows, corresponding to fire. Now that science has unravelled the mysteries of these quite different atmospheric effects, the collective term has become restricted in meaning to only one of them: a METEOR is now specifically a shooting star, and if it lands on Earth without burning up in the atmosphere it becomes a METEORITE. But the study of atmospheric conditions in general is still called METEOROLOGY. Shooting stars are not really stars at all, rather they are tiny pieces of debris which occasionally chance upon the Earth's atmosphere. The heat generated by friction makes them appear to glow as brightly as stars and so each one is 'star-like', or using a word of Greek derivation *asteroides*, an ASTEROID.

Stars which wander rather than shoot around the heavens were known to the Greeks as *planetes asteres*. The equivalent Latin term for wandering stars was *stellae errantes* but the Romans also used the Greek expression which they reduced to *planetae*, the origin and counterpart of the English term PLANETS. Nine planets which orbit the sun are now known and all except the Earth are named after Roman gods and goddesses. They are Mercury, Venus, Earth (a word of Teutonic origin), Mars, Jupiter, Saturn, Uranus, Neptune and Pluto, the last three of which were unknown in medieval times. On the other hand the moon, which is a satellite of the Earth, and the sun, which is really a star, were included in the list of planets to give a total of seven: Mercury, Venus, Mars, Jupiter, Saturn, the Sun (identified with the god Apollo) and the Moon (which was identified with one of three goddesses, depending on its phase). These seven planets were thought to transmit their influence to the Earth through a medium composed of an element other than water, air, earth or fire. It was thus a fifth essence or in the Latin of the alchemists in the Middle Ages *quinta essentia*, an expression now more familiar as the term QUINTESSENCE; still a viable concept for physicists, the quintessence is now known as the AETHER, a Greek word meaning 'upper air'.

The behaviour of the heavens was thought to mirror human behaviour and so the arrangement of the planets within the houses of the zodiac would reveal information about worldly affairs. On a large scale there was the MACROCOSM, the name of which is derived from the Greek *makrokosmos*, large-world, and on a more modest scale there was the MICROCOSM, the *mikrokosmos* or small-world. Because of the close relationship between these dual worlds, many parallels were thought to exist between 'planets' and worldly objects. Quicksilver is still called Mercury but similar cosmic names for other metals have fallen into disuse and alternatives have prevailed: copper was known as Venus; iron was Mars; tin was Jupiter; lead was Saturn; gold corresponded to the Sun, and silver to the Moon. Perhaps coincidentally, the main tinctures and metals of heraldry correspond to the colours associated with these planets: Mercury was matched with *purpure*, purple; Venus with *vert*, green; Mars with *gules*, red; Jupiter with *azure*, blue; Saturn with *sable*, black; the Sun with *or*, gold; and the Moon with *argent*, silver. Relationships were also found with the days of the week, precious stones and parts of the hand which were important in palmistry. But the most lasting association is retained in the English language: those under the influence of Mercury are changeable or MERCURIAL; Venus makes people loving or VENEREAL (a usage which is now open to ambiguity because of the association with the phrase 'venereal disease'); those most affected by Mars are warlike or MARTIAL; Jupiter, also known as

Jove, confers JOVIALITY and Saturn makes people depressed or SATURNINE; the Sun causes a SUNNY disposition but the influence of the Moon may result in LUNACY, the Latin name for the Earth's only natural satellite being *luna*.

People or animals who were thought to be under the influence of a planet were PLANET STRUCK and those affected by stars were STAR STRUCK. Fortunate individuals, whose stars are in the ascendant, THANK THEIR LUCKY STARS and unfortunate ones are said to be BORN UNDER UNLUCKY STARS; they might be ILL-STARRED or, like Romeo and Juliet, STAR-CROSSED. An object of DESIRE should really be a lucky star, since the word is made up from the Latin *de*, from, and *sidus*, star. Another Latin word for star, derived from the Greek *aster*, was *astrum*; together with the prefix *dis* meaning 'away', it shows what will happen if the desire is not fulfilled – DISASTER. In order to know the worst it was wise to inspect the night sky and think about the relative positions of the stars. From *con*, together, and *sidus* comes the word CONSIDER which well describes the action of thinking about desires and disasters.

The Romans had yet another word for a star, *stella*, which, like *sidus*, could be prefixed with *con* to produce a new compound. *Con*, *stella* and an appropriate suffix give the modern English CONSTELLATION which is applied to groups of stars, or rather to stars which from Earth appear to lie together. The most important constellations in the Northern Hemisphere are those which can be used to identify the pole star and thus enable navigation. Indeed the word STAR, Anglo-Saxon *steorra*, is a very close relative of the word STEER and of STARBOARD and STERN, the names of the parts of the ship from which early sailors steered. It is no coincidence that the German word for star is *stern*, the distinction between navigating and steering having hardly existed in early times. The Pole Star is in a constellation usually called the Little Bear, a partner of the Great Bear which is also known as the Plough, King Charles's Wain, or, in America, the Big Dipper. Using two bright stars in the Great Bear it is also easy to identify Polaris, the Pole Star which lies at the end of the Little Bear's tail. The Greek *arktos*,

This rather unusual comet was seen in 1528 although the drawing dates from
almost seventy years later. There can be little wonder that comets were
regarded as divine warnings if they looked anything at all like this. One
suspects that the popular press of today could have learned a thing or two from
the reporter who recorded the incident at the time.

    The Greeks, who presumably had comets more in line with the ones that we
are accustomed to, thought of them as long-haired stars. Their phrase for a
star with long hair was *aster kometes* from which, indirectly, we have the name
COMET.

meaning 'bear', has provided the English word ARCTIC for the far
north and ANTARCTIC for the 'anti-arctic', the corresponding
area in the far south which is as far away as possible from the two
bears.

    Like alchemy, the practice of astrology as it was known in the

Middle Ages has acquired an undeserved reputation. Because its modern exponents have the reputation of being cranks or charlatans, and because the Church never approved of scientific research which might undermine its authority, the founders of modern chemistry, the alchemists, and of astronomy go largely unrecognised. The distinction between ASTRONOMY, *astronomia*, star arranging, and ASTROLOGY, *astrologia*, star discoursing, is a relatively recent one. Previously the distinction would have been between natural astrology and judicial astrology: natural astrology concerned itself with the timing of Easter, eclipses, planetary conjunctions, the phases of the moon and time measurement, while judicial astrology was concerned with occult influences. The word INFLUENCE, from Latin *in*, in, and *fluere*, to flow, originally referred to flows of occult power such as those which were thought to cause INFLUENZA. This 'judicial' variety is the nearest to the modern understanding of astrology, a sad remnant of its former self. The transition from ancient to modern science did not occur overnight, for each new theory had to prove itself before displacing its predecessor. Sir Isaac Newton knew as much about astrology, alchemy and other occult sciences as he did about the scientific disciplines for which he is now so well known.

Newspaper astrology has not helped the image of the unfortunate proto-scientists who once sought to unlock the secrets of the universe. Hardly worth a glance today, the HOROSCOPE once involved precise observation of the hour as the word itself shows: in Greek *hora* meant 'an hour' and *skopos* meant 'an observer'. Both ancient and modern astrologers note the arrangement of the planets along a circular path called the zodiac. Now with twelve signs, the original zodiac had only six, all of which were named after animals. Each of the twelve signs corresponds to a constellation, but it is the original six animal ones that are responsible for the word ZODIAC; Aristotle referred to them as the Circle of *Zoidion*, meaning the circle of small animals. If ever the zodiac was of use in predicting the future it is difficult to see how the modern newspaper horoscopes could ever be. Since ancient times the position of the houses of the

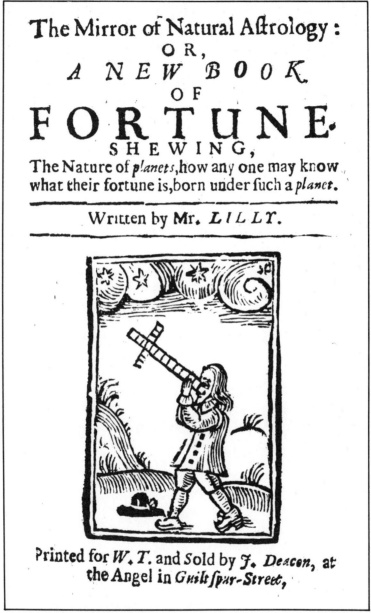

The Mirror of Natural Astrology:
OR,
A NEW BOOK
OF
FORTUNE·
SHEWING,
The Nature of *planets*, how any one may know what their fortune is, born under such a *planet*.

Written by Mr. *LILLY*.

Printed for *W. T.* and Sold by *J. Deacon*, at the Angel in *Guiltspur-Street*,

Seventeenth-century Mr. Lilly added to the confusion by calling a chap-book on ASTROLOGY 'Natural Astrology' which at that time meant ASTRONOMY.

zodiac and the dates upon which the corresponding birth signs are determined have gradually lost their close relationship. For reasons similar to those which have resulted in such an unlikely tax year, dates and astrological signs have been dislocated. Any astral significance that there might have been has now been lost. Even though their arguments no longer make sense in the light of modern knowledge, it is clear that people of ancient times used the information available to them in a rational manner. For example, the Romans, like the Greeks before them, were aware that the appearance of Sirius corresponded to the hottest time of year. Being the brightest star in the sky, Sirius was thought to supplement the power of the Sun at this time and so cause the additional warmth which characterised a number of days in July. Indeed the name of Sirius comes from the Latin *sirius*, from the Greek *seirios*, scorching. Like so many other theories, this one lasted into the Middle Ages, and the time of year noted by the Romans became in English the DOG DAYS because Sirius, the DOG STAR, lies in the constellation called *canis major*, the Great Dog.

Given that the heavenly macrocosm mirrors the worldly microcosm, and further that the movements of the stars and planets can be predicted, it follows that human affairs are predetermined. In the next chapter it will become apparent that our ancestors read a great deal into aspects of the universe which were beyond their control. It will also become apparent that their ideas can properly be described as weird.

5

Che sarà, sarà

For many centuries it has been a common belief that certain days are inherently lucky and others unlucky. The Romans marked the lucky days on their calendars in white and the unlucky ones in black. Adapting this idea Church calendars were marked in red to show special days, so producing the phrase RED LETTER DAY to describe a special occasion. By contrast BLACK LETTER DAY is an unlucky or unfortunate one. Many lucky and unlucky days continue to be recognised by various groups, the best known example being the thirteenth day of any month which happens also to be a Friday. Unlucky days to the Romans were *dies mal* and in Old French they became *dis mal*: in English the expression became DISMAL, a term applied to the results of unfortunate happenings. From the Latin *fas*, the divine word, comes the modern FATE; and anything not in accordance with the divine was *nefastus* or as we now say NEFARIOUS. Whether we believe in fate or not we can be sure that our end will be FATAL.

The Anglo-Saxon equivalent of the Latin word *fas* was *wyrd*. Almost obsolete, the word was rescued by Shakespeare who used it in *Macbeth*. When he wrote of the three WEIRD sisters on the blasted heath, he almost certainly had in mind three supernatural beings resembling the Fates of mythology, rather than the witches that have only existed in the popular imagination of recent times. Also concerned with one's fate was the SORCERER whose name is derived from the Latin *sors*, chance or lot in life; and another word for fate, FORTUNE, has developed from a similar root, *fors*. To the Anglo-Saxons one's LOT was a *hlot*, literally a portion or choice; the word was applied to the pieces of wood traditionally used to forecast the future. Life must have been as much of a lottery to the Anglo-Saxons as it is to their descendants over a thousand years later.

By throwing sticks, bones or dice on to the ground many people in different parts of the world have tried to read the secrets of the future. Presumably because they thought that there was a chance of success, Church leaders in Europe banned such practices, or at least tried to. Cards and dice have both been used extensively in order to gain forbidden knowledge and it is this aspect rather than the innocent pleasure of gambling which accounts for puritanical denunciations. Terms such as the Devil's Bible for a deck of cards and the Devil's Bones for dice were designed to discourage their use. But tarot cards are still popular, as are playing cards and dice; and when the inevitable becomes apparent it is as though the ancient dice have been thrown and the future seen: if two bones are scattered the dice are cast; if only one, the DIE IS CAST. Either way the future is settled. To forecast is literally to cast before, as the dice or a plan might be thrown down for inspection before an event. The Latin words *pro-*, forward and *jacere*, to throw, produced a word which meant the same as forecast, PROJECT. Similarly the term CONJECTURE is formed from *con-*, together, and *jacere*, for the first conjectures were about the meanings of lots and dice throws.

As to forecast is to cast before so to foretell is to tell before. Again there is a parallel word formed from Latin: *prae-* means before and *dicere* means to tell or say; together they form the word *praedicere* from which we have the term PREDICT. One who sees rather than tells is a SEER and, specifically, one who can see into the future enjoys the gift of FORESIGHT. The word 'foresight' means exactly the same as a word of Latin origin, 'prevision', and also the same as one of Greek origin, 'providence'. In much the same way one who has knowledge of an event before it happens is said to have foreknowledge, and foreknowledge is simply *prae*, before, *scientia*, knowledge, PRESCIENCE; the word PROGNOSIS, of Greek origin, has the same structure again, 'before-know'; in fact the terms prognosis and prognostication have precisely the same origin, and a medical prognosis is merely a better sounding description of what is really a prognostication. Yet another term with a similar 'fore-know' structure is the word PRECOGNITION, *'pre-cognition'*. This game of matching words from different languages could go on for a long time but some of the terms are rather obscure. Nevertheless there are many expressions in common use which imply knowledge of the future and which have this 'fore-' or *'pre-'* element. To FOREBODE is to foretell since the word BODE, Anglo-Saxon *bodian*, means 'to announce'. A token of an event in the future is a FORETOKEN, and a feeling or sentiment beforehand is a PRESENTIMENT. What is destined for the future is predestined, and what is set in order, or ordained, in advance is PREORDAINED. One who is discerning is a sage and that which enables the future to be discerned is said to PRESAGE it. When the future stretches out into the present like a shadow we say that the future is FORESHADOWED. A figurative shadow is in a sense a portent since the word PORTEND comes from the Latin *portendere*, *por-*, towards, and *tendere*, to stretch out. By extension, as it were, the shadow of the future gives a warning. A specific type of supernatural warning was a MONSTER; originally signifying no more than a portent the word monster attached itself to abnormal animals or humans which were thought to exist for the sole purpose of communicating messages from God. The ideas of warning and showing are close relatives as the Latin words for them confirm. The verb 'to warn' is *monare* and 'to show' is *monstrare* so that the appearance of a MONSTER could be interpreted as a forewarning or PREMONITION, or as a DEMON-

STRATION of divine ADMONITION. Having followed a route similar to that of the unfortunate monster is the word PRODIGY, a
disguised member of the 'fore-tell', 'fore-bode', 'predict' class.
Originally it, too, denoted only a warning, but then the word
was applied to anything out of the ordinary, and since extra-
ordinary occurrences were often feared, the innocent prodigy
became another monster. These dual old and new meanings,
'exceptional' and 'monstrous', allow fond parents to refer to their
precocious children as prodigies while also permitting more
objective observers to agree without compromise of honesty.

The Romans required more specific information than could
be gleaned from everyday monstrosities so they relied heavily
upon the inspection of animals' entrails for additional details.
Not all Romans believed in this method of divination; indeed
Cato, a man renowned for his good common sense, once said of
the *haruspices* – the men who performed the ritual sacrifices and
inspections – that he did not know how they could pass each
other in the street without laughing. As the *haruspices* looked at
entrails, so the *auspices* looked at birds, and it is the latter who
have left the greater impression upon the English language.
From the Latin *avis*, a bird, and *specere*, to see, came the term
AUSPICES as used by the Romans to describe bird-watching
prophets and adopted into English with a more general meaning. If the auspices are right then the occasion is AUSPICIOUS.
With a function similar to that of the *auspix* was the *augur*, part
of whose name also comes ultimately from the word *avis*. The
birds of ancient Rome now have little connection with the
meaning of the modern term AUGURY, although INAUGUR-
ATIONS are still held to be auspicious occasions. Nowadays
though, we often neglect to watch the birds in the sky to check
that the gods approve of our major projects. In order to observe
birds during the day, and stars during the night, it is sensible to
watch from an elevated place such as a hill. In Rome a hill
chosen for this purpose was the *mons vaticanus* and from there
the prophet or *vates* made his observations. The word VATICI-
NATOR is a term for a prophet, and the place where divine
information was interpreted is still known as the VATICAN HILL,

This character was born in 1512 and understandably caused some consterna-
tion at the time. It is easy to see how monstrous births might be interpreted as
divine warnings, even though the sixteenth century artist responsible for this
picture probably enjoyed a fair degree of artistic licence.

Monsters were not necessarily warnings of ill-fortune; some deformities
were thought to bring luck since they conveyed messages from God. Even
now it is considered to be lucky to have, or to touch, a hunchback. To feel
lucky is to have a HUNCH.

the palace upon it being the VATICAN. Within resides the
PONTIFF who fulfils a similar role to his pre-Christian counterpart, the chief *pontifex* or *pontifex maximus*. But one should
really expect there to be a TEMPLE on top of the hill since the
heavenly space marked off for observation by the vaticinator
was known as a *templum*. Another method of obtaining information was to consult the *oraculum* or, as it would now be called,
the ORACLE. Like many a fortune-teller the *oraculum* or 'little
mouth' usually managed to make its utterances as general or
ambiguous as possible. Also ambiguous is the origin of the word
'omen' which may be related to a Latin word meaning 'to speak'
or alternatively to one meaning 'to hear'; either way *omen*,
disguised as '*omin*' has found a home in the words OMINOUS and
ABOMINABLE.

In modern England the counterpart of a Roman *oraculum* is a
reader of palms. To PALMISTS, as to medieval alchemists, the
parts of the hand correspond to the planets. The thumb belongs
to Mars, the index finger to the Sun and the little finger to
Venus, while two bumps or mounts on the palm itself are
associated with Mercury and the Moon. The ring finger was
called by the Romans *digitus annularis* which means exactly the
same thing – 'ring finger'. Rings were originally worn upon that
finger because it was believed that a nerve ran from it directly to
the heart; for this reason marriage and engagement rings are
traditionally worn there. Also because of this belief the ring
finger was thought of as the medical finger; it was a sort of probe
which communicated immediately with the all important car-
diac control centre. To the Anglo-Saxons, therefore, it was the
lech man, healing finger. The name is no longer used but the
word LEECH is still applied to healers, whether they be blood-
suckers or medical practitioners, or both. Other Anglo-Saxon
names for the fingers have also fallen into disuse. The little
finger or pinkie, was known as the *ear man* for obvious reasons;
the middle finger was simply the *long man* and the index finger
the *scite man*, shooting finger. The thumb, however, has retained its name almost unchanged; it was originally called a
thuma, literally a 'swollen' finger.

As a chirurgeon or surgeon is one who works using his or her hands and a chiropodist is one who cares for hands and (more commonly) feet, so the less respectable CHIROMANCER is a 'hand diviner'. CHIROMANCY, derived from the Greek *cheir* meaning hand and *manteia*, divination, is a more explicit synonym for PALMISTRY. In English there are dozens of words which incorporate the Greek word for divination, the best known of which is NECROMANCY, the name applied to the doubtful practice of obtaining information from a corpse or *necros*. In the Middle Ages it was thought that the word was formed from the Latin *neger*, black, and it was thus spelt NEGROMANCY; as a result of the confusion we now talk about the 'black art' and 'black magic'. Using a magic wand the technique of divination is rhabdomancy and employing an oracle it is theomancy; the communication implied is from the gods because DIVINATION implies *divine* agency. Watching the flight of birds is now popular as ornithology but to the Romans it was a more serious business already mentioned and known as ornithomancy. Reading the future from animals' entrails is called HIEROMANCY because the sacrificial victim is holy: the first part of the word is from the Greek *hieros* meaning 'sacred', as in the words HIEROglyph, meaning sacred writing, and HIERarchy, literally 'sacred rule'. If the sacrificial victim is human the practice is anthropomancy; less drastic is the use of dice, cleromancy, or of playing cards; cartomancy.

Almost every aspect of the occult mentioned in these last two chapters has, at one time or another, played a part in divination. Even the four elements of the Middle Ages could be employed in such practices: geomancy, using earth, austromancy, using air, pyromancy, fire, and hydromancy, water. Paralleling meteorology and astrology (now astronomy) are meteoromancy and astromancy; and there are other such terms for dowsing, tea-leaf reading, crystal gazing and a host of practices which, to the disbeliever, seem even more bizarre. Although few of these words are in common use they serve to demonstrate how important various forms of divination have been in the past, when people were almost as gullible as they are today.

6

Say the magic word

The idea that fate can be affected by divine intervention on behalf of mere human beings is thought to be almost as old as mankind. Details of the supposed mechanics change from time to time, however; current methods of supposed intercession and agency are called religion while the discarded techniques, often half forgotten, are collectively known as magic. Having served time in the domain of magic, old religious words tend to drift into new areas of usage and it is sometimes possible to trace a word's progress from ancient religion through medieval superstition all the way to modern lay usage. Thus, for example, the Ancient Hebrew word *qabbalah* meaning 'received divine law' developed into the English term CABBALA, sometimes spelled CABALA: it is applied to more or less the same thing, but that law is now regarded as a secret magical doctrine. Later the English word also produced a clipped form, CABAL, without the final vowel. When first used this word denoted a small number of initiates such as those who possessed knowledge of the Cabbala. By coincidence a group of seventeenth century government ministers had surnames or titles with the initial letters C, A, B, A and L. So it is that the word cabal has now come to be applied to any small group of secret schemers whose intrigues parallel those of Clifford, Ashley, Buckingham, Arlington and Lauderdale.

The best known cabalistic word must surely be ABRACADABRA: now virtually meaningless, it was once believed to be a powerful invocation, being made up of parts of various Hebrew names for the Deity. The Christian god later provided another magical term, HOCUS POCUS. Formerly uttered while a supposedly magical trick was being performed, it is a corruption of *hoc est Corpus*, the opening Latin words of consecration in the Roman Catholic Mass. Another derivative is the word HOAX which seems to suggest that the supposedly superstitious masses were not too naïvely credulous after all. Both hocus pocus and abracadabra were part of the PATTER. This word has a similar derivation. It also comes from the Church and is derived from the Latin *pater noster*, 'Our Father', the opening words of the Lord's Prayer. Another example of patter, still in common use, is the word 'presto' as in 'Hey presto!'; it was used in order to make an object disappear, just as the formula 'Hey jingo!' was used to make such an object reappear. From jingo came the exclamation 'by jingo!' which was included in a popular music hall song during the Russo–Turkish War of the 1870s. At the time there was a danger of Great Britain becoming involved and patriotic fervour ran high. From the lines,

> We don't want to fight, but by *Jingo* if we do,
> We've got the ships, we've got the men, we've got the money
> too . . .

came the new word JINGOISM meaning aggressive patriotism. The earlier usage of the word jingo has become obsolete, probably because of the useful function performed by its later derivative, but some of the other occult terms have retained at least a vague association with stage magic. The modern illusionist may literally have something up his sleeve but, metaphorically the trickster also has something up his. Even without a long sleeve it is still possible to 'palm off' fraud as truth.

Illusionists are often referred to as magicians or conjurers but rarely as sorcerers. In fact none of these latter three titles originally carried implications of deception. MAGICIAN comes from the word *magi*, the plural of *magus*, originally denoting a member of an ancient Persian priestly caste. The three wise men referred to in the Bible were not kings at all, merely magi. CONJURERS were originally only conspirators who swore an oath together: their name being formed from the Latin *con*, together, and *jurare*, to swear. Because of the attendant secrecy and sacred oaths used, suspicions were aroused and the word attached itself to those who secretly tried to summon good or evil spirits. Another Latin word *sors*, meaning 'one's lot in life', produced the word SORCER and then SORCERER to describe one who tried to influence fate. The same root also provided the word SORT, to arrange, and the phrase OUT OF SORTS, out of proper arrangement.

Popular modern ideas of ancient magic bear little relationship to historical fact; the professional illusionist, the film industry and the Church have seen to that. In order to gain popularity, the practices of the early Church were sufficiently flexible to adopt any important traditions which it encountered. Popular festivals of pagan gods were happily encompassed and then, if possible, later abandoned. Pagan gods were cobbled together to produce that ultimate incarnate evil: the Devil, with cloven hooves, horns and a tail. The idea that witches worshipped the Devil is a pure invention of the Christian religion. The Anglo-Saxons originally worshipped the gods of their Germanic fore-fathers and it was this Old Religion which, in early times, rivalled Christianity in England. As Christianity gained the upper hand, the Old Religion was represented as a parody of all that was holy. Thus witchcraft, Anglo-Saxon *wiccecraeft*, eventually became punishable by death in the fifteenth century, when the Christian Church had become sufficiently powerful to enforce its repressive ideas. Originally denoting one who knows, foretells or averts, the word WITCH was applied to those who knew and followed the Old Religion. Now it is usually used of women, and more rarely of men, although the original

Anglo-Saxon forms distinguish between *wicce*, feminine, and *wicca*, masculine. A wise man is specifically known as a *'wise-ard'* or WIZARD: again the underlying sin is nothing more than knowledge. The same unfavourable association of ability and supposed abuse of that ability has affected the present meanings of the words ARTFUL, CRAFTY, CUNNING, KNOWING and SLY, all of which originally meant only 'skilful' or 'informed'.

An enchanter is one who enchants and enchantment is accomplished by incantation: the words INCANT and ENCHANT are both derived in the same way, from the Latin *in*, into, and *cantare*, to chant or sing. The song itself is a CHANT or CHANTY or, as we usually spell it now, SHANTY. As an enchanter enchants by singing so a caster of spells SPELLBINDS and a witch BE-WITCHES. The PRESTIDIGITATOR looks as though his name is derived from *presto* and *digitator*, meaning something like 'finger manipulator', but curiously the word has a different derivation: it comes from a Latin word meaning 'to blindfold' and thence 'hoodwink'. The prestidigitator's dazzling tricks literally gave him PRESTIGE, although the word is now applied to those who dazzle by their other accomplishments. GLAMOUR has undergone a similar transformation: in medieval works on witchcraft the word is used to describe spectral appearances and disappearances. One particularly upsetting application seems to have been the use of a glamour to deprive a man of his 'virile member': the subject warranted a whole chapter in a work entitled *Malleus Malificarum*, literally 'The Hammer of the Witches'. From the spectral appearances, rather than dis-appearances, comes the later meaning of deceptive beauty. Again the connection with knowledge is striking for GLAMOUR and GRAMMAR share the same root, the Greek word *grammatike*. Another related term, GRIMOIRE, shows the connection between them because it is the name of a learned book (like a grammar) on magic (or glamour). The same association of ideas is con-tained in the word SPELL, Anglo-Saxon *spellian*. To recite letters is to spell and to recite certain words might be to cast a spell. Another word which has followed the course similar to that of the glamour is CHARM. Like ENCHANT and INCANT it is related to the Latin word for song; from there it has provided a verb meaning to bewitch and, more usually, to captivate or delight; as a noun it also keeps its magical properties, being used as the name of an object with magical influence, a CHARM. A TALISMAN is another object with occult power; through Arabic its name comes from the Greek word *telesma* which meant 'mystery'. From the Provençal *masco*, a sorcerer, comes the modern MASCOT and from Latin via Portuguese and French comes the word *fetiche*, or more commonly FETISH. Such magical objects were often worn to ward off evil; in particular evil spirits and even death could be kept at bay by their judicious use. In order to minimise infant mortality a mother might employ the powers of an AMULET; named directly from the Latin *amuletum*, the word ultimately derives from *amolire letum* which means 'to turn away death'.

Belief in supernatural beings such as elves seems to have been remarkably widespread and the English language has adopted names from a number of sources: as well as brownies from Scotland and piskies (also known as pixies) from the West Country, there are FAIRIES from fairyland, the land of the 'fey'. Actually their name is probably derived indirectly from the Latin *fata*, meaning the Fates. From various Teutonic words come the names of the familiar dwarf, troll and goblin. These beings were believed to live underground and not to welcome the intrusion of human miners into their domain. Various mining mishaps were attributed to their malign influence and in particular they were blamed when ores did not yield the metals being sought. *Kupfernickel* was the name for the German goblin thought to be responsible for preventing the extraction of copper, but in reality there was no copper to be smelted: the element eventually found to be responsible for the deception was named after *Kupfernickel* and is now known simply as NICKEL. In a similar way another goblin, *Kobald*, gave his name to the element COBALT. In England, goblins were often named *Robin* and from this came the term ROB-GOBLIN which has since been corrupted to HOB-GOBLIN. A similar creature was ROBIN GOODFELLOW who was so called in order to appease him, for he may not have been such a good fellow after all. In the same way GOODMANS CROFT was, and perhaps still is, a term applied to part of a field left unploughed in deference to the original fairy owner.

The word GNOME is formed from the Greek elements *ge*, earth, and *nomos*, a dweller. Because a favourite pastime of gnomes was supposed to be counting treasure which they kept in dark recesses underground, the phrase 'gnomes of Zurich' provides a vivid mental picture of modern Swiss bankers who similarly dwell in secret underground vaults and have stacks of money to count. Also from the underworld is the OGRE, but he appears to have been the invention of a Frenchman in the seventeenth century. Perhaps the word is fashioned after the name *orcus*, a god of the underworld. A more recent addition to the language is the word GREMLIN which seems to have been coined by members of the RAF soon after World War I. Just as the goblins made things go wrong in the mines, so GREMLINS caused problems to occur in aeroplanes; the name probably derives from *Fremlin's*, a Kentish brewery which provided the airmen's supply of bottled beer. Other words which have acquired a connection with the supernatural are many and varied. An IMP was once no more than a graft or offshoot but, perhaps from phrases such as 'imps of Satan' and unrelated words such as impious, the word came to be associated with a small demon or mischievous sprite. A medium is a conveyor of news but the plural forms show two separate developments: the MEDIA convey information from the living and MEDIUMS convey it from the dead. A GENIUS was once a guiding spirit which stayed with a man throughout his life; the word is now used to indicate a person of exceptional ability but the plural GENII is sometimes confused with the word GENIE which comes from JINN, the Arabic *jinni*, a spirit which can be trapped in a bottle (but not to be confused with gin). A variation of the original Roman belief was that each man had a good genius and an evil genius: the EVIL GENIUS is still busy but the other one seems to be redundant.

Some supernatural creatures are deliberately invented and

some have continued to exist within the human mind down the ages since the dawn of history. Others survived for centuries until they were distorted beyond recognition. Films based upon Robert Louis Stevenson's *Dr Jekyll and Mr Hyde*, first published in 1886, have completely altered the concept of a WERE-WOLF which dates back at least to Anglo-Saxon times; then *wer* meant 'man' and a werewolf was literally a man-wolf, a man who could change into a wolf at will. Bram Stoker's *Dracula*, published in 1897, introduced the modern idea of a vampire which is really a composite creature whose characteristics are drawn from a number of sources. The man upon whom the Count in the book was based was almost certainly Vlad V, also called 'Vlad the Impaler', who died (permanently) in the fifteenth century. Before the Victorian Age, literary monsters contented themselves with the destruction of things other than ancient beliefs. Mary Wollstonecraft Shelley wrote *Frankenstein* in order to compete in an informal horror story competition with, amongst others, her poet husband. It was published in 1818 and is notable for having provided an entirely new and useful word to the language. A FRANKENSTEIN is properly one who creates a monster which cannot be controlled, not the monster itself.

The outrages perpetrated by Hollywood have been far worse than anything that werewolves, vampires or Frankenstein's monster could ever have accomplished. Distorting the truth beyond recognition is an art form in itself and the supreme masters, the ones who invented Satanism and gave witchcraft a bad name, have caused a great deal of change in the English language. Their activities, fictions and propaganda are more than enough to fill a book. Like Dr Frankenstein's monster, those created by the Church tend to cause their inventors more trouble than could ever have been expected and in the next few chapters words like dogma, nepotism, propaganda, pontificate and sinecure will tell their own revealing stories.

Vlad V, otherwise known as Vlad the Impaler. He is enjoying breakfast in conducive surroundings.

Vlad V's father seems to have been the first Walachian ruler to bear the title *Dracul*, which in Romanian means 'devil'. The suffix '-a' has been used in this part of the world to mean 'son of' so the name DRACULA probably means son of the Evil One.

7

Holy . . .

Magic bears the same relationship to religion that superstition bears to taboo; the religious taboos of yesterday are only the magical superstitions of today and the religious taboos of today will be the magical superstitions of tomorrow – for what seems obvious to one generation is inexplicable to the next, and what is venerated in one culture may be laughable in another. To follow the supernatural path from the realm of religion to the domain of magic has been the fate of many words and phrases. Once *Mumbo Jumbo* was the name of a god, now the expression signifies little more than nonsense: the path is downhill all the way.

Many religions have contributed vocabulary to the English language and beliefs to the established Church. Amongst the contributors are the old religions which once flourished in Western Europe, for they have provided the Evil One along with his malign cohorts. Other important contributors are the gods of Greece and Rome but most important is the Middle Eastern religion whence comes the Christian god: identical with the Islamic deity, the Jewish god is also the Christian one. Some words with religious associations are taken directly from the ancient Jewish language: for example, SABBATH. Others have been translated into Greek and Latin and then taken into English from those languages, while yet others have been translated into English and still produced new words. How this can happen is well illustrated by the word SCAPEGOAT. English already had the terms 'escape' and 'goat' but an '*escapegoat*' was unknown; hardly surprising since the ancient practice of trans-ferring sin on to an animal, and then allowing it to run off into the wilderness, was unknown to the Old Religion.

Yet another way in which English words have been created is by mis-translation of the original Hebrew, and thus it is that the

divine protagonist and antagonist of Christianity are both misnamed. JEHOVAH is the more interesting mistake: to the Jews the name of God, *Jhvh* pronounced something like 'Jahweh', was thought to be too dreadful to speak out loud so the word *adonai*, approximating in meaning to 'lord', was used instead. In order to show that the word *Jhvh* was meant, but that the word *adonai* was to be substituted, the scribes created a compound of the letters JHVH with the vowels, or equivalent marks, of *adonai*, and this accounts for the form of the made-up word JAHOVAH or JEHOVAH. Another way to avoid saying the word *Jhvh* was to speak of it as 'the four letter word', or in Greek, the TETRAGRAMMATION. The word for god in many Indo-European languages has four letters: in Sanskrit it is *diva*; in French, *dieu*; in Spanish it is *dios*; in Latin, *deus* and in Greek, *theos* (in Greek a single letter, Θ, stands for the sound now represented in English as 'th') and all these words are thought to be derived ultimately from a single source. Specific names of chief gods also tend to be four-lettered: for example, the Scandinavian *Odin*, Roman *Jove* and Greek *Zeus*. The English word 'God' is very old and related to similar terms in other Teutonic tongues; although it has only three letters its German cousin *Gott* follows the more usual pattern of having four.

The abode of God is heaven, a haven for the angelic armies. Originally this was thought to be above the sky, for the word 'sky' meant cloud and 'heaven' meant the firmament overhead. Also resident there are the Seraphim, Cherubim, Thrones, Dominions, Virtues, Powers, Principalities, Archangels and Angels, ranked in decreasing order of importance. The terms SERAPHIM and CHERUBIM, plural forms of SERAPH and CHERUB, have come to England along the well-worn Hebrew–Greek–Latin–Old English route. Like the fairies, they were originally more or less the same size as human beings, but in the last few hundred years they seem to have regressed into childhood. Each of the nine orders is mentioned in the Apocrypha, although little is heard of them nowadays and only the angels and archangels play a significant part in the New Testament. Here Jesus is referred to as the anointed one: in Greek this is rendered *Christos* and in Latin *Christus* from which we have the title CHRIST; but the Hebrew equivalent was *mashiah*, a word which has become an alternative epithet MESSIAH.

As the Christian religion absorbed other, older faiths, the indigenous gods had to be evicted. This might be a slow process and, for a while, old and new gods would co-exist. Gradual eviction can be observed today in South and Central America; and just how bizarre the resulting hybrid religion can be is demonstrated by cults such as voodoo which are still at an intermediate stage. If precedents are followed then the non-Christian elements will eventually become Satanic, then they will be played down, and finally, if possible, abandoned. But sometimes the Church has not been able to destroy the monsters which it has created. Like Frankenstein's monster, the Church's are fashioned from corpses and the Devil himself is made up of dismembered parts of ancient, dead gods which have been put together to terrorise the credulous.

The nearest that the Rabbinical scribes got to a carnal devil was *Seirizzim* which meant 'goat'. This poor old goat was crossed with the Greek god Pan who was not generally approved of for various reasons – for one thing he had a reputation for enjoying himself, and for another, he had a habit of scaring travellers. The terror which he induced was called PANIC FEAR and is now termed simply PANIC. Pan, being half-goat, made an ideal prototype devil complete with horns, a tail, shaggy hair and cloven hooves. Borrowing Neptune's TRIDENT, the name of which means literally 'three teeth', and some of the characteristics of the Norse god Loki, he was almost complete. Various names for this composite creature are also drawn from a number of sources: DEVIL comes from the Greek *diabolos*, traducer or slanderer, which has also provided the word DIABOLICAL. SATAN sounds less evil for that name is the Hebrew *Satan*, an adversary or enemy. Less threatening still is LUCIFER: named from the Latin word *lucifer*, light bringer, and generally applied to the 'morning star' which is now known as the planet Venus. The use of the word as a synonym for the Devil arose through one of the many mistakes made when translating the Bible; it seems to have arisen because a king of Babylon once called himself 'day star' (Isaiah XIV, 4). The word for 'day star' was translated as Lucifer, a fact which seems to have been rationalised to produce the story of an archangel falling from Heaven. The expulsion of a god or demi-god from Paradise is a common theme in mythology and makes a much better tale than having a pre-sumptuous mortal fall off a tower. A better use of the word Lucifer in Victorian times was to describe a match, which really does bring light.

One of Jhvh's early competitors was called *baal*. This semitic word meant 'possessor' or 'lord of' and could thus be prefixed to another word. *Baalzebub* or *Beelzebub* was probably a god who was the 'Lord of the high dwelling' but, perhaps to make him less appealing, his title has often been rendered as 'Lord of the flies'. The Greek gods were also seen as a threat so the minor deities, or *daimon*, were conscripted as DEMONS into the evil hordes. To the Greeks they had been relatively harmless but now DEMONS are indistinguishable from the equally imaginary Satanic devils. There are a large number of other names for the Devil; some of their origins are known, some are not. DEUCE seems to be related to throwing an unlucky number (two) at dice. OLD NICK is reputedly derived from the name of Niccolo Machiavelli who seems not to have been universally popular. The original possessor of the epithet is much more likely to have been the German goblin known as Nickel, but *Macchiavelli* is certainly responsible for the term MACCHIAVELLIAN. OLD SCRATT is related to the Norse supernatural being called *Skratte* and OLD HORNEY may or may not have an obvious derivation, but DICKENS is a mystery: perhaps related to DICKON and thus Richard, it is certainly nothing to do with Charles Dickens who was born centuries after the first use of the phrase 'what the Dickens . . .' – in the sense of 'what the Devil . . .'

Ideas of heaven and hell developed as the character of the Devil was cobbled together from a rag bag of old religions. PARADISE was originally no more than a walled garden or enclosed park: the Old Persian word *pairidaeza* being adopted by the Greeks from whom it has passed into English. The abode of the dead, according to Teutonic mythology, was called *hele*; the word indicating a hidden or covered place (related to it is the modern word HELMET which covers the head and also the word for a large covered building, a HALL). The goddess who ruled this domain was *hel* and she originally had charge of all the dead irrespective of how they had lived or died. Later the belief grew up that those who had died in battle would be rewarded with a place in VALHALLA or *valhöll*, literally the hall of the slain. *Hele*, like the Greek underworld, was not necessarily an unpleasant place in which to find oneself – until it was ceded to the Christians. HELL was then used to translate the word GEHENNA, another arrival from the Hebrew language through Greece and Rome. The original form *gehinnom* meant merely the 'valley of Hinnom', a place where the god Moloch was worshipped. Later imaginations produced such stirring concepts as LIMBO refer- ring to the supposed borders of hell and named after the Latin expression *in limbo*, itself formed from the word *limbus* mean- ing simply 'border'; and from the Latin verb *purgare*, to clean or purge, came the name of the place where sins are supposed to be PURGED, PURGATORY.

SAINTS, who are so-named from the Latin *sanctus* because they are supposed to be holy, like their superiors are not always who they appear to be. *St Audrey*, for example, whose name provided the word TAWDRY, was really called Etheldrida. St Valentine was several different people, at least two of whom have 14 February as their special day. This day was celebrated as *Lupercalia* by the Romans who noted that birds mate at around this time of year. The association is the source of the Valentine's day customs still observed, or rather recently in- vented, and it also seems to have influenced the saint's name: the Old French *Galantine*, meaning a lover, has produced VALENTINE as well as GALLANT. Another saint with even less convincing credentials is St Vitus. He was originally a European god known to the Slavs as *Scanto-vid*, a name which became SAINT VITUS without too much effort on the part of those who converted him. The worship of this god involved wild and ecstatic dancing on the part of adherents and this revelry gave

In the good old days, before social workers had been invented, the 'jaws of Hell' really were the jaws of Hell.

Hell was the place of all the demons, and Milton coined another word for the infernal regions which meant exactly that: from the Greek elements *pan*, all, and *daemon*, DEMON, we have the term PANDEMONIUM.

its name to a medical condition, one symptom of which is uncontrolled jerking of the limbs; the condition is commonly known as ST VITUS'S DANCE but to medical practitioners it is CHOREA, so-called from the Latin phrase *chorea Sancti Viti* which again means no more than 'dance of St Vitus'. Readopting pagan ways, St Nicholas, another saint with a suspiciously pagan history has had his German name *Santa Nikolaus* anglicised to SANTA CLAUS; like those other survivors from ancient times, the fairies, he still has to be appeased by the offer of a vestigial sacrifice – usually a mince pie and a glass of milk.

Lighting fires under unfortunate old women, dead soldiers or corpses of plague victims resulted in *bone-fires* or, as the modern form has it, BONFIRES. But the earlier reason for lighting huge fires each autumn was to help the weakening sun-god through the winter. The festival was actually celebrated at the beginning of the Old Celtic year (1 November) which the Church adopted as All Saints' Day or All Hallow's Day. The fires were moved to 5 November after the Gunpowder Plot but the Church has never been altogether happy about the end of the Old Celtic year when natural laws were thought to be suspended. Thus it is that the day before All Hallow's Day, All Hallow's Eve or HALLOWE'EN, still has its evil connotations. Three months after All Hallow's Day comes Candlemas corresponding to another Celtic festival; three months after that day is May Day, corresponding to another one; and three months after that is Lammas, matching yet another. It is interesting to note how closely these days correlate with the Scottish quarter days; in the same way Anglo-Saxon festivals match up with other Christian festivals and with the English quarter days.

Old gods never die they only fade into sainthood.

8

. . . Holy . . .

Just as the Church took over the most popular festivals of older religions, so the churches took over their holy sites. The most spectacular example of this occurred at Knowleton in Dorset where the local church was built inside a Neolithic stone circle, but other examples are many and varied. A number of Celtic gods feature on early altars and fonts, and the cult of the ancient 'green man' or woodland spirit is reflected in more recent churches as well as modern public houses. Often sacred yew groves provided a suitable site for new buildings and this explains why, even now, yew trees feature in so many church-yards. In early Anglo-Saxon times it was not unknown for churches to have two altars: one for the Christian god and one for another, older deity. Blood sacrifices certainly occurred in churches at this time, and until relatively recent times (the last recorded is 1897) the ancient practice of burying animal sacri-fices under new constructions was continued for new churches as well as for other buildings. Often the deity to whom the site was sacred later became a saint to whom the church was dedicated. Where this happened it is not uncommon to find that the church does not lie on an accurate East–West axis, but rather along an axis directed towards the point on the horizon where the sun rises on the appropriate god's or saint's day.

Saints are, by definition, supposed to be holy but angels are merely functional as their title shows, for the word ANGEL is ultimately derived from the Greek *aggelos* which meant 'messenger'. In the Bible angels are divine messengers, more modest earthly couriers being APOSTLES so-called from the Greek *apostolos* meaning 'one who is sent away'. They were sent to convey news and this they did by carrying an *epistole*, or as we might now say in English an EPISTLE. A number of such epistles or letters are included in the New Testament. The Bible itself takes its name from the Greek word for a book; it is related to *biblos* meaning the inner bark of papyrus. An early medium for writing upon, the Greek *papyros* was simply a primitive form of PAPER, the name of which has also provided the English word PAPYRUS. Even though peppered with errors, mistranslations and self-contradictions, the Bible was held to be literally and absolutely true; this belief has resulted in the expression GOSPEL TRUTH, the first word of which is descended from the Old English *godspel* meaning 'good news'. After the Reformation, the Protestants realised that some books of the Bible which had previously been included in the vulgate version were of extremely doubtful validity. Those of the most dubious authenticity were relegated to the APOCRYPHA, a collection whose name is derived from the Greek *apokrypto* meaning 'hide away'. Because of the nature of the material included in the Apocrypha the word APOCRYPHAL can now be applied to any unlikely or obviously false story. Other Biblical words which have found their way into the English language include a number of personal names such as JONAH, applied to people who bring bad luck, and CAIN, as in the phrase TO RAISE CAIN meaning 'to raise the Devil'.

From the city known as Sodom comes the name of the practice of SODOMY and of its practitioners, SODOMITES or simply SODS. Ephraimites, however, lead more mundane lives: their only claim to fame resulted from an inability to pronounce the sound 'sh'. When the Gileadites wanted to identify an enemy from Ephraim the suspect would be required to say SHIBBOLETH, the name of a river chosen merely because it contains the 'sh' sound. Ephraimites could not pronounce the word properly, the nearest they could get being something like 'sibboleth', and so it was that the term SHIBBOLETH came to denote a test-word or pass-word and thus an obstacle.

Not to be confused with the mother of Jesus is another biblical Mary, Mary Magdalene, traditionally depicted in Church art as weeping after the crucifixion. Because of this characterisation the unfortunate woman has given her name to the word MAUDLIN which is now used to describe *mawkish* states such as hers. Bearing testament to the connection are the Oxford and Cambridge colleges whose names are spelled 'Magdalen' and 'Magdalene', respectively, but both pronounced 'Maudlin'. Because of ambiguous wording in Luke's gospel Mary Magdalene is often thought to have been a reformed prostitute; hence the term MAGDALENE meaning either a reformed prostitute or a home for fallen women. Also from the Bible comes the title of the modern PHILISTINES who acquired their unenviable title in Germany as a result of a university pun on the word *philister*, a term applied to the uneducated townspeople. Another biblical group, the *Maccabees* seem to have given their family name to the English language where it lives on as the term MACABRE.

The fate of the word 'apocryphal' is similar to that of LEGEND, derived from the Latin *legenda* meaning 'what is read'. Originally a legend was a collection of stories such as the ones which dealt with the lives of saints, but these stories were so obviously exaggerated or patently untrue that the word LEGEND acquired a secondary meaning of myth. What was not fit to be read by Roman Catholics was, until 1966, decided by a Papal body, the free flow of knowledge being too much of a threat when in competition with legend, dogma and propaganda. Even the word BAN shows, through its development, how changes in meaning reflect the changing role of the Church. The Teutonic *bannan* meant 'to summon' and this old usage is retained in the name of the marriage BANNS, but the singular word BAN attached itself to a curse, then to an interdict, then to a supernatural invocation, to an execration and finally to a prohibition. To take another example, the word ANATHEMA has come to be applied to anything accursed; from the Greek *ana*, up, and *tithenai*, to set, the word was originally used in connection with offerings which were 'set up' or devoted to a god. Such offerings were regarded as fortunate, but if they were living animals then they were doomed, and thus the word became associated with those who were beyond salvation. Anathema was eventually regarded as even worse than EXCOMMUNICATION, the cutting off of someone from communication with the Church. Incidentally the ceremony of excommunication, or one version of it, involved the use of bell, book and candle: the bell would be tolled as for one who was dead, the book closed and the candle extinguished. Hence the association between the supernatural and the phrase BELL, BOOK AND CANDLE.

During the history of the Catholic Church it has not been unknown for rival popes to excommunicate each other. Kings, whole countries and schismatic sects were also popular recipients of the treatment and even comets have been excommunicated in the past. Although there are hundreds of Christian sects it is quite common for them to incorporate the word 'catholic' into their titles. This use of the word might have had some justification before the Great Schism of 1054 when the Eastern and Western Churches separated, but is now coloured with irony. The original Greek word *katholikos*, which literally meant 'concerning the whole', produced the word CATHOLIC, meaning general, universal, comprehensive and thus broadminded and tolerant. Many English words serve as their own opposites and in this respect it is sometimes important to distinguish between the terms 'catholic' and 'Catholic'. The PROTESTANT Churches are so-called because of their original *protests* concerning Roman Catholic practices, and protesting more than most, at a later date, were the PURITANS, a group who have done more than anyone to give the pursuit of *purity* a bad name.

At the head of the Roman Catholic Church is the POPE who

takes his name from the Greek children's word for father, *pappas*. Similarly the more junior ABBOT takes his name from a word of the same meaning, *abba*, which arrived in Greece having been originally invented by babies in the Middle East. Popes are elected from the College of CARDINALS upon whom the Church hinges, as their title shows for the Latin word *cardo* means simply 'hinge'. A BISHOP takes his title from a Teutonic form of the Greek *episkopos*, literally meaning 'overseer'. Had the word EPISCOPAL not already found a place in the English language, the familiar submarine periscope (so-called because it looks around) might well have been called an 'episcope' since it also looks over or 'oversees'. The Latin word for a seat, *sedes*, provides the bishop with the name of his SEE; and the Greek word for the same thing, *kathedra*, is used to distinguish a bishop's church from any other, for a place of worship which possesses a bishop's throne is a CATHEDRAL church or more usually simply a CATHEDRAL.

PRIESTS are so-called from the Old English *preost*; this word is related to the Greek *presbyteros* which means 'elder' and from the same source come the words PRESBYTERIAN and PRESTER. RECTORS get their titles from the Latin word *rector*, a ruler; they are distinguished from vicars who are technically only 'stand-ins' and so not entitled to all of the tithes due to the church. The word VICAR, like VICARIOUS, comes from the Latin *vicarius* which means 'deputy'. The DEAN and DEACON, like the Roman *decanus*, obtained their titles by virtue of having ten underlings, but the more humble PARSON is only an ecclesiastical *'person'*. More humble still is the MINISTER, a servant of the Crown or of the Church, whose Roman superior or *magister* has provided both of the titles MASTER and MISTER. Like the abbot and Pope, the PADRE is really a father: the Spanish, Italian and Portuguese word *padre* corresponding to the Latin *pater*, the source of PATRONAGE, itself often to be found in the hands of PATRIARCHS. FRIARS derive their title from the Latin word for brother, *frater*, while PASTORS get theirs from their function. Both the PASTOR and the PASTORAL shepherd are responsible for the well-being of their flocks, a responsibility taken over from the great god Pan

This is what happens to SIMONISTS: people who, like the biblical Simon Magus, traffic in supernatural powers or church offices. Simon tried to buy the power of blessing (Acts 8, 9–24).

whose name is related to theirs and to the Latin verb *pascere*, to feed. Also named after his function is the CURATE who has the *cure* (i.e. care) of souls; but a post which involves no work because there are no parishioners is 'without care' or *sine cure*. This Latin phrase accounts for the modern English word SINECURE, a term applied to any office which provides benefits for no effort. Within the last few hundred years church offices, especially sinecures, could openly be bought as investments or distributed as bribes.

The CLERGYMAN is really an inheritor, for the title comes from the Greek *kleros*, a lot or inheritance. Because the CLERGY of the Middle Ages enjoyed a virtual monopoly in the fields of education and writing, the CLERIC developed into the modern CLERK. Since clerics provided virtually the only outlet for vendors of writing equipment, it became customary for suppliers' stands to be set up outside religious establishments. As these stalls became permanent fixtures, they were said to be STATIONARY, from the Latin *statio*, to stand, and a similar word, STATIONERY, came to be used to describe the sort of things that they sold. From the Latin *scribere*, to write, came a host of English words such as SCRIBE, SCRIBBLE and SCRIPT along with derivatives like ASCRIBE, SUBSCRIBE (literally to underwrite), INSCRIBE, TRANSCRIBE, PROSCRIBE, PRESCRIBE and DESCRIBE, as well as the terms MANUSCRIPT (written by hand), NONDESCRIPT (literally 'not written down', figuratively not worth writing home about) and the trailing POSTSCRIPT, written after the bulk of the script. From the same ultimate source came the Old English *scrifan*, to decree in writing; later the word came to be applied to written judgements, then to the penance imposed and finally to the absolution subsequently granted; the modern form SHRIVE is more commonly encountered in the guise of SHROVE (as in SHROVE Tuesday) and another form features in the expression SHORT SHRIFT, which is literally what condemned prisoners used to get, being allowed a brief confession before their execution. Also related is the Old English word *scrin* which has developed into the modern English SHRINE. Originally it denoted the chest or box in which expensive writing materials were locked, but other valuables could also be stored there and, in particular, sacred relics could be kept safe. In numerous such shrines throughout Europe were preserved tons of timber from the one true cross, gallons of holy blood, heaps of dismembered saintly limbs and a volume of bones greater than each of their legendary owners could reasonably have fitted into an elephant.

Competition was strong when it came to claims about exactly what shrines contained. The more outrageous the claim, the better the prospect of making money out of credulous pilgrims who would be tempted to visit the holy place. Saintly flesh was supposed to smell rather pleasant as it decomposed and thus was born the phrase THE ODOUR OF SANCTITY contrasting to the more usual STENCH OF CORRUPTION which resulted from ordinary putrefying flesh. From the practice of placing relics and icons on plinths comes the phrase TO PUT ON A PEDESTAL and from the custom of lighting candles in front of these idols came the phrase TO HOLD A CANDLE TO . . .

Those who travelled through the country to visit such shrines were called PILGRIMS, their name having come into English by way of France and Italy from Rome where *peregrinus* meant foreigner. Made up from *per*, through, and *ager*, a field or countryside, the word is still used in English as a man's name PEREGRINE, a bird's name PEREGRINE falcon and also as part of the word PEREGRINATION. At one time the word peregrine was used almost interchangeably with the alternative pilgrim. Those who peregrinated to *Rome* are at least partially responsible for the verb to ROAM, while those who rode to Thomas à Becket's shrine at Canterbury did so at a *Canterbury gallop*, a practice which produced the word CANTER. Pilgrims to the Holy Land apparently travelled slower as the word SAUNTER demonstrates for it seems to be a corruption of the Old French for Holy Land, *Saincte Terre*.

The sanctuary in which St Martin's cloak, or what was left of it, was kept became known to the French as the *chapelle*. This word, derived from the Latin *capella*, a little cloak, gave to the English a similar form CHAPEL, now used to denote a place of worship, and also the name of one who officiates there: a CHAPLAIN. Much older than the chapel is the CHURCH; to the Anglo-Saxons a *circe*, or *cirice*, was a holy place the name of which, despite the spelling shows its close relationship to the Northern version, KIRK. Ultimately related to the Greek *kuriakon*, it was not favoured by the early Church whose leaders preferred the word ECCLESIA, itself derived from the verb *ekkalein*, to call out; the *ekklesia* was originally the name given to the General Assembly of Athens. Although the word ECCLESIA failed to displace the naturalised *circe*, a derivative of the word later established itself as ECCLESIASTIC.

An ALTAR, a raised block or table used for sacrifices, takes its name from the Latin *altare* which is related to *altus*, high, and high places were favourite sacrificial sites. Derived from the Latin *sacer*, holy, and *facere*, to make, the word SACRIFICE means just that, to make holy. Since the word HOLY is derived from *halig* meaning whole, and thus perfect, the underlying idea seems to be that the sacrificial victim is made perfect by a ceremonial act. The Anglo-Saxon word *blod* produced the derivative *bledsian* meaning 'to consecrate with blood'; a relative is the French word *blesser*, to wound, but the direct English descendant is the verb to BLESS. That which is sacrificed on the high altar is, or was, indeed blessed. Primitive concepts gradually change and, to fit in with current ideas, are often carefully disguised; but underneath the modern veneer ancient memories still remain.

9

. . . Holy

Very few traditions, such as the delightful one of stoning wrens to death on St Stephen's day, were actually invented by the Church. Most were adopted from existing practices of other religions. For example, Christmas corresponds not only to the Anglo-Saxon Yule but also to the Roman *Saturnalia* and to equivalent festivals in almost every ancient religion. In the Middle Ages it was customary at this time of year to appoint Lords of Misrule to preside over festivities at the Royal Court, in the City of London, at the Universities and elsewhere; similarly cathedrals, churches and schools appointed Boy Bishops who reigned for three weeks over Christmas before the normal order was restored. These customs date from a time when their purpose and consequence were rather more serious. In ancient times the chosen one would enjoy all the rights of his exalted, king-like position for a short time – often only a day – and afterwards would be ritually murdered to ensure the return of the sun or the fertility of the crops in the coming year. In Victorian times vestiges of the custom remained: on Twelfth Night a BEAN KING and a BEAN QUEEN were selected by finding beans in the specially prepared Twelfth Night cake. Now money is substituted for beans and the cake used is a Christmas cake: the reasons are lost but the ancient practices continue. Saturnalian exchanging of roles still occurs in the armed forces where the officers traditionally serve the men on Christmas Day, and ancient sacrificial selection rites are preserved in the procedures associated with children's rhymes such as *London Bridge is falling down* and *Oranges and Lemons*.

During Saturnalia the Romans used sprigs of holly for decoration and, in order to prevent drunkenness, leaves of ivy. Both still play a part in Christmas decorations, as does the Druidic mistletoe which, perhaps because of its ancient fertility associations, is still excluded from churches. A goddess of fertility gave her name to the other great Christian festival, Easter, which is also associated with moon worship, as demonstrated by the method of calculating the dates upon which it falls, for its occurrence is determined by the first full moon on or after the Spring equinox. But the connection with fertility and birth is also strong, as demonstrated by the still-popular Easter eggs and prolific rabbits. Yet another festival which echoes the ancient past is SHROVE TUESDAY, the last day of SHRIVENTIDE when it was customary to have confessions heard, that is, to be *shriven*, but earlier it had been a day of celebrations in imitation of a Roman sacrificial procession. The French name for Shrove Tuesday, MARDI GRAS, means, literally, 'fat Tuesday' and, because this day was the last before the beginning of Lenten fasting, all meat had to be removed or eaten by the end of it. For this reason the season was known as *carnelevarium* from the Latin elements *carno*, flesh, and *levare*, to remove or put away, and from this compound word comes the shorter, modern English term CARNIVAL.

Those who did not follow the main course of Christian thought were generally lucky to survive for very long in the Middle Ages. Whether they did or not, the names given to them invariably tended to acquire uncomplimentary overtones. Those who lived in the countryside were less likely to follow the latest religious fashions than were the fashion-conscious town dwellers, so the people who lived on the heathland were literally HEATHENS. Similarly the Latin word *paganus*, a villager or rustic, was applied to those who continued to follow the old ways, so giving the word PAGAN. But this usage was initially due to early Christians who thought of themselves as members of a sort of early Salvation Army and so called themselves *Milites Christi*, 'soldiers of Christ'. The Roman soldiers had used the word *paganus* in a contemptuous way when referring to civilians and so the soldiers of Christ did likewise. Later, free-thinkers on matters of religion were called LIBERTINES; but thinking for oneself was not encouraged by the Church so the term, which had been derived from the Latin term *libertinus* denoting a freedman, came to be applied to licentious or debauched individuals. More generally those who chose to worship as they pleased were called HERETICS, a word which is derived from the Greek word *hairesis* meaning simply 'choice'. Bulgarians, because they chose to follow the Eastern Orthodox Church, were regarded as particularly unpleasant heretics so that the eleventh century Latin name for a BULGARIAN, Bulgarus, gave rise to the Old French *bougre* and hence the English BUGGER. Those who abandoned the Christian faith, having once adopted it, were called RENEGADES, this description being from the Latin *re*, back, and *negare*, to deny. But those who never adopted the Christian faith in the first place were called MISCREANTS from the Old French description *mescreant*, disbeliever. The words renegade and miscreant were both employed initially to describe people of the Islamic faith as, ironically enough, was the word INFIDEL which comes from the Latin *in*, not, *fidel*, faithful.

Although its origin is not known for certain, the word BULL as applied to an absurd or ludicrous statement may well be derived from the title of a papal BULL or edict, which, in turn, takes its name from the *bulla* or seal attached to it; from the same Latin root come the words BILL and BULLETIN. The Pope's title, Supreme Pontiff, has provided the word PONTIFICATE which usually describes what people do when they are full of 'bull'. To the Greeks the word DOGMA meant only an opinion but from its

A few of the many thousands who met their deaths at the hands of the Inquisition. Burning was favoured because the Church preferred not to spill blood; the civil authorities usually did the messier dirty work on their behalf.

These fifteenth century victims of the Inquisition appear to display an admirably casual attitude towards death by burning. They provided the essential elements of a *bone-fire*, which we now know as a BONFIRE.

religious use it has acquired more than a hint of arrogance. The doctrine of papal infallibility, proclaimed in 1870, cannot have helped to discourage the connection. Also associated with the Roman Catholic Church is the INQUISITION: its name is derived from the Latin *inquisitio* meaning simply 'an enquiry', but it had acquired such appalling connotations that the Congregation of the Inquisition was renamed the 'Holy Office' in 1908. Another papal organisation set up in order to encourage the spread of the official faith has provided the word PROPAGANDA for that body was called the *congregatio de propaganda fide*, the 'congregation for the propagation of the faith'. PATRONAGE is literally due from a father, since the word is related to the Latin *pater*, father, but popes were not supposed to marry and so their illegitimate children were referred to as nephews. These 'nephews' enjoyed disproportionate advantages and so the practice of advancing one's own near relatives became known as NEPOTISM from the Latin word for nephew, *nepos*.

Matters relating to a PARISH are, by definition, PAROCHIAL. Both words are derived from the Greek element *para*, around, and *oikos*, a house; although only the second has acquired a figurative meaning: because parishes are small areas the word parochial has attached itself to people of limited outlook as a description of their views. The inventor of the word MUMPSIMUS seems to have been afflicted with something similar to a parochial attitude; he was a clergyman who consistently used the meaningless word MUMPSIMUS instead of the Latin *sumpsimus* when reading the Mass. When the error was pointed out to him he still preferred his own familiar nonsense word to the real one: thus it has now come to be applied to any erroneous belief which is adhered to, even when disproved.

In the late thirteenth century the theologian John Duns Scotus (from *Duns*, in Scotland) had acquired a reputation for his narrow-minded prejudices which resulted in a modification of his name, DUNCE, being used to describe any exceptionally stupid person. Another churchman who also donated his name to the language was *Lambert le Bègue*; a monastic order was named after him, a lay brother of which was a *beghard*. Since brothers of this order survived by soliciting alms, the words BEGGAR and later BEG came into being to describe them and their activities. Another word which may well be related is BIGOT, but it has also been suggested that this is a corruption of the phrase 'by God'.

Like the Jews before them, the Christians imagined that it was wrong to pronounce the name of their deity except in certain permitted circumstances. In order to avoid the sin of taking the lord's name in vain, the following device was resorted to: one or more letters of the word 'God' could be changed or dropped altogether so no harm was done. This device, known as mincing oaths or cheating the Devil, has been in use for many centuries but was most popular in the seventeenth century. Even in the twentieth century new forms such as GORDON BENNETT and GORDON HIGHLANDERS follow the same fundamental rule that the word must be disguised, in this case by adding further sounds after the initial 'gawd'. Some forms have survived better than others and modern English still possesses many old corruptions: BEGAD, EGAD and GAD are obvious enough, but GADZOOKS (*God's hooks*, i.e. nails) and GADZOONS or GADSWOONS (*God's wounds*) are less so. *God's wounds* also gave ZOUNDS and *God's truth* produced STRUTH or STREWTH. By dropping the initial letter *God's pittikins* (dear pity), *God's bodkins* (dear body) and *God's flesh* became OD'S PITTIKINS, OD'S BODKINS and OD'S FISH, this latter apparently being a particular favourite of Charles II. Changing GOD to COCK produced forms such as COCK'S BONES, COCK'S MOTHER and COCK'S PASSION but possibly the only survivor of this family is COCKSURE, a word for which alternative derivations are easy to find. More certain are the origins of GOLLY and GOSH which are just corruptions of the word GOD; DRAT IT is derived from the phrase (*may*) *God rot it*, and GOR BLIMEY which is really (*may*) *God blind me*.

Disguised as English expressions are DEAR ME and FIDDLE DE DEE both of which seem to derive from Italian phrases. FIDDLE DE DEE is really *fedidio, fe di Dio* which means 'by the faith of God' and DEAR ME is probably a corrupted form of *Dio mi (salvi)* which translated is 'God (save) me'. Echoing the primitive taboos concerning the names of supernatural beings it was also thought necessary to avoid using the names of Jesus and of Mary. Thus Jesus becomes the American JEEZ and GEEWHIZ, reflecting the Shakespearian GIS and the even earlier GYSE, while the Latin term *Jesu Domine* becomes JIMINY and Christ turns into CRIKEY, CRIMINY or CRIPES. Jesus Christ becomes JIMINY CRICKET or even, amazingly, JEEPERS CREEPERS. The derivation of the anaemic form of the word BLOODY is not known for certain but is likely to have been influenced by a contraction of the phrase *by our Lady* just as LAKIN is a shortened version of BY'R LAKIN or *by our Ladykin*. The expression *by our Lady, Hail!* might simply become BLOODY HELL! But even the meaningless

BLOODY was too strong a word for the Victorians so they resorted to words such as BALLY and RUDDY as substitutes; instead of *damn!* we have minced oaths like DARN! and in place of *damnation* we have TARNATION. Again *Hell* turns into HECK by a similar process. An early expression of despair which avoided any appeal to the supernatural was *alack a day*. From it is derived LACKADAISICAL, a term which is still appropriate for the type of people who habitually do little but rue the day on which they were born. Alas and alack, all this hypocrisy has changed the meaning of the word sanctimonious from 'saintly' to something less complimentary.

10

The naughty bits

In ancient times it was, and in primitive societies it still is, common to find certain words being endowed with super- natural power. These are usually the names of animal spirits, peoples or gods, for there is a tendency to confuse an object with its name or symbol. It seems that in prehistoric times hunting was thought to be aided by making use of cave drawings; later, people believed that enemies could be harmed by abusing their effigies or their names and, for this reason, many societies developed dual naming systems: each person would have a general name known to all and of little importance, but also a private secret one, known only to the trustworthy. Closely connected to this sort of belief is the idea that by calling a god's name the god would be automatically invoked and, unless there was a good reason for disturbing the divine repose, retribution would assuredly follow. Primitive superstition dies hard, so we still disguise the name 'God' as 'Od', 'Cod', 'Gad' or 'Cock' in various compound words; and sometimes, as in 'strewth' and 'zounds', the dreadful word is lost altogether. Swearing, or making an oath, whether done by a legal witness or an army trooper continues a tradition which stretches back into prehistory. Only the divine titles themselves have changed.

Now the restrictions on the use of names have been relaxed. But the taboos have not disappeared; rather, they have been shifted on to perfectly ordinary expressions with honourable ancient ancestries, with the result that there are now no acceptable everyday words for what are technically known by the terms testicle, penis, vagina, copulation, anus, flatulence, excrement and urine. To the Anglo-Saxons there was nothing special about parts of the body or bodily functions: everyone was well-accustomed to the workings of nature for, until the coming of so-called civilisation, they were treated as everyday facets of existence: whole families and friends slept naked together each night and answered the various calls of nature without embarrassment. Their practical, healthy attitudes contrast starkly with modern humbug. Now we are obliged to use alien words which properly belong to Latin, or employ absurd euphemisms such as 'pooh-pooh', 'grunties', 'big jobs', 'number twos' and 'do-dos'. Alternatively one can risk punishment by the courts for using the words which everyone still knows, and most people continue to use in private. One of the ironies is that, in all probability, some of the puritans and hypocrites who perpetuate this state of affairs have surnames which are, themselves, slightly disguised versions of those forbidden words.

To the Anglo-Saxons the word for a testicle was *bealluc*. From it comes the modern BOLLOCK which, like the words BALL, BOLL, BALLON and BOWL, is ultimately derived from an ancient word meaning 'round'. Like the terms for other physical attributes, the word BOLLOCK was liable to provide a man with a convenient secondary name; what would now be a surname or NICKNAME – an *eke-name*, literally 'another name'. As well as BOLLOCK and BALLOCK, the names WHITEBALLOC, GILDEN-BALLOKES and BLAKEBALLOC have been recorded. Sadly they have been abandoned or corrupted, but at least some of the people now surnamed BULLOCK provide a link with the past. Having abandoned the word BOLLOCK in the early nineteenth century, the prudes have been quite happy to accept foreign words which originally denoted the same thing. Among them are ORCHID, from the Greek *orchis*, and AVOCADO, amended by the Spanish from the Aztec word *ahvacatl*. Ironically the flowers which are now known as orchids were once called *dogstones* (i.e. dog's testicles) or less ambiguously *sweet ballocks*.

Now little-used except in dialect, the Anglo-Saxon word *pintel* has evolved into PINTLE. It was standard English until the early part of the eighteenth century and is related to the words PIN and PENCIL. It means penis and occurs in the, now obsolete, names of Messrs COLTEPINTEL and DOGGEPINTEL and also in still thriving plant names such as that of the 'Cuckoo Pintel', or Cuckoo Pint, with its suggestive spadix. The Latin word *penis* means, or rather originally meant, 'tail': it was an ironic choice for a new acceptable term because, until about 1750, the word TAIL was, itself, used in respectable English to mean penis. *Taegel*, the Anglo-Saxon form of TAIL, seems to have been used since ancient times for the hindquarters (male or female, human or animal) as well as for what is now more usually referred to as the tail. But the old meanings continue and, in the USA at least, have recently enjoyed a new lease of life. Another Anglo-Saxon word for tail, *steort*, having since become START and fallen into disuse, has been altered to STARK in the expression STARK NAKED, although START has been retained in REDSTART, the name of a bird with a red tail. In the Middle Ages the words 'cock' and 'prick' became acceptable terms for what was already called a pintel. The former seems to be derived from the word cock as used for a water tap, and the latter from the idea of piercing or penetrating. Both are suggestive of preparing for action as in the verbs 'to cock' and 'to prick up', and both are widely used despite having supposedly become vulgar in about 1830 and 1700 respectively. Prick seems to have been used in this sense earlier than cock; although both were first recorded around 1600, the existence of one John PRIKEHARD who lived in the early thirteenth century suggests that the meaning was already well understood. Perhaps his descendants are now called PRICHARD or PRITCHARD. ('Prick' also had the additional Chaucerian meaning of 'to ride'.)

Presumably derived from the same ancient root are the Latin *cunnus*, Greek *kusthos*, Persian and Hittite *kun*, Old Norse *kunta* and Anglo-Saxon *kunte*. In each, the first two letters are essentially identical and in each case the meaning is similar although varying slightly between 'tail', 'rump' and 'female genitals'. The Anglo-Saxon form has, of course, become CUNT, a word which was the first to suffer from prudery; it started to fall out of use as early as the sixteenth century but did not become altogether unacceptable until 1700 or so. As a term of abuse, it is first recorded only in this century. Like all the words which have been debased in this way, its insulting and offensive nature has developed only since it dropped out of standard English. Also gone are the names FILLECUNT, CLEVECUNT, WYDECUNTHE and the picturesque SITBETHECUNTE, but the Cockneys get around this modern prudery by the use of rhyming slang: a cunt is a 'Berkeley Hunt' and thus more concisely a 'berk'.

Sex and violence are commonly associated themes, and it is interesting that in many languages the verb meaning 'to strike' has been adapted to mean 'to copulate'. Two of them, Latin *futuere* and Germanic *ficken*, seem to have coupled together to provide the English word FUCK. Also with this dual nature are the French descendant of *futuere*, *foutre*, and the unchanged German *ficken*: what is news to psychiatrists has long been known to etymologists. It is not obvious why evolutionary pressures should have so closely connected mammalian excretary and reproductive organs. But since they are interconnected it is not surprising that as one has become unmentionable so likewise has the other. Also with relatives in a number of languages is the word ARSE which dropped out of polite use in the seventeenth century. Earlier it was Anglo-Saxon *aers* and was, of course, perfectably acceptable to all, just as it is now quite permissible to use terms such as FUNDAMENT and BASE, meaning 'bottom'; and REAR, HINDQUARTERS, BACKSIDE, DERRIÈRE and POSTERIOR, all meaning 'behind'. Also dropped from general use are expressions such as 'arse upwards' and 'he would lose his arse if it were loose': they have been replaced by similar phrases, equally innocent but less expressive. Even when the word was used extensively it was still possible to employ it in a less than complimentary manner. People with the surname BAYSERS have to content themselves with the knowledge that their forefathers earned it many generations ago, for it comes from the Old French *baise* meaning 'kiss' compounded with the Anglo-Saxon *aers*.

A bird with a white rump is really a *'white-arse'* but with disarming ingenuousness we now call it a WHEATEAR. One is almost tempted to speculate about the surname Whitehouse. Before the word ARSE became supposedly obsolete, the alternative term BUM was already gaining favour; it arrived from an uncertain source in Middle English and lived a blameless life until the nineteenth century. It is not a contraction of 'bottom' but rather seems to be related to the word BOOM, and was echoic, originally indicating a buzzing noise. Wherever it came from, the word was soon used in compounds such as BUM CARD and BUM-FODDER; they are now enjoying wider use again, although their modern alternative names 'marked card' and 'toilet paper' are still more common. Curiously, the word BUTTOCK has retained its acceptability. Perhaps this is because it is used of an area near, but not actually part of, a taboo region of the body. In any event, it is of good ancestry being to the Anglo-Saxons *buttoc*, a close relative of the word BUTT simply meaning 'end'.

First recorded in Middle English, but almost certainly much older, the word FART is, like BUM, probably echoic in origin. A corresponding French word meaning to fart is *péter*. The older form, *peter*, certainly accounts for many French surnames and may be the origin of the now infamous one, *Pétain*; certainly the thirteenth century Roland le Fartere was also known during his lifetime as Rolland le Pettour. Also derived from the French word was the stage name of Pétomane, a Frenchman who made a good living in the late nineteenth century by entertaining European audiences with the versatility of his farting. In Cockney rhyming slang a fart is a 'raspberry tart' and hence simply a raspberry.

The Anglo-Saxons had a word *sceotan* which was derived

An Eighteenth Century print entitled *The Bum Shop*.

from an older, similar Germanic word meaning to project, or move quickly. Ultimately, from this word, either through the Anglo-Saxon form, or the Old Norse *skytta*, or one of the several other variations, come a host of English words which retain a hint of the early meaning. Amongst them are SHOOT, SHOUT (projecting words), SKEET and SCOOT (originally projecting water), SCOUT (rejecting contemptuously or throwing away), SHUT (originally shooting the bolt of a door), SHUTTLE (an article thrown from one side to the other), SKIT (to dart about), SKITTER and SKITTLE. Other related words, like SCOTER, the name of a darting sea bird, are not widely used and some have fallen out of use altogether: for example, the bowman's shooting finger was a *skite* finger, and a hole in a castle wall through which arrows could be shot was, before it became known as a loophole, a *skitebrook*. Some are not recorded at all although they are likely to have been used at some time in the British Isles; for example, an Old Norse word *skutill* meaning harpoon might reasonably be expected to have had a parallel in English. Some associated words like SCOT and SHEET have lost any obvious connection with the idea of throwing, darting or projecting, although specialist jargon sometimes gives the game away: for example, a SHEET anchor is one designed specifically to be shot overboard in an emergency. Yet other words appear to be related but cannot be proved to be so. SCUTTLE, SCUT, SCUD and SKID are certainly related to each other but cannot be definitely tied up with the rest, and the origin of SKEDADDLE is likewise doubtful. Despite the missing links, all this tends to confirm that the word SHIT, with the Middle English form *schitte* and Anglo-Saxon *scitta*, would originally have been applied specifically to diarrhoea, as indeed it seems to have been until the fifteenth century. Even now the closely related terms SQUIT and SQUIT-TERS are used specifically to describe diarrhoea, although another related word SQUIRT is now used in a more general sense.

The word shit remained in general use until the nineteenth century, but nevertheless it is difficult to believe that people had taken kindly to being named, as they certainly were, SCITTE-BAGGE, SCHITBROCH ('shit breeches'), SHITPOT and SHITFACE. Not surprisingly, these appellations have fallen into disuse, at least as conventional surnames. In North America there is a type of heron still known, for obvious reasons, as a shitepoke. *Shitteborwelane*, 'shit-bowel-lane', in the City of London has succumbed to misplaced delicacy for it is now known as SHERBORNE LANE. Towns such as 'shit-brook', *schitebroc*, now called SKIDBROOK have disguised their origins; and even plants, such as the one known to the Germans as the *kuhscheisse* ('cow-shit'), have acquired more refined names: but even '*ox slop*' and '*cow slop*' have proved too much for sensitive southern ears so now they are known as the OXSLIP and COWSLIP respectively. In the North, however, people are more matter-of-fact. There, one who talks blatant nonsense is thought of as 'talking shit', for such an individual is likened to a windbag full of shit and so called a BLATHERSKITE or BLETHERSKATE. The Victorian moralists never really had a chance of stopping this expression, for the very existence of such people and their excessive willingness to express their views ensured that the term should become indispensable.

Oddly enough, the word PISS is derived from an Old French verb *pisser* rather than its Anglo-Saxon equivalent. Nevertheless, the word has fallen victim to those who prefer more learned

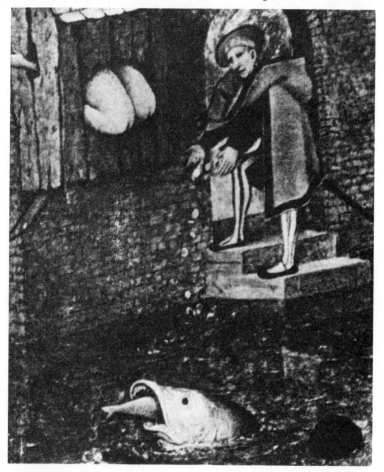

This detail from Bruegel's Netherlandish Proverbs illustrates a phrase well known in England. The squanderer is literally 'pouring money down the drain'.

terms; urinate and micturate are quite acceptable, probably for no better reason than that they are derived from classical words and have more than four letters in them. Before dropping out of polite use in the mid-eighteenth century, the shorter word featured in many catch-phrases and well-known sayings. From the fifteenth century onwards, people who squandered money on drink were said to 'piss money against the wall'. In the next century, the term PISS-POT was applied to medical men as well as to chamber pots, a short time was a PISSING-WHILE, and a dandelion was, because of its diuretic properties, a PISSABED. Later, a sour person became a PISS-VINEGAR and braggarts were said to piss more than they drank. A common and obvious method of putting out small fires provided another term for a boaster PISS-FIRE; and there was also a common saying 'money will make the pot boil though the Devil piss in the fire'. Even the translators of the Bible had no qualms about reporting what Rabshakeh said (II Kings 18, 27 and Isaiah 36, 12): 'Hath my master sent me to thy master and to thee to speak these words? hath he not sent me to the men that sit upon the wall, that they may eat their own dung and drink their own piss with you?'

Ironically those who try to impose their own values on others usually achieve exactly the opposite of their declared intentions. Thus, for example, missionaries preach cleanliness but introduce previously unknown European diseases to their converts; they intend to spread Culture but instead succeed in destroying entire cultures; they teach only acceptable, 'nice' English words for parts of the body, but even this sometimes backfires. In Nigeria the missionaries' acceptable Latin words became associated with their prurient views on sexual matters. Other more practical Europeans, like sailors and traders, introduced common English terms and these became associated with a more reasonable down-to-earth attitude to life. Thus it is that in some parts of Africa words like penis, vagina and sexual intercourse are regarded as obscene; the acceptable alternatives, used on television for example, are cock, cunt and fuck. As beauty exists in the eye of the beholder, so obscenity can exist only in the ear of the auditor.

Ye Goode Olde Dayes

It is inevitable that during the course of fifteen hundred years some words should drop out of general use in any living language. Having numerous sources of new words and a correspondingly large vocabulary, English has lost a large portion of its Anglo-Saxon inheritance. Undoubtedly some words which were never used extensively have disappeared without trace and it is clearly impossible to discover how many have vanished in this way. Occasionally it is safe to deduce the existence of an Old English word simply because it exists in other closely related languages: since these languages were originally only dialects of the same language the question is one of when, rather than whether, the word became obsolete. Fortunately the words preserved by early literature are sufficiently comprehensive to give an adequate representation of the Old English language. Apart from the words that have vanished altogether there are three broad groups: those which have retained their original meanings; those which have found entirely new ones; and those which sustain a ghost-like existence, half way between existence and total oblivion, trapped like flies in amber.

It is paradoxical that a word can be almost obsolete and yet still enjoy extensive use. How this can arise is demonstrated by the twilight worlds of specialist jargon, slang and dialect, and by apparently meaningless modern compounds such as LODE-STONE, WALNUT, COBWEB and NICKNAME. In each of these Anglo-Saxon compounds the first part represents a word which is almost dead while the second is a living, thriving one. A LODESTONE is really a LODE STONE, literally a 'way stone' or magnet. The Anglo-Saxon *lad* or *lode*, meaning way, course or path, also appears in the word LODESTAR, a star such as the pole-star, which shows the way. The course of one's life is really a LIVELIHOOD, this word having been corrupted from LIFELOAD, originally *liflad*, literally a 'life course'. Although the word LODE still finds an application in mining it is hardly ever encountered elsewhere. Close relatives, however, continue to be useful to the modern traveller who may still be LADEN with a LOAD and LED by a LEADER.

The Anglo-Saxons had a word *wealh* which meant 'foreign' and which was applied specifically to the Celtic people. In Britain the Saxons displaced the Celts who, retreating west-ward, settled in an area known as the land of the *wealas* or foreigners. The area is now known, to the English, as WALES; and another region to the South and West became known as West Wales although, being shaped like a horn or '*corn*', we now know it as CORNWALL. Welsh people, not being trusted by the English, gave their collective name to the verb WELSH meaning 'to cheat' and individuals from Wales acquired names such as WELSH and WALSH. On the other hand, Celts who were driven northwards towards Scotland acquired names like WAL-LACE, and those who stayed in England in small communities are responsible for place names such as WALCOT ('Welsh' cottage); WALTON ('Welsh' town); WALFORD ('Welsh' ford); WALBROOK ('Welsh' brook) and SAFFRON WALDEN (a dene or valley of the 'Welsh' where saffron was grown). On mainland Europe the Saxons encountered other foreigners who have come to be known as WALLOONS (in southern Belgium) and WALACHIANS (in Rumania); and all the way from Persia came the foreign nut or *wealh hnutu* now more familiar as a WALNUT.

A NICKNAME is really *an eke name*, literally 'an also name', but in the course of time the *eke* has become *ick* and the initial 'n' has been transferred from the previous word. This sort of migrating 'n' has also affected *an ewte* and *an otch* which are now more familiar as A NEWT and A NOTCH. Other words have suffered from emigrating rather than immigrating letters so that AN APRON is really *a napron*; AN AUGER (the tool) is *a nauger*; AN ORANGE, *a norange*; AN UMPIRE, *a numpire*; and UMBLES are more properly *numbles*. This last word which means the 'entrails of a deer', has lost its initial 'n' but gained an 'h' to make it like the already existing HUMBLE. As umbles became less popular and the word less well-known, the practice of 'eating humble pie' would seem to make more sense than 'eating umble pie', the fare of humble peasants. Another word which has lost its initial 'n' is the Old Saxon word *nadra* which meant a viper; its close relation, the German *natter*, is similar to the Anglo-Saxon *attor*, meaning poison. The word *nadra* is the ancestor of the modern ADDER and *nattor* probably features in that well-known phrase AS MAD AS A NATTER meaning 'as angry as a viper', but the practice of hatters sending themselves mad by using poisonous compounds of mercury has, along with Lewis Carroll's mad hatter, altered the phrase to its more usual form, AS MAD AS A HATTER. The Saxons knew that some spiders were also poisonous and so called such a creature an *attercoppe*, which means literally a 'poison-head'. The *coppe* of *coppeweb* later became *cop* and then *cob* which accounts for the modern COBWEB.

As words start to drop out of use their meanings are forgotten and their eventual disappearance is almost assured. There are, however, words which have been kept in suspended animation within popular usage: the word stays on, but does no real work because it is supported by another which does. For example, the word *lewk*, tepid, may stand alone in dialects but to most users it is a sleeping partner in the compound LUKEWARM. Blacksmiths still use large hammers called SLEDGES but to many other users they have become SLEDGEHAMMERS. Likewise the old *causey*, a word from Norman French which is still used in some dialects has attached itself to another word of almost the same meaning to give the modern CAUSEWAY.

Meanings of words are often preserved in phrases, whether the words themselves have survived or not. A 'pig in a poke', for example, is simply a pig in a bag; the origin of the phrase can be traced to medieval times when the equivalent of the modern market conman would sell piglets in closed bags. Buyers could not be sure of what they were buying until too late, then they might LET THE CAT OUT OF THE BAG or find that they had been SOLD A PUP. Derived from the Old Norman French word *poque*, the English POKE has little other use than in this single phrase and the dialect term POKE-PUDDING which is the name of a pudding made in a bag. By contrast there are numerous closely-related terms which continue to flourish: the diminutive POCKET, the name of a little bag; the POUCH, another small bag; POACHING, the actions of cooking in a bag-shaped device and of 'bagging' game illegally; and even the word PUCKER, to crumple up like the top of a bag (just as to PURSE is to crease up like the top of a purse when the purse strings are drawn). From the small bag-shaped indentations or POCK marks which charac-terised some diseases come the name of those afflictions: the POCKS or POX. (The word poke, meaning to prod, is unrelated, at least from an etymological point of view.)

The word QUICK has also left reminders of its old meaning scattered around the language. Unlike it, however, the word itself still exists, albeit with a changed meaning. It is easy to see how the word and its meaning have both developed from the Anglo-Saxon word *cwic* which meant 'living'. Echoing the older usage are phrases such as 'the quick and the dead' and 'look quick!' which are alternatives for 'the live and the dead' and 'look alive!' To 'cut to the quick' is to cut to the living flesh such as that found under the dead finger nail. When the quick of the finger end becomes infected it may develop into a quickflaw; the word is retained in some dialects, though most speakers prefer the corrupted form WHITLOW. The change of initial letter also explains the name of the wood now known as witch hazel. The idea that witches used the wood probably resulted from its use

Nowadays the English have strange ideas about Scotland, having forgotten that until not so long ago bagpipes, haggis and porridge were as popular in England as anywhere else. Shakespeare had particular misgivings about Lincolnshire bagpipes; HAGGIS is probably named after a French word for that dish and PORRIDGE is another form of POTTAGE, as in the biblical 'mess of pottage'.

Kilts, on the other hand, are relatively recent inventions as are the numerous distinctive clan tartans. In England the smocks commonly worn by the majority of people had two slightly different names: one from an Anglo-Saxon (West Germanic) word and one from the corresponding and closely related Old Norse (North Germanic) word. Now we make rather more of a distinction for the former has developed into the word SHIRT and the latter into SKIRT.

in water divining or dowsing: when the divining twig moved spontaneously it seemed to be alive and was thus 'quick' or *wick* hazel, now WITCH hazel. Amongst other remnants of the earlier meaning is the word COUCH, a form of QUITCH which is related to QUICK, COUCH grass being renowned for its vitality and still known in some places as quick-grass. COUCH is hardly recognisable as a relation of the original *cwic* but more obvious relatives are the QUICKSET hedge composed of living wood; QUICKSAND which seems to be alive; QUICKLIME, an alternative name for calcium oxide which behaves as though alive when in contact with water; and of course QUICKSILVER, living silver which to the Anglo-Saxons was *cwic seolfor*.

By changing a letter or two it is easy to disguise almost any word. This is especially true of short ones and even more so when the change makes them look like another unrelated word; the relationship between CHAR and AJAR may not be immediately obvious, but the old practice of prefixing an 'a' to verbs (still done, for example, in some Southern states of the USA) provides the missing link, A-CHAR. To char is to turn away or turn aside, and so a door which is 'a-turning' can be said to be A-CHAR; not all doors stay closed properly and not all letters stay fixed, so partially open doors are now said to be AJAR. Derived from an Anglo-Saxon word of the same meaning, CHAR may well be related to the dialect CHARK which, like its more common alternative CREAK, echoes the sound of a closing door. By analogy doing a *turn* of work could be described as a 'char', a fact which accounts for the term CHARLADY and the American word CHORE. The memorial cross in London where the Thames turns aside is CHARING CROSS; and wood which is turned into another form by burning is 'turned-coal' or CHARCOAL. At one time charcoal was simply called coal, and what we now call coal was known as sea-coal because it was so often shipped around and was therefore associated with ports rather than mines. The word CHAR meaning to burn has developed as a consequence of the association of CHARCOAL with burning.

Many words which are still widely used have changed their meanings over the centuries and most seem to leave some trace of the earlier ones. The 'merry' of Robin Hood's Merry Men, Merry England and the merry month of May, for example, means pleasant or contented rather than happy or joyful. The same is true of the word when used in the well-known Christmas carol which contains the line 'God rest ye merry, gentlemen' (with the comma after, not before, the word merry). By contrast, the word 'sad', another Anglo-Saxon survivor, has enjoyed many different meanings, being successively used as a synonym for sated, tired, heavy, solid, trustworthy, serious, sorrowful and, finally, generally distressing. Even though the early meanings have long been obsolete in general usage it is still quite common to hear the word used in connection with 'heavy' bread which has failed to rise properly. It is surprising how closely some dialects keep to the language of hundreds of years ago despite the popularity of new meanings elsewhere. The word SILLY and its twin SEELY are both derived from the Anglo-Saxon *saelig* and both have developed along the same lines while retaining their earliest meanings in some areas. SEELY is now used only in dialects and the early meanings of SILLY are found only in Northern England and Scotland. During the last thousand years or so it has meant: deserving of pity, helpless, weak, simple, blessed, simple-minded, foolish, stunned and dazed. One wonders which meaning cricketers had in mind when 'silly-mid-on' and 'silly-mid-off' were first named in 1900.

Usually it is easy to see how a word has gradually shifted its meaning. The Anglo-Saxon *hosa*, which meant a leg-covering, shows a logical progression in its development which, bearing in mind the changes in fashion, seems almost inevitable. Originally applied to stockings, the word later transferred itself to breeches when they came into vogue in the fifteenth century. Now that the male apparel known as doublet and HOSE is no longer worn, the term has dropped out of general usage except in its derivative form HOSIERY, the recent panty-HOSE and the five-hundred-year-old HOSE pipe. The only surprise here is that trousers are not known as *hose* or *hosen* as they are in modern German. Another word which shows how changes in meaning can occur is SHAMBLES. The Anglo-Saxon *sceamul* was simply a bench; later the form *scamel* was used specifically for a market bench upon which meat was displayed. From this meaning of SHAMBLES comes the modern usage as a scene of carnage and thus a mess, but the streets of ancient cities where these market stalls once stood are often still called the SHAMBLES.

Human nature is often reflected in the way that words and phrases develop. In many countries which were once part of the British Empire, the word PRESENTLY still means 'immediately', but in England it has come to indicate some indefinite time in the future. Presumably the need to do something 'presently' implied different degrees of urgency in different places. This theory is more convincing still when it is realised that the phrase 'BY AND BY' and the words 'SOON' and 'ANON' have all changed their meanings in exactly the same way. Urgency has given way to procrastination. The word ANON is one of many expressions in English which has been formed by compressing together two simpler words, in this case *on* and *ane*. Literally 'on one', the term originally meant 'on one course' and thus directly or 'straightway'; the reasoning may seem convoluted but other similar compounds are easier to disentangle: HANDICAP, for example, is '*hand in cap*' the name of a betting game; ALONE is '*all one*'; ALSO is '*all so*'; ATONE is '*at one*'; UNLESS is '*on less*'; DON is '*do on*'; DOFF is '*do off*'. Other compounds in common use include SHILLY SHALLY, '*Shill I? Shall I?*'; WILLY NILLY, '*Will I? Nill I?*' and even the word HOBNOB, *hab-nab*, '*have, not-have*', the idea being that those who hobnob should stay friends come what may. It might be necessary for the 'have-nots' to dress up in order to hobnob with the right people: to be 'dressed up to the eyes' was once to be 'dressed up to *then eyne*', a turn of phrase which is preserved in the alternative modern version 'dressed up to the nines' since our Old English inflections have fallen into disuse and the meaning of *then* ('thine') and *eyne* (eyes) forgotten.

Some words are more tenacious than others and even when they have died out in England they may continue to thrive elsewhere. Countries which were colonised in Elizabethan times have provided a safe haven for a considerable amount of vocabulary which is lost to standard English. Occasionally such words have been reintroduced to their parent language from their foster parents, perhaps with a new meaning. Although still used in parts of Northern England and Scotland the word JOUK (or JOOK) has fallen out of general use in England. In the USA, however, the word survived with its original meaning of dodge, evade or duck; in fact the word itself may well be related to the very similar term DUCK. During the years of Prohibition, the word JOUK was applied to illicit drinking places which evaded the law, and when new music machines were introduced to such places it seems that they also adopted the name. Hence the title of the now-familiar JUKE box.

12

Take a letter

About 3,500 years ago the Semitic people of the Middle East made a significant breakthrough in the development of writing. It was the Canaanites who, at this time, first developed an alphabet similar to the ones in use throughout most of the world today. Indeed all the letters of the English alphabet are, directly or indirectly, related to this Canaanite prototype. Most of our letters come directly from the Roman alphabet, the Romans having acquired them from the Etruscans who had, in turn, taken them from a script of the archaic Greeks. The Greeks had borrowed their letters from the Phoenicians – the race who provided the final link to the ancient Semites. As well as the Roman alphabet, this same ultimate source also provided the Arabic, Hebrew, Classical Greek and Cyrillic alphabets which superficially look so very different. During their long histories letters have changed considerably: invariably they have been simplified, but some are still recognisably the same as their ancestors of thirty-five centuries ago. The most revolutionary simplifications occurred within the first few hundred years of the alphabet's development, and thus the Greek alphabet of the eighth century BC is easily recognisable as a relation of the Modern English one. Looking at each letter in turn, it is interesting to observe the early association of everyday objects with the names and shapes of the letters.

The Canaanite word for an ox was *'alp* and it was a drawing of an ox's head which formed the first letter 'A'. The orientation of the letter was irrelevant in the early scripts so that this modern letter looks more like an ox's head if drawn on its side rather than in the English fashion, with its nose uppermost. The Greeks of the eighth century BC would have been as happy with the symbols ∠ or even ∀ as with the now familiar A.

The letter B was originally drawn like a box and represented a house, the Canaanite word for which was *bet*. In archaic Greek the letter could be written ᖯ, which, when turned around, resembles the modern version. In Greek the Canaanite *'alp* became *alpha* and *bet* became *beta*: these two words were used to describe the whole collection of letters and '*alpha-beta*' requires little alteration to give the word ALPHABET, another name for the 'ABC'.

From the Canaanite word *gimel* comes the Modern English CAMEL and a drawing of this animal provided the next letter which the archaic Greeks simplified to < or Γ. From the latter form the classical Greeks produced their letter *gamma* which is now written Γ and corresponds to the modern English G. But the Etruscans had no use for a letter G so they used the other form of the letter, <, to represent a sound corresponding to our 'K' thus creating what is now the letter C, a letter which the Romans adopted in preference to the rarely used K.

A picture of a fish was simplified to a triangle in order to represent the next letter. The archaic Greek version, △, became the classical Greek Δ, *delta*, while the Roman ▷ became our D. Triangular aeroplane wings and areas at the mouths of rivers are known as DELTA wings and river DELTAS, respectively.

The letter E acquired its form at an early stage and is thus identical in the Greek and Roman alphabets; it had originally been the figure of a praying man. F was, in early times, drawn as a mace or peg but it had acquired its modern form 3,000 years ago as the Greek *digamma*, written as one gamma on top of another: Ⅎ. This letter was dropped from the classical Greek alphabet but was recovered by the Romans who passed it on indirectly to English. In the past a capital letter F was written ff and, mistaking it for two small 'f's, some illiterate families with names like Foulkes styled themselves ffoulkes, or even Ffoulkes. Classical Greek having already lost the *digamma* developed another letter to represent a similar sound; the letter was Φ, *phi*, which accounts for the fact that the Greek words adopted into English are almost invariably spelt with 'ph' where an 'f' might otherwise be expected.

Because the letter *gimel* had provided the Romans with a C instead of a G, another symbol was required to deal with the omission. Rather than adopt the Greek symbol Γ the Romans solved their problem by adding a bar to the lower end of the letter C, so creating a new letter G, which we now recognise as G. In Middle English there was another letter representing a sound like a guttural 'g'; it was written ȝ and is now known as 'yogh'. Nowadays, in English, it is usually replaced by 'g', 'y' or 'gh', but in Scotland its use continued for longer than in England and the letter came to be written like a 'z' – although the earlier pronunciation was retained. For this reason there is a considerable difference between the Scottish and the usual English pronunciations of surnames like Menzies, Mackenzie and Dalziel.

H originally represented a fence but it had acquired the form 目 sufficiently early to provide the Roman and Greek alphabets with the same letter; although in Latin it represents a consonant, in Greek a vowel. As well as representing a 'breathing' noise in English, the letter also serves to amend the sound of its neighbours (as it once did in Greek). Thus 'th' is now used for the single Greek letter Θ, *theta*, just as 'ph' is used for the Greek letter Φ, *phi*. The Greeks had originally used 'kh' for the sound later represented by χ, *chi*, but in English this is often transliterated as 'ch'. In order to fill in other gaps in the alphabet a number of combinations such as 'gh', 'sh' and 'wh' have been developed since the Norman Conquest.

The letter I was, in early times, a rather more complicated symbol, representing as it did a forearm and outstretched hand. When it became simplified it was a small letter known as *yod* in Hebrew and *iota* in Greek. From the Hebrew form comes the phrase 'not to give a JOT' and from its Greek cousin the phrase 'not to care one IOTA'. As a TITLE, so-called from the Latin word *titulus* meaning 'superscription', is placed above a piece of writing, so a TITTLE is a mark placed above a letter such as the dot over a small I. The 'jot' in the above phrase is, therefore, often extended to 'jot or tittle'. Because the letter i is a small letter it has also given its name to the action of writing a short note and thus it is possible to 'JOT down a few words'. Dotting the small Is was a habit developed in the eleventh century in order to avoid confusion between two 'i's together and the single letter 'u'. Being punctilious, in this respect, or now in any other, is to dot the 'i's and cross the 't's.

Another innovation of the Middle Ages was the invention of a letter which could take over the function of I when used as a consonant. This letter was J, the small form of which had already been used but for different purposes. It was, and still is in some places, customary to write the last 'i' in Roman numerals with a tail; thus, for example, a three would be iij. It was also a common practice to write the second of two consecutive 'i's with a tail when the letters occurred in Latin words such as *filij*. Like the use of dots this practice helped to differentiate between two 'i's and a single 'u'. Furthermore capital Is, often representing consonants at the beginning of Latin words, were sometimes written with an extended tail, so – *J*. By the seventeenth century it was becoming usual to employ the letter I as a vowel and J as a consonant. However, the two letters were not fully distinguished for a considerable time: up until the nineteenth century J was regarded as only a variation of the letter I. Thus it would not necessarily warrant a separate section in a dictionary and words beginning with I and J would be mixed up together in the same section.

The Greeks borrowed from the Phoenicians a letter written Я which, reversed as K, was subsequently learned by the

Romans. As well as this letter the Greeks also had one to represent a similar sound, something like the 'ch' in the Scottish pronunciation of the word loch. This letter was χ, *chi*, and in English it is represented in words of Greek origin by the letters 'ch': for example, we have the word CHRIST rather than 'Krist'. We dimly remember the Greek letter in the abbreviation Xmas for Christmas, since the initial X is really a '*chi*'.

In very early times the orientation of the letters was a matter of convenience: personal preference or limitations imposed by the materials available would determine whether a letter was drawn in the manner now accepted or upside down or back to front or even at an oblique angle. Thus in archaic Greek the letter L could be written ╲ or ╲, symbols derived from a picture of the implement used for goading oxen. From the first form came the Roman L and from the other came the Greek letter *lambda*, Λ.

M and N acquired their form at an early stage and are thus identical in Roman and Greek scripts. They were originally symbols for water and for a serpent respectively and have changed remarkably little since the Canaanites first drew them as the symbols ∿ and ∿. Another survivor is the symbol for an eye. It is now rounder than it was and has lost its pupil since becoming Greek, but it is still recognisable as the modern O. In classical times the Greeks decided that they required a second O; they therefore called the one that they already had 'O-little', *omicron*, and the new one 'O-big', *omega*. The new letter was placed at the end of the Greek alphabet so the phrase 'from alpha to omega' has come to mean from beginning to end.

The ancestor of the letter P was used for the sounds represented by both P and F, as the Hebrew equivalent still is. The Greeks, however, did not need to use it as an F since they had, in archaic Greek at least, the *digamma* corresponding to the modern F. Although this was not used in Classical Greek, it was replaced by another letter *phi* Φ and so, as in Latin which did retain the F, the letter P could be used exclusively for its function as a P. Early forms of the letter were ⌐ and Γ, the second variety of which became the symbol P simply by closing its loop. But extending both vertical bars to equal length produced the Greek letter *pi*, now written Π.

As archaic Greek developed into classical Greek three of the letters became redundant, although two of them were retained for numerical purposes. One of them, the *digamma*, has already been mentioned: the others were *san* and *quoppa*, the latter being the equivalent of the modern Q which like the *digamma* resurfaced in Roman times. In English it was superfluous since it could invariably be replaced by another combination of letters, usually 'cw', nevertheless the letter Q seems to be here to stay. R, on the other hand, is genuinely useful: it originally looked like a simple picture of a head and became even more simplified to look like ꟼ or a modern P. It still looks like this in modern Greek but our version is differentiated from a P by an extra leg, so providing the symbol R or R.

The letter S comes from a pictograph of a hunting bow which, in archaic Greek, could be represented as ⟨ , ⟩ or later as Ϟ . This latter form gave the modern S and the former gave the classical Greek *sigma*, Σ. Almost obsolete is the long 's' written ʃ which is so easy to confuse with an f: depending upon its position in a sentence the letter was written s or ʃ. This distinction is lost in English but the Germans still retain it: in some circumstances when two 's's lie together the first is ʃ and the second s. Together the symbols would look like ʃs, but the Germans have a special composite figure β which, to the untrained eye, is easily mistaken for a B. Even the single ʃ seems to have caused some misunderstandings: the word SNEEZE, for example, almost certainly echoic, was earlier spelt fneeze but must at some time have been mistaken for ʃneeze. In England, and the rest of the world, the symbol ʃ enjoys a vestigial existence in the language of mathematics. Like the Greek Σ it stands for the initial S of the word summation; specifically, Σ is reserved for a discrete, and ʃ for a continuous, summation.

The last letter of the ancient alphabet corresponded to the modern T. It was originally written as a simple cross × or +, a fact which gives the corresponding Hebrew symbol its name, for *taw* means, simply, 'sign' or 'mark'. Its present European shape, T, has not changed since the archaic Greeks first wrote it, almost 3,000 years ago.

As previously mentioned, the Greeks dropped three letters from the alphabet, but they introduced another five which they tacked on to the end of it. Only one of these letters, *upsilon*, Υ, was adopted by the Romans and that became the letter V, although it is ultimately derived from the same symbol as the modern F. V could be either a consonant or a vowel, a fact which made words more difficult to read than they needed to be. So, just as J was introduced in the Middle Ages to take over the role of the consonant I, at about the same time U was introduced in order to relieve V of its function as a vowel; previously V had simply been the capital form of the small 'u'. In order to write an 'oo-oo' sound the scribes put together two 'u's to create a double-U or W which, as a capital letter, is actually written as a double-V: W, or W. Thus F, U, V and W are all ultimately derived from the same ancient symbol. In fact the Anglo-Saxons had had a perfectly serviceable letter for the sound now represented by a W. It was written Υ and is generally called 'wyn' or 'wen'; but it is hardly ever used now, even in modern publications of Anglo-Saxon texts.

The Romans were responsible for introducing the modern letter X about 2,000 years ago. They first called it *ultima nostrarum*, 'the last of ours' since it was then the last letter of their alphabet. Derived from the Greek letter *ksi*, Ξ which had locally been written X it had originally come between the letters N (nu) and O (omicron), but had not found its way into the Roman alphabet along with its neighbours and had had to be added later in order to cope with Greek names such as Xenophon. Later the letter Y was also introduced by the Romans who based it upon the Greek *upsilon* Υ, the origin, also, of V and thence U and W. Z, now pronounced 'zed', 'zee', 'ezod' or 'izard', was another letter borrowed from the Greeks by the Romans in order to represent Greek words; an example of such a word being *zodiacus* or in English ZODIAC. The original Greek letter *zeta* had appeared in the alphabet immediately following the *digamma*, but since this letter had been aban-

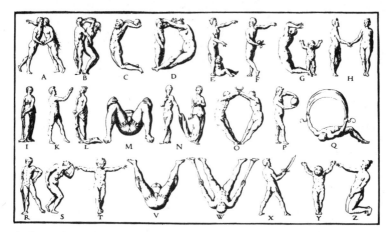

A sixteenth century representation of the English alphabet. J and U are not yet accepted as separate letters although W is well established.

doned in classical Greek, the *zeta* fell between E (epsilon) and H (eta). Because the Romans had, at first, no need of the *zeta* they filled the vacant space with an additional letter which they did need: that is why G falls where it does in the modern alphabet, while the reintroduced Z has had to be tacked onto the end.

The Greeks had another letter which the Romans did not adopt: the letter *theta*, Θ, representing the sound which is now written 'th'. If the Romans had needed it then undoubtedly it would have been introduced into England and so provided a useful English letter. As it was the Norman scribes had no way of representing the two English sounds 'th' as in 'then' and 'th' as in 'thin', so two new symbols were adopted from the Saxons: the letter *thorn*, written þ and the letter *etha*, written ð. Later these two symbols dropped out of use in England, although they are both still used in other languages, for example, Icelandic. The scribes found two ways to compensate for the loss of these letters: one was to use 'th' as we still do, the other was to employ the letter Y. Thus in old texts it is quite common to see, for example, Y^e meaning 'the' and Y^t meaning 'that'; this also explains the rather silly modern misunderstanding about tea shops. 'Ye Olde Englishe Teashoppe' is simply 'The Old English Teashop' not a variation of 'You old English teashop'.

As 'th' was used to represent a sound for which no letter existed, so it was necessary to invent other pairs for other such sounds; thus there are 'ng' as in 'sing', 'ti' (usually with a French derivation) as in 'nation', 'sh' (usually with a Teutonic derivation) as in 'sheep', and 'ch' as in 'church'. There used to be in English a sound similar to the Scottish 'ch' in loch. It was, like the German 'ch', a fairly soft sound but over the course of centuries it has faded away altogether much as the rolled 'R' is now gradually disappearing and the 'wh' in which is becoming indistinguishable from the 'w' in witch. The soft 'ch' sound resembling that in the word 'loch' was represented in English by 'gh' and thus many words with this combination are quickly recognisable as relations of their German cousins; a few examples show how close the relationship is: 'light' corresponds to *licht*; 'night' to *nacht*; 'right' to *recht* and 'might' to *macht*.

Running parallel to the development of the alphabet was the development of the present system of punctuation. The word PUNCTUATION like PUNCTURE is related to a Latin word meaning 'to prick': to punctuate (and to puncture) is simply to put in a point. Early writing did not distinguish the ends of sentences or even the ends of words, so letters followed in a continuous stream which made reading a rather slow process. The Greeks introduced a mark, used to identify a change in the sense of a text, which corresponds to the modern ¶, denoting a new paragraph. Indeed the word PARAGRAPH comes from the Greek *para*, beside, and *graphein*, to write: a PARAGRAPH being the symbol written beside the text to identify the change of sense. Now a change of sense in the text is noted by the writer starting a new line, so the word is now applied to blocks of text rather than to punctuation marks.

Taking the opposite course of development to the paragraph, a full stop or PERIOD was originally a section of writing rather than its punctuation mark. *Periodos* is made up of the Greek *peri*, around, and *odos*, way: a *periodos* being a circuit of thought. Similarly, a smaller section of a passage was called a COMMA, a word which is related to the Greek *coptein*, to cut: even now the word comma is applied to the symbol which cuts up a sentence. The APOSTROPHE used in punctuation takes its name from the Greek phrase *he apostrophos prosodia* which was used to indicate a deliberate omission made for the sake of rhyme. An ASTERISK is just a small star ($\star$); the diminutive form of the Greek *aster*, star, being *asteriskos*. Similarly a small roasting spit or *obelos* was an *obeliskos* so that the OBELISK known as Cleopatra's Needle is really a spit, not a needle. Thus also a long-cross or dagger (†) is called an OBELUS.

The question mark is simply a small q written over a small o thus ^q_o, these letters being the first and the last in the Latin word *quaesto* meaning a question; but is it not relatively easy to see how the letters have become corrupted to the present form? In much the same way, the Latin *Io*, an exclamation of joy, became ^I_o and thus the modern exclamation mark !. The pioneer of shorthand, a Roman called Tiro, invented the symbol '&' which in its italicised form *&* shows its derivation: it is simply the Latin word *et* meaning 'and', a fact which explains why etc. (an abbreviation of '*et cetera*') is sometimes written *&*c. For centuries English school children carried around hornbooks (covered with a thin layer of transparent horn) which had inscribed upon them, amongst other things, the alphabet. At the end of the letters, by itself, was the symbol '&', and, in order to emphasize that it was not part of the alphabet the phrase 'and per se' was placed after the 'Z' and before the '&'. Writing after the Z would, therefore, be read '*and per se, and*', which accounts for the present name of the symbol '&', AMPERSAND. Before and sometimes after the alphabet another symbol, like a Maltese Cross, called a Christ-Cross, was written: the rows of letters were thus *christ-cross* rows or, as the modern version has it, CHRISS-CROSS or CRISS-CROSS.

All Western European alphabets have been virtually identical since the introduction of printing, although some letters, like W, are not found in all of them. Sometimes, however, letters take on unfamiliar shapes: for example, Z may become ʒ , a cedilla under the c in French words such as *garçon*; and n may become ~, a tilde over another n in Spanish words such as *doña* (or as we would spell it DONNA). In Eastern Europe there is another alphabet altogether. Introduced by St Cyril, a Greek Christian theologian in the ninth century, it takes its name from his, and is called CYRILLIC.

Another alphabet, now obsolete, was used by the Anglo-Saxons before the Roman one was introduced. Actually this runic alphabet had ultimately the same source as the modern English one and it acquired its name in a similar way. The first two Greek letters produced the name of our alphabet in much the same way that the first six letters f, u, þ (i.e. th), o, r and k produced the name FUTHORC for that alphabet. Fifteen hundred years ago we had a symbol, þ, in the futhorc to represent the sound which we now have to use two letters for. Such is progress.

13

A little learning . . .

The words READ and WRITE are both of Anglo-Saxon derivation: READ has developed from *raedan*, meaning to make out, and WRITE from *writan*, to scratch on tree bark or stone. Much of the vocabulary of learning is however, like the learning itself, firmly rooted in ancient Greece. In school and university the ancients have a great influence still: for we cast ideas in the moulds of language which have been used for well over two thousand years. Not only that, but many words have passed into everyday language, their academic origins and originators largely forgotten. In ancient Greece, wise men were called *sophoi*, their name translating into English as SOPHISTS. Pythagoras thought the term a little presumptuous so he called himself instead a 'lover of wisdom', a PHILOSOPHER. Nevertheless he clearly had a relatively high opinion of himself for some of his students were not allowed even to see him when he was lecturing. Standing behind a curtain, he imparted EXOTERIC or 'outside' knowledge to those who could only listen; but those who were admitted behind the veil were favoured with ESOTERIC or special, secret, 'inside' knowledge. Now worldly knowledge is available to all and those who take advantage of it are said to be SOPHISTICATED.

In Athens there was a garden called *academeia* which had been named after a man called *Academus*; in it Plato taught followers about human nature just as modern philosophers teach in ACADEMIES, or in the GROVES OF ACADEME. Ironically the name of *Plato* is remembered in the phrase PLATONIC LOVE, an expression which is usually applied to innocent love between the sexes although when first used it was, more accurately, a description of homosexual love. Zeno taught in a porch, or *stoa*, in Athens so his school of philosophy became known as the STOIC school; and, since part of his teachings were that the workings of fate should be accepted without fuss, the description STOIC can now be used of any austere uncomplaining person. The followers of Pyro of Elis went even further and doubted the very existence of what they could not verify for themselves: the Greek verb *skeptesthai* meaning 'to look about' provided the name of their school, each follower being a SCEPTIC; so now any doubter is said to be SCEPTICAL. Epicurus held that the ultimate goal in life was the achievement of happiness and pleasurable sensations, which is why people who enjoy life, and good food in particular, are now known as EPICURES. Epicurus's teacher had held similar beliefs, his school of Philosophy being the HEDONIST school, so-called from the Greek word for pleasure, *hedone*. Athens has long since lost its pre-eminence in the field of scientific enquiry but philosophers have continued to contribute useful words to the English language. Now used in a looser sense the words realism and idealism, for example, were both used originally to describe philosophical beliefs.

The Greek word *schole* meant 'leisure', a meaning which many children might find surprising since it has provided the English word SCHOOL. PUBLIC schools were originally set up for the benefit of the *public* but have now become mostly private, and similarly GRAMMAR schools no longer concentrate on teaching *grammar*. In Germany the educational establishment comparable to the English grammar school is called a *gymnasium*, the same as the English word GYMNASIUM. In both

Having little regard for worldly things, the followers of Diogenes became known as CYNICS, the word apparently being applied to them because they were *kynikos*, dog-like. Diogenes himself is said to have lived in a barrel and could still be said to have been CYNICAL, even though the word has acquired a slightly extended meaning.

countries the word denotes a place of training but in both an essential feature is lacking: nakedness. Exercise, both mental and physical, is now undertaken by clothed participants but the Greeks saw no point in such coyness and one who undertook physical exercise was invariably a *gymnos*, a naked person. So those who use gymnasia are generally overdressed nowadays.

An Anglo-Saxon word which meant 'to show' has developed into the modern word TEACH. A teacher may also be called a PEDAGOGUE although the original bearers of that title held a rather more lowly position in life. With a name derived from the

Greek elements *paidos*, boy, and *agogos*, leading, a PEDAGOGUE
was a slave who took a well-born boy to and from school. The
word is hardly complimentary, carrying as it now does a
suggestion of severity, and the same sort of implications are
inherent in another word which the Italians formed from the
same source: applied specifically to those who overestimate the
value of book learning, the English word PEDANT is recognisably the same as the Italian version *pedante*. But those with no
learning have also been subject to mass abuse: the word LEWD,
for example, originally meant 'lay' as opposed to 'clerical' and,
therefore, unlettered rather than educated.

In Latin the word *doctor* means teacher and is associated with
the verb *docere*, to lead. In universities the teachers are still real
DOCTORS but in general usage the word has been taken over by
the medical fraternity. Now the title is used by anyone with a
medical degree, however lowly, but the original university
doctors were highly-qualified teachers of Divinity, Law or
Medicine. Although medical practitioners have appropriated
the title for themselves, the lawyers still call legal teachings
DOCTRINES and the Church is a past master when it comes to
INDOCTRINATION. Those who taught Arts were called MASTERS,
their title being derived from a Latin word for a man in
authority, *magister*. The word ART, from the Latin *ars*, denoted
skill acquired by study and practice; still with this meaning it is
used in phrases such as the 'black art' but the subjects of study
covered in the medieval universities were the trivium: Grammar, Logic and Rhetoric, then the quadrivium: Arithmetic,
Geometry, Music and Astronomy. All of them were pioneered
by the ancient Greeks. The words TRIVIUM and QUADRIVIUM,
however, are of Latin origin and mean 'three-way' and 'four-
way' respectively. Having graduated to the quadrivium, the
trivium seemed with hindsight to have been relatively simple,
TRIVIAL in fact. Trivia such as Grammar, Logic and Rhetoric
are now out of favour, there being much more important
subjects to study nowadays: Sociology and Economics, for
example.

One who PROFESSES knowledge is a PROFESSOR, both words

being derived from the Latin verb *profiteri* meaning 'to declare out loud'; and from the same word we have a description of those who are versed in esoteric knowledge, PROFESSIONAL. Having a *diploma*, professionals can also be said to be DIPLO-MATS; the first diplomas were folded sheets, a fact which explains their name, for the word *diploma* in Greek could be applied to anything folded in two or doubled over.

A university should like the universe turn as one, since the terms UNIVERSITY and UNIVERSE are both derived from Latin words which mean exactly that – *unum*, one and *vertere*, to turn. VARSITY is a corrupted form of *university*; no longer in common use in England (although it is elsewhere) the word is generally restricted to the names of competitions between the ancient universities, the intervarsity boat-race, for example. Older universities are made up of separate colleges, each of which is, itself, made up of fellows and scholars: the Latin word for a fellow is *collega*, from which we have the word COLLEAGUE, the Latin word being made up from the elements *col*, together, and *legere*, to choose. The word COLLEGE, which comes from the same source, originally denoted a body of people who as-sembled together for a specific purpose. At the universities this purpose was the pursuit of learning, as it still is in most modern colleges, but the original more general meaning is also pre-served in the names of the College of Arms and the College of Cardinals, and also in the expression, electoral college.

The word TRIPOD means the same as the Latin one from which it is derived: *tripus*. Another form of the word now used only at Cambridge University is TRIPOS, and its meaning has changed considerably: originally denoting a three-legged stool upon which a disputant sat while wrangling, arguing, discus-sing or reading satirical verse, the word subsequently attached itself to the disputant as well as his stool. Later the satirical verses of the TRIPOS also became known by that name and then, since the list of new Mathematics graduates was printed on the back of the TRIPOS paper, that list also became known as a TRIPOS. Then the word attached itself to the Mathematics examination as well as to the pass list and finally it has come to be applied to other examinations. Because of the arguing skills originally necessary to gain a degree in Mathematics, those mathematicians who gained a first class honours degree became known as WRANGLERS; their name appeared at the top of the tripos list when the results were published, and at the very bottom of the list was the name of the student whose performance only just qualified him for the degree. For no obvious reason he received a spoon made out of wood as a sort of booby prize: the origin of the custom is obscure but those who come last are still said to win a WOODEN SPOON.

The Universities of Oxford and Cambridge have tended to generate their own names for a large range of objects and practices. Thus a university friend at Cambridge was called a CRONY, originally a *chrony*, from the Greek word for time, *chronos*; the reference being to the fact that the friends were contemporaries. In Oxford, however, close friends and those who shared sets of rooms have, for hundreds of years, been known as CHUMS; the word CHUM being derived apparently from the expression *chamber fellow*. Often the origins of university slang are lost to posterity because, like much slang until relatively recently, the words were rarely written down, and were used only orally and in informal circumstances. It is not, therefore, certain that the word SNOB is taken from the abbreviation *s.nob* which stands for the Latin expression *sine nobilitate* and means literally 'without nobility'. The abbreviation was once used after the names of students not of noble birth and it is tempting to imagine that those who were noblemen came to be known as NOBS for similar reasons. Whatever the truth, it is certain that the gold tassels worn on the mortar boards of noble undergraduates were called 'tufts', and that other students who had pretensions to be counted amongst the aristocracy came to be known as TUFT HUNTERS. Now the expression is slightly old-fashioned although still applied to certain society hosts and hostesses; and a corrupted form of 'tuft', TOFF, is still used occasionally, especially by taxi drivers who use it as though it means 'one who tips heavily'.

It seems that in France the students were given to wrangling and disputing in places other than those specifically designed for that purpose. The Latin word *quamquam* which means 'although' was a favourite introduction to an argument and seems to have been overworked to the extent that it came to be applied to any piece of entertaining nonsense. In particular, the word is now associated with the sort of dance performed in the places of which the students were especially fond: but to disguise its academic background the word has changed from *quamquam* into CAN CAN.

14

Time to reflect

In any agrarian society people are more interested in time periods like days and months, rather than smaller intervals like seconds and minutes or longer ones like decades and centuries. Apart from anything else periods like days, months and years are natural units of time in that they can be measured by observation of the sun and moon. It is no surprise, therefore, to find that time periods greater than a day but less than a year mostly have ancient names which can be traced back at least to Anglo-Saxon times, while smaller and larger time units generally have more recent English names, often borrowed, directly or indirectly, from Greek or Latin.

The words Spring, Summer, Fall and Winter all have long ancestries which can be traced back to the distant past. SPRING the season, the source of water, the mechanical device and the action of jumping all retain the meaning of the word's ancient root: to burst forth. Springtime is the season when new plants burst forth. The name of SUMMER, Anglo-Saxon *sumer*, is also derived from an ancient root and like many such words has a readily identifiable parallel in other Indo-European languages;

Sanskrit *sama*, for example, means half-year. In England the word FALL as the name of a season gave way, for some reason, to AUTUMN, a word of Latin derivation, although the Americans have retained the shorter alternative to describe the time of year when the leaves fall from the trees. The last season of the year, WINTER, also has a long history; its name, unchanged since Saxon times, is ultimately derived from a word meaning to be wet. Indeed 'Winter' is almost certainly related to the words 'water' and 'wet'.

Just as the words Autumn and Fall were, at one time, contenders for the name of a season, so too were the words Spring and Lent. A shortened form of LENTEN, LENT comes directly from the Anglo-Saxon word *Lencten* meaning to lengthen, which is exactly what the days do in springtime. Easter, like Lent, has become associated with Christianity although it has an older significance: it was originally a festival held around April and named after the goddess Eastre or Eostre but, like many pagan practices, it was gradually absorbed into the Church's calendar. Another victim was the festival called Yule; originally related to the Anglo-Saxon verb *gylan*, meaning to make merry, the day now called Christmas Day was known as *geola*. The latter term later became YULE, a relative of the word JOLLY, and of the Old Norse word *jol*, the name of a pre-Christian feast which lasted twelve days and which is remembered in the Twelve Days of Christmas.

Christmas was a holy day and since no labour was expected on a *holy day* the language formed the word HOLIDAY to describe a period when no work was done. Christmas was also one of the four quarter days, the days on which quarterly rents were due. The others were, and still are: Lady Day, 25 March; Midsummer's Day, 24 June; and Michaelmas, 29 September. In Scotland, however, different dates are used: CANDLEMAS, the mass or festival when candles are blessed, 2 February; WHITSUNDAY, which was originally 'white Sunday', but is now dissociated from the religious festival of the same name, 15 May; LAMMAS, named from the Old English *hlaf*, bread, and *masse*, mass, 1 August; and Martinmas, St Martins Day, 11

November. Interestingly the English quarter days fall just after the equinoxes and solstices which mark the changes of season. The Spring equinox falls on about 21 March; the Summer solstice, 21 June; the Autumn equinox, 23 September; and the Winter solstice, 22 December. The words Equinox and Solstice, both of Latin derivation, appeared in English during the late sixteenth century and early seventeenth century respectively. The component parts of EQUINOX, *equi* and *nox*, mean 'equal night', that is, when night and day are of equal duration; and similarly SOLSTICE can be rendered 'sun-still', that is, when the sun reaches the extremes of the ecliptic and thus appears to stand still in the sense that it appears to follow the same path on successive days.

Like Latin, Greek has contributed many technical terms to the English language over the years. The names of the three divisions of the Stone Age, for example, are all of Greek derivation: *palaios*, old and *lithos*, stone, give PALEOLITHIC, the name of the Old Stone Age; *mesos*, middle, and *lithos* give MESOLITHIC, the Middle Stone Age; *neos*, new, and *lithos* give NEOLITHIC, the New Stone Age. EPOCH is another Greek word; literally it means a stop or pause and was applied to significant points in time; the interval between two successive epochs later became known as an ERA from a Latin word *æra* meaning 'a number expressed in figures'. The distinction between epoch and era has been lost although both words retain a suggestion of a long period of time with a definite beginning and end. The Greek word for time was CHRONOS and echoes of this term occur in many words: for example a CHRONOMETER measures time, an ANACHRONISM occurs at the wrong time, to SYNCHRONISE is to set to the same time, a CHRONICLE is a record in CHRONOLOGICAL order, and a disease which lasts a long time is said to be CHRONIC.

From *Shabath*, the ancient Hebrew word for rest, came SABBATH, the name of the Jewish day of relaxation. Just as every seventh day was one of rest, so every seventh year was a SABBATICAL year to the Israelites – and still is to some university lecturers. After the Reformation, the word SABBATH came to be used for the Christian day of rest (Sunday rather than Saturday) and then, in the seventeenth century, the largely imaginary witches' SABBATH acquired its name. Seven was an important number to the Israelites: after every seventh set of seven years, that is, each fiftieth year, there would be great festivities, the ground would be left fallow, debts would be forgiven and slaves set free. This occasion was marked by the blowing of a ram's horn and from the Hebrew *jobel*, the word for a ram's horn and thus a trumpeting sound, is derived the word JUBILEE. The fifty-year cycle is remembered in the expression golden jubilee and now we have a large selection of similar names, such as silver and diamond jubilee, to describe other periods of time. It is tempting to link the word jubilee to JUBILATION but this word is connected to the Latin verb *jubilare* meaning 'to shout for joy' and may be unrelated to the Hebrew. Events which are celebrated each year on the same date are called ANNIVERSARIES from the Latin words *annus*, meaning 'year', and a verb meaning 'to turn'; the seasons turn through a full cycle during the year. The Latin word *annus* also features, with different endings, in the words ANNUAL, 'occurring yearly' like the publication of some books, ANNUITY, a sum paid yearly, and ANNAL, a record of events year by year. Periods of more than a year generally have names which are also of Latin, or ultimately Greek, derivation. Thus the word DECADE, denoting a period of ten years, is related to the Greek word for ten, *deka*; CENTURY is derived from the Latin word for a hundred, *centum*; and MILLENNIUM comes from the Latin word for a thousand, *mille*. Small time intervals also tend to have names which are of classical origin. Thus the word HOUR comes from the Latin *hora* which in turn comes from a Greek word for season: the Greeks, it seems, thought of the hours as being the seasons of the day. Latin also gives minute and second: *minutus* meaning 'small' is the source of the word MINUTE, a minute being a small part of an hour or of a degree; and the expression *secunda minuta*, 'second minute', abbreviated to SECOND, simply denotes a second order of smallness.

In the Middle Ages small intervals of time could be measured

Wordly wise

by mechanical devices of relatively recent origin. Since the time had previously been announced by the church bell, the new time-pieces were called by the alternative name for such bells – CLOCKS, the Anglo-Saxon word for a bell being *clugga*. The names MORNING and EVENING both have Anglo-Saxon origins, *morgen* and *aefnung*, and AFTERNOON is self-explanatory, but NOON holds a surprise: its name comes from the Latin *nona hora*, the ninth hour, for noon used to be at what is now 3 p.m., nine hours after the start of the day at 6 a.m. Six hours after the start of the day comes the *sexta hora* when the Portuguese have their *sesta* and the Spanish their SIESTA. The word MERIDIAN broken down into its constituent parts literally means 'mid-day'; hence a.m., *ante meridiem*, means before midday and p.m., *post meridiem*, means after midday. In modern English the word 'time' has taken the place of 'tide', a term which has now been relegated to the sea except in old compounds such as Yuletide and eventide. It also lives on disguised in the word TIDY which originally meant the same as timely; but from the idea of the appropriate time came the present meaning of the appropriate, and thus appropriately prepared, place.

In general, the Romance languages have played only a small part in donating words to describe periods of time greater than a day but less than a year. The word DAY, itself, is a direct descendant of the Anglo-Saxon form *daeg* and similarly NIGHT comes from the Anglo-Saxon word *niht*. Ancient Greek has made a small inroad into the language, however, in the form of EPHEMERAL, a word which literally means 'of one day's duration'. Latin has made a larger intrusion: from *diurnus* comes another word for daily, DIURNAL; but via the French it has also provided JOURNAL (a daily record); SOJOURN (to spend a day); JOURNEY (to travel or work for a day); JOURNEYMAN (one who earns a full day's wage); ADJOURN (to put off until another day) and JOURNEY CAKE which is now often corrupted to JOHNNY CAKE. Other possible corrupted forms are JERRY-built (built to last only a day); JURY mast (a temporary mast); JURY rig (a temporary rig) and JURY leg (a temporary wooden leg).

Returning to more common words for periods of time, WEEK,

from the Anglo-Saxon *wicu*, has outlasted SE'NNIGHT, 'seven night', although its sibling FORTNIGHT, earlier FORTE'NNIGHT, 'fourteen nights', has survived. The word MONTH, Anglo-Saxon *monath*, is closely related to the word moon; the phases of the moon being indicators of each month's progression. Until they were usurped by their Latin counterparts the names of the months reflected the agricultural year very closely. JANUARY is named after *Janus*, the two-headed god who looked forward to the new year and backwards into the old. The name *Janus* is related to the Latin word for a door, *janua*, hence the term JANITOR meaning doorkeeper. But the original Anglo-Saxon name for the month was *se æfterra geola*, the 'after Yule', or alternatively *wulf-monath*, the month when hungry wolves would have presented more problems than usual. The Roman purification festival held on 15 FEBRUARY gave that month its present name, for *februare* meant to cleanse or expiate; the Anglo-Saxon name had been *Sol-monath* or 'mud-month'. MARCH is named after *Mars*, the god of war, because military campaigns were restarted in that month having been abandoned for the Winter. The Saxons called it *hreth-monath*, the 'rough month', and it was also known as *lencten-monath* for the same reason that Lent was so-called, that is, because the days grow longer at this time. *Aperire*, the Latin verb meaning 'to open', gave the word APRIL for the time of year when the flowers open, but to the Anglo-Saxons it had been *Easter-monath*, the festival of the goddess Eostre. MAY is so-called after the Roman goddess *Maia*; the Anglo-Saxon equivalent was *thri-milce*, the month when '*three milkings*' were possible each day. The origin of the word JUNE is a Roman clan or family name *Junius* but to the Anglo-Saxons it was *seærra litha*, 'the joy time', or *sere-monath*, the dry month. JULY was *se æfterra litha*, 'the second joy time', or *mæd-monath*, the month when cattle were put into the meadows; the original Roman name had been *Quinctilis*, meaning the fifth month, but Mark Anthony renamed it *Julius* in honour of *Julius Caesar* who was born in this month. Similarly *Augustus* Caesar gave his name to AUGUST replacing the earlier name *Sextilis* which meant the sixth month. Augustus thought that his month should not have fewer days in it than his uncle's, so he took an extra one from February which partially explains why that month is so short. The indigenous English name for August had been *weod-monath*, the month when vegetation flourished. SEPTEMBER, the seventh month named from the Latin *septem* meaning seven, had been *gerst-monath*, 'barley month', *hæfest-monath*, 'harvest month', or later *halig-monath*, 'holy month'. Because the original Roman calendar had started two months after the Anglo-Saxon one, OCTOBER, the Roman's eighth month named from the Latin for eight, *octe*, corresponds to the Anglo-Saxon *teo-monath*, literally the tenth month. NOVEMBER, the Roman's ninth month, so-called because the Latin word for nine is *novus*, was known to the Anglo-Saxons as *wind-monath* or *blot-monath*, 'blood month', the time when cattle were slaughtered for the winter. DECEMBER, the Roman's tenth month, was to the Anglo-Saxons *se aerra geola*, 'before Yule' in contrast to January which was 'after Yule'; since the Anglo-Saxon year actually started on what we now call Christmas Day these names were more accurate than they might now seem, the date of the English new year having been moved first to 25 March and then to 1 January. Before Julius Caesar reformed the Roman calendar in 46 BC, March had been the first month of the year and hence *Quintilis* really had been the 'fifth month', *Sextilis* the 'sixth', September the 'seventh', October the 'eighth', November the 'ninth', December the 'tenth'. In the reformed calendar, however, January became the first month, and so could be thought of as looking backwards to the old year and forward to the new.

When the Norman French arrived in 1066 they brought with them their own new year. One quarter day, Yule, 25 December, gave way to another, Lady Day, 25 March, as the first day of the new year. Lady Day was dedicated to the Virgin *Mary* so this annual cycle became known as the MARIAN year. It continued to be used in England until 1752 when the calendar was finally reformed. As early as 1582, Pope Gregory XIII had altered the continental calendar by losing ten days from October and refining the occurrence of leap years. This change had become necessary because the dates and seasons no longer matched up in the traditional way: too many leap years had resulted in a loss of synchrony between dates and seasons. But Protestant England waited a further 170 years before relenting, falling into line by losing 11 days from September and abolishing leap years for every round century not divisible by 400. This change was not universally popular: the ignorant imagined that they would lose 11 days of their lives and the more sophisticated spotted the effect on taxation and interest payments. For this latter reason the fiscal year continued to end on the old 25 March which is 11 days later than the present 25 March. This explains why, even now, the tax year runs from 6 April to the 5 April. The Russian calendar incidentally was not reformed until 1918.

As Mary gave her name to the Marian Calendar so Julius Caesar gave his name to the JULIAN Calendar and Pope Gregory XIII his to the GREGORIAN. The word CALENDAR, itself, comes from *calendarium*, the name of an account book, which had, in turn, taken its name from the Roman calends: the first day of each month when accounts became due for payment. Roman habits also provided the word DATE: letters would start *datum Romae*, 'given at Rome', followed by the time, and from this association of data and time comes the modern word DATE. The word DATUM, along with its plural DATA, has also been appropriated by the English language to denote given information.

Although the Roman influence had such a sweeping effect on the months of the year, the days of the week, with one exception, have Teutonic names; even if they are translations of the Roman names. SUNDAY comes from the Old English *sunnen dæg*, the day of the sun, while MONDAY, *monan dæg*, was the day of the moon. Tiw, also called Tiu and Tyr, was the Norse god of war who gave his name to TUESDAY which in Old English was *Tiwes dæg*. The variations of Tiw's name come from a much older, Indo-European root which also gave the Greeks the name *Zeus* and the Romans the word *Deus*. Another Norse god, Wodin, Woden or Odin provided WEDNESDAY, earlier *Wodnes dæg*, and Thor donated his name to THURSDAY, *Thures dæg*. FRIDAY, Old English *frige dæg*, is named after the goddess Friya, Frigga or

Freyja but Saturday is an interloper from Rome: from *Saturni Dies*, 'the day of Saturn', came the corresponding English form *sæten dæg* and subsequently the present form SATURDAY.

Words often disguise their ancestry by changes in spelling and pronunciation, and sometimes they change in different ways depending upon time and place. Thus, for example, the Anglo-Saxon word *wer*, meaning 'man', survives in a number of forms in different compounds, although the word itself has died out. VERMOUTH and WORMWOOD both mean 'man-mood'; a WEREWOLF is a 'man-wolf'; WER-GELD was 'man-money', what we now usually call blood money; and CANTERBURY is '*cant-ware-burgh*', the Kent man's town. Our ancestors called their existence on Earth 'the age of man', or using an ancient meaning of the word 'old', 'man-old'. To the Anglo-Saxons the whole of existence was '*wer-old*', what we now call the WORLD.

15

The root of all evil

I Timothy 6, 10 'For the love of money is the root of all evil . . .'

New inventions require new words to describe them, and occasionally an innovation comes along which is so important that a whole host of new descriptions is required. Some terms are freshly coined when first needed and some are borrowed permanently from their previous owners. The world of finance, for example, has begged, stolen and borrowed its vocabulary from other spheres ever since the first monetary token was put into circulation.

Since cattle provided one of the earliest mediums of exchange it is not surprising that words for cattle have transferred to monetary tokens. Thus the Anglo-Saxon word *feoh*, originally applied to livestock, has developed into the modern word FEE. At one time, not so long ago, the term 'fee house' could be applied equally well to either a treasury or a cattle shed. So, too, a system based upon ownership is a FEUDAL one and a business partner, who laid his money together with another's, was a 'fee layer', *feolaga*, what we now call a FELLOW. A similar association of cattle and wealth occurs in Latin where the word *pecu* meant 'cattle' and *pecunia* meant 'money'. Thus in English the word PECUNIARY means 'concerning money' and IMPECU-NIOUS means 'without money'. As we talk of so many 'head' of cattle so the Latin word for 'head', *caput*, is also connected with cattle and hence wealth: as well as the word CAPITAL, meaning a store of wealth, we have the word CATTLE itself as well as its sibling CHATTEL which is applied to more general possessions. The word capital has kept its meaning of 'head' in most of its other applications: a country's head city is its capital, at the head of a sentence is a capital letter, the head of a column is called its capital, and one form of capital punishment is behead-ing, i.e. decapitation.

Monata was an epithet of the Roman goddess Juno whose functions included the giving of warnings; the Latin word *monata* comes from the verb *monere*, to warn. The epithet also provided a name for Juno's temple and since the first Roman mint was situated next to it the word was applied to that too. Passing through Old French, *monata* became the modern English MONEY but taking another route, via the Old English form *mynet*, it also gave the word MINT. CASH, a term which until the late sixteenth century was applied to a money box, comes ultimately from a Latin word meaning a case, *capsa*. The word WEALTH is an Anglo-Saxon resident; derived from *wela* it originally meant well-being – as it still does in the compound COMMONWEALTH and in phrases such as 'the wealth of nations'. Other words have had a longer journey: for example, the Greek word for a peg, *konos*, gave the Romans a word for a wedge which has since provided builders with the term QUOIN, applied to wedge-shaped stones. The Latin form also went on in French to become a term for a die, then specifically a stamp for impressing money; English made another slight change to give itself the word COIN, a word which in French can mean die, stamp, wedge or corner but which in English is more common as a word for metal currency. In appearance it is not unlike that of its distant cousin the word CONE. In fact conical dies were for a long time used for coining metal currency.

In many ways coining money is similar to coining phrases. As new money gains currency so too does a new expression. 'To utter' was originally to put into circulation, as specifically goods and money might be; later, less material objects like words were said to be uttered when they too were put into circulation. As a metal coin might be tested to see if it 'rings true' so, too, might the latest rumour.

Monetary terms have been selected by an eclectic process. Although many different sources have been tapped there are a few common themes which recur again and again. One such is the connection between money and weight; traders soon recognised that the value of a chunk of metal could be found simply by weighing it, as long as it was pure. The word POUND is the most obvious example of this association; it still retains its meaning of a measure of weight as well as that of a monetary unit. In Anglo-Saxon times the pound was divided into mancuses, mancuses into shillings and shillings into pennies. The mancus has been lost but the word shilling still seems to reflect its role as a division of a division of a pound: with its double diminutive ending 'lling' it is literally a 'little little part'. The PENNY, Anglo-Saxon *pening*, was a silver coin until as late as 1797 when it was replaced by a copper one. Small change is still sometimes referred to as COPPER, although bronze has been used since 1860 (Maundy pennies, however, are still silver). The abbreviations for pounds, shillings and pence were £, s, and d; £ or L stands for the Latin word *libra*, meaning a balance, which is another reminder of the connection with weighing; 's' is from *solidus*, the name of a Roman coin, and similarly 'd' is from *denarius*. From the East of Germany came the *Easterlings*, the first reputable money-makers in England; their reputation may have produced the terms STERLING silver and later the expression 'pounds STERLING'. Since decimalisation, the pound and the reformed penny have continued their ancient roles. The English shilling however has gone, presumably for ever, although its relative, the Austrian schilling, survives. Also lost are the FLORIN, replaced by the 10p piece; it was originally a coin from *Florence* which bore a *floral* design*; the FARTHING,

*The crown, which bore the design of a royal crown.

literally a '*fourthling*', a quarter of a penny; the GUINEA, a coin made of gold imported from *Guinea*; the sovereign, originally a coin showing the Sovereign, Henry VII, on one face; and the long-gone GROAT – literally a '*great*' coin. The 'bit' as in 'threepenny bit' has also gone west, but only as far as America where it is now part of a dollar. Dollars were first minted in sixteenth century Europe: specifically, they were produced in Joachim's Dale and were thus called *Joachimsthaler*. But this name was too long for popular use so it contracted to *thaler* and then changed to DOLLAR. Americans also call dollars BUCKS because their early ones literally were *buck* skins (rather than less valuable doe skins). The name of the American coin known as a DIME comes from the French and corresponds to the English word tithe, meaning a tenth part, just as a CENT(ime) is literally a hundredth part. A small coin known in Ireland as a rap has provided the phrase 'NOT TO GIVE A RAP' just as the Indian coin *dam* has at least influenced the parallel expression 'NOT TO GIVE A DAMN'. A SEQUIN or *Zecchino* was originally a small Italian coin and a *gazetta*, another small coin, was the price of an Italian newspaper sold during the wars between Venice and Turkey. The name of the coin was transferred to the publication and thus gave the word GAZETTE. Earlier the city of Byzantium (Constantinople), now Turkish Istanbul, has produced a coin known as a BEZANT which has maintained a precarious existence in heraldic jargon. Another survivor is the TALENT, so-called from the Greek *talanton* which denoted a sum of money and, as might be expected, also a weight. From the biblical parable of the talents (Matt. 25, 14–30) comes the present meaning of the word TALENT, 'aptitude' or 'faculty'. From the action of weighing comes another word, STIPEND which literally means to weigh alms: its second part, derived from the Latin verb *pendere*, to weigh, has also provided the word PENSION. It is also associated with the Old English word *pund*, and hence the modern English POUND.

As a stipend is a sum paid to a clergyman or to a stipendiary magistrate, so an emolument was the profit of a miller. The word EMOLUMENT comes from the Latin verb *emolere*, to grind out. Roman soldiers did not make profits; they were paid by the state and part of their allowance was made in salt. Later this part of their allowance came to be paid in money although its name continued to reflect its purpose: *salarium* means literally 'salt money'. From this term comes the word SALARY and also the phrase 'worth one's salt'. A wage was originally a pledge or a declaration that payment would be made; it has since come to mean payment but retains a hint of its earlier meaning in phrases such as 'waging war'. A surprising number of words have both military and monetary associations: 'mercenary' is an obvious example and 'reserve' is another. The word SUBSIDY is less obvious: it was originally applied to Roman soldiers who were held in reserve waiting for action. The word soldier itself comes from the Latin *solidus*. GARNISHEE is a noun derived from the verb 'to garnish', to serve notice for the purpose of attaching money. The word GARNISH comes from the Old French verb *garnir* or *warnir* meaning 'to take warning'. Later it came to mean 'equip with arms'; later still it was applied to the armour itself and then specifically to fancy armour; thus the word GARNISH has also acquired the present sense of decoration or embellishment. 'To pay' is literally to 'pacify' but the word COMMISSION has a more interesting history: derived from a Latin word *commissus* meaning 'sent together', it first denoted the authority to act together, then the group so authorised (like a royal commission); then it came to be applied to the warrant giving such authorisation (as in an army officer's COMMISSION) and then to the subject of the warrant. Finally it associated itself with the monetary allowance made for the execution of the warrant and now it can be applied to other allowances, such as a broker's COMMISSION.

The words COMPUTE, COUNT, ACCOUNT and DISCOUNT are all derived from the Latin verb *computare* meaning 'to reckon together'. Computing sounds less distressing than engaging in BUSINESS, this word being derived from the Old English *bisigness*, meaning 'to occupy' or 'to worry'. FINANCE was originally a payment to settle a debt in full; the Latin *finare* meant to pay a FINE and *finis* was a settled debt, i.e. one that had been

FINISHED. Debts which are not settled attract INTEREST in more ways than one, but both senses derive from yet another Latin word *interesse*, 'to be concerned with'. Wise creditors ensure that money lent by them has been adequately secured; this practice is very old and is reflected in the word BORROW which comes from the Old English noun *borg*, meaning a pledge or security. Loans which are not secured are fiduciary – given in trust. Banks, of course, attempt to obtain adequate security whenever possible; they have been in business long enough to have learned how to minimise their own risk. An Anglo-Saxon *banke* was anything flat, like the banks of a river; money dealers used to trade over flat benches so that they became known as BANKERS. Insolvent dealers stood a good chance of having violence directed towards both them and their places of work; if their benches or '*banks*' were broken up then they would be literally BANKRUPT. One type of secured loan is the mortgage; technically the word should be applied to the document which gives the security for a loan but, as the constituent parts of the word show, it was once a '*mort-gage* (or wage)', literally a death pledge. An impoverished heir could raise a loan on the security of his father's estate then later, when the father died and the heir inherited, the loan could be repaid. At least it could be if there were sufficient funds left after the dead man's debts had been repaid. The fourteenth century term *aseth* was used to describe that part of a dead man's estate which was to be used to discharge his debts: it is easily recognisable as the modern word ASSET.

As a mortgage was a death pledge, so mortmain was a 'dead hand'. Feudal obligations in the thirteenth century could be avoided by making over land to the Church (the 'dead hand') and then leasing it back. This tax dodge was severely limited by the Statute of Mortmain in 1279. By then tax avoidance was less harshly treated than it had been previously: the Danes had earlier imposed a nose tax in Ireland. It is said to have been so-called because the penalty for not paying up was having one's nostrils split open, hence, possibly, the phrase 'paying through the nose'.

Another Danish tax, in the North of England, had been danegeld which was effectively no more than protection money. Blackmail was another form of protection money payable near the Scottish border; it was paid in labour or cattle, while properly authorised 'white rent' was paid in silver. Another form of tax was the SCOT, named after an Anglo-Saxon coin the *sceat*, and its name survives in the phrase SCOT FREE. TARIFF was originally yet another form of blackmail, this time charged by Mediterranean pirates from the North African port of *Tarifa*. Even paying homage once involved literally dipping into one's purse as an integral part of feudal service. A vassal's service was called HOMAGE because it was the service of a man and the Latin word for a man is *homo*. Originally homage had been a man's public act of pledging allegiance to his lord.

Income tax is a relatively recent form of taxation and was introduced 'temporarily' in order to finance the Napoleonic wars. Tax revenue has, since well before Napoleonic times, been dealt with by the Exchequer, a government department with a truly chequered history. The Persian title *shah*, meaning king, passed through Arabic into Old French where it took the form *esches* and gave the game of CHESS its name. When, in that game, the king was threatened, the attacker would call *eschec*, whence the word CHECK meaning 'to hold in place'. The black and white chequered board on which the game was played was an *eschequier*; this was a convenient surface upon which to count government revenues and thus the EXCHEQUER got its name. An official of the Exchequer was the *escheater* whose practices provided the language with the word CHEATER and thus the verb to CHEAT. As some words with financial connotations have come down in the world so others have risen. The word economy, for example, originally meant merely 'household management', but has gained in status in much the same way as the word BUDGET; this word comes from the Old French *bougette*, a wallet, and is ultimately derived, via Latin, from a Celtic word for a bag. In order to finance its activities the government raises money by borrowing as well as by taxation. Until the last century, government loans were acknowledged in the following manner: a piece of wood was marked with the details of the loan, the sum borrowed being indicated by notches. Such notches had been used since ancient times as a method of recording numbers and it is no coincidence that the word SCORE means both 'notch' and 'twenty'. Once marked, the piece of wood was split along its length: the lender retained one half of it, the 'stock', and the Exchequer kept the other half, the 'counter stock'. When repayment was due the two halves were matched up in order to confirm that the redemption was valid. From the French word *taille*, meaning a cut or incision, came the name for the wooden sticks, TALLIES or tally sticks, and also the verb to TALLY, meaning to match up. From the same ultimate source come the titles of TELLERS (who were originally in charge of the tallies) and TALLYMEN (hawkers who also keep tallies). Tally sticks had been used for a very long time before their popularity declined in the last century; their one-time importance is demonstrated by the number of words that have been absorbed into the language as a result of their use: for example, stocks are still issued by governments and other financial institutions, teller's figures must still tally, and scores are still notched up.

Over the centuries the government's tally stick records accumulated until they took up more space in the parliament building than could be justified. Accordingly, in 1834 the stores of the House of Lords were used as a convenient method of disposal. Unfortunately the resulting fire also disposed of most of the Palace of Westminster; which explains why a large proportion of the present parliament buildings dates from the nineteenth century. As is so often the case, the intentions of government policy did not quite tally with actual results.

16

The turn of the screw

Our forefathers recognised very few crimes, but the perpetrators of those crimes which they did recognise were severely punished. By contrast modern penal codes identify many more illegal acts and inflict much lighter sentences upon supposed wrongdoers. In Saxon times a youth could ride to the house of a brewer who might sell beer until any hour of the day or night. There he could gamble, dance, eat and drink to his heart's content; upon leaving he might answer a call of nature by the roadside and then ride home. Should he try it a thousand years on he would almost certainly break the law: not just one law but probably dozens, and with only a little effort hundreds. On the other hand, committing serious crime is not such a risky business as it once was. Torture, dismemberment and judicial execution, once common, are now quite rare in the civilised world, and the first-time thief may well get a lighter sentence than the motorist who parks on a yellow line.

Punishments may change but many crimes continue down the centuries hardly altered. PICKPOCKETS are criminals who do exactly that, pick pockets. But before pockets, or little bags, were sewn into the clothing they were hung on strings from the belt where they could easily be removed by the dexterous use of a knife; so instead of worrying about pickpockets, honest citizens were obliged to watch out for CUTPURSES. Sneakthieves must operate stealthily, and indeed the word STEALTH was originally applied to the practice or action of stealing. The word steal still possesses an underlying idea of unnoticed action, especially when applied to sleep or darkness which steal over, not from, their victims. With this association of sneakiness was the Anglo-Saxon term *thiof*, which has become the modern THIEF. In a crowd it was, and is, a common practice to create a disturbance during which a theft could be carried out. In the

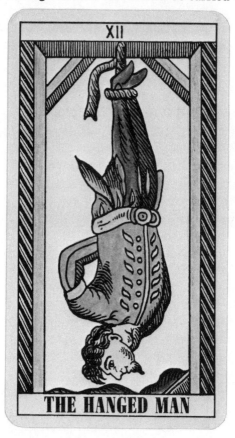

commotion physical contact might easily go unnoticed and, even if the stolen item were missed, the thief would still stand a good chance of escape. The commotion of the mob caused a noise or racket and the organisers of crime are thus called RACKETEERS; in the USA they moved into blackmail and extortion and so these operations also became known as RACKETS or euphemistically as 'protection' RACKETS. The fickle crowd, incidentally, being so changeable, was known to the Latin-loving upper classes as a *mobile vulgus*, then simply as a *mobile*, and finally as a MOB.

Whether or not it is justified, the Irish have developed a close linguistic association with civil disturbance, commotion and troublemaking. The term BALLYHOO, for example, seems to be derived from the name of the Irish village called Ballyhooly; but the range of influence is far greater than that. In London the Houlihan family created so much trouble that they gave their common surname to the language as HOOLIGAN. At about the same time the Australians were suffering from the activities of an individual who left his name as the term LARRIKIN, and in the USA it was a young man called Muldoon. Apparently a newspaper reporting his activities disguised his surname by reversing the letters to give the fictitious name 'Noodlum' which, because of a typesetting error, ended up as HOODLUM. Other Irishmen were busy creating trouble at the same time, for the word BARNEY, which also seems to have arisen from a common Irish name, was, like the rest, first recorded in the nineteenth century soon after the main Irish migrations to England, the USA and Australia. However much trouble the Irish caused, they were hardly in the same league as the Indian sect known as the *thugs* whose title, derived from the Hindi word *thag*, a cheat, has developed into the English term THUG. They were originally called cheats or deceivers because they would pretend to make friends with their victims before strangling them. On an even larger scale, the Barbarian hordes, and in particular a Germanic tribe known as the VANDALS, had already gained a reputation for causing widespread destruction in Roman times. The original tribe has passed into history but vandalism lives on. Back in Ireland the supposedly barbarous natives of the sixteenth century were separated from the civilised inhabitants by stockades. These stockades were made of stakes or PALES, from the Latin word *palus* meaning a pointed stick. Those who lived outside the stockade were literally 'beyond the pale' and those who tried to get in risked IMPALING themselves. Similar earlier PALISADES in Rome may well account ultimately for the title of a grand building within the defensive works: a PALACE (like Augustus's on the PALATINE hill in Rome). More modest buildings may manage with smaller stakes or PALINGS around them.

Those beyond the pale were outside the law in that they were physically removed from the jurisdiction of the courts. But in medieval times it was possible to be without the protection of the law wherever one lived. A court could, and often did, declare a criminal to be outside the law: to be, in other words, an OUTLAW; thenceforth as far as the state was concerned that person did not exist. Forfeiting all rights to justice, such a one could not own land or goods, and if injured by another could have no recourse to the courts. As a consequence of this principle it was perfectly legal for people to kill outlaws without themselves being guilty of murder. Remarkably a sentence of outlawry was passed by an American judge as recently as the latter half of this century. Some American states have retained other archaic punishments into this century despite their abolition long ago in Europe. Metaphorically we might still pillory people for their unconventional views, or alternatively treat them as a laughing stock. But the pillory and the stocks, in which wrongdoer's hands and feet were trapped, provide literal memories for some living Americans.

Some punishments and related techniques live on only in name: for example, a man may be 'branded' as a criminal without bearing any physical mark; in earlier times he might really have been branded on the cheek or chest, B for a Blasphemer, V for a Vagabond, F for a Fray-maker in church and K for what, to the Romans, had been a *Kalumnia* or *Calumnia*, a false accuser, guilty of CALUMNY. Those in Church

The stocks are so-called because they, or part of them, are made of pieces of wood. A STOCK is just a wooden post or log and takes its name from the Anglo-Saxon word *stocc* which had the same meaning. Thus the phrase STOCK STILL means simply as still as a log.

Being put into the stocks or pillory was not quite as harmless and picturesque as sometimes imagined. Punishments like those shown above might be combined to provide additional suffering; and the public could contribute rotting vegetables, dead animals and assorted excrement to make the environment even more unpleasant.

orders could plead benefit of clergy; at one time they would not suffer at all for their misdeeds simply because of their status. But abuse of this privilege was widespread and small concessions were eventually made: for example, a T brand on the left thumb for Theft and an M for Man-slaughter. Even so the system provided rather good value for numerous ecclesiastical criminals who would have been executed but for their position. Similarly, privileged children could usually avoid any real punishment for their wrongdoings. Another child could be paid to take any beating due to the real culprit and, usually being a boy and suffering a whipping, though innocent, such a one was a WHIPPING-BOY.

The death penalty was first abolished in England by William the Conqueror, but capital offences were soon creeping back on to the statute books. Even after its supposed abolition in this century the ultimate deterrent still endures for some crimes: arson in Her Majesty's dockyards, piracy with violence and, of course, the crime of treason. Historically the usual punishment for those found guilty of treason was to be drawn through the streets at the tail of a horse, hanged until almost dead and then dismembered, various parts of the body being subsequently displayed at key points throughout the kingdom. The unfortunate victim was thus drawn, hanged and quartered but, perhaps because there was also a practice of disembowelment or 'withdrawing' the entrails (and sometimes burning them) at some stage during the proceedings, the usual phrase has become 'hanged, drawn and quartered' rather than 'drawn, hanged and quartered'.

Hanging was, until recent times, reserved for the lower classes, high ranking men and women generally being beheaded by the axe or, as in Anne Boleyn's case, by the sword. But if for any reason a Peer of the Realm was hanged rather than beheaded it was customary to allow the luxury of a silk, instead of a hemp, rope for the purpose. The best remembered English hangman and executioner is probably JACK KETCH whose name has become synonymous with the title of his trade. But some fifty years before he was appointed there was another famous hangman who worked at Tyburn, near the place in London now known as Marble Arch. Gibbets, and later similar mechanical devices, were named after him; but now his name is more generally applied specifically to cranes: it was DERRICK.

Before the police force was formed in the first half of the last century, a body of men known as 'the watch' were responsible for preventing crime and catching criminals. They have gone but their passwords live on as WATCHWORDS. Sir Robert Peel introduced the first constabulary in Ireland, when he was Chief Secretary there; a few years later, in 1829, as the Home Secretary he started a similar force in London. Because he was responsible for their introduction policemen are still occasionally known by one of his names: they are sometimes called BOBBIES, and sometimes, though rarely, PEELERS. The word

COP may be related to the Latin *capere*, to take; spelled *cap*, it has existed in English for hundreds of years and from it comes the common name for a policeman, a 'captor', *'capper'* or COPPER, which the Americans have shortened again back to COP. A detective, like his dog, is a bloodhound who follows a trail. But if a red herring has been drawn across the trail then the hunter might be thrown off the scent, the smell of smoked herring being enough to divert any animal. The bloodhound or tracker-dog used to be called a SLEUTH-HOUND because it followed a track: the word SLEUTH being derived from the Old Norse *sloth* meaning a track or trail. By extension detectives are now called sleuths as well, since they also follow trails. Animal hunters remember the original meaning of the word more precisely when they speak of a slot, for in this sense the word SLOT, applied to animal footprints, has changed little since it took the form *sloth* well over a thousand years ago.

The keep of a Norman castle was a *donjon*, merely a tower belonging to the master. Gaining a sinister reputation and inexplicably moving underground it has become a modern DUNGEON. Here, according to popular belief, various tortures were applied throughout the centuries. Doubtless some were, but until the eighteenth century it was the practice to send state prisoners across the Scottish border to have their tongues loosened: torture being legal in Scotland but not in England. Many tortures rely upon a gradual turning motion to inflict the most exquisite agony: metaphorically we still apply the 'thumb-screws' and we may still be 'racked' with pain though no physical handle is turned. The TURNKEY is named after the tools of his trade, the keys to the cells; and for a similar reason modern prison warders have come to be known as SCREWS: in this context the word screw is a shortened version of 'screw-driver', this in turn being a slang term for a key, especially a skeleton key. From a Latin verb *torquere* meaning 'to twist' or 'to turn' come the words TORTURE and TORMENT (originally applied to an engine of war which worked by using TORSION). Tortured features may be twisted together or CONTORTED, while the limbs were twisted out of place or DISTORTED. Not too harsh

This is a detail of a print from 1833 which shows that the introduction of the Metropolitan Police did not meet with universal approval. At least the uniforms have changed.

The word POLICE comes from the same source as POLICY and POLITICIAN, by way of Rome and France, from Greece where *polis* meant city or city-state. A 'mother-city' is a '*metro-polis*' or METROPOLIS, so the Metropolitan Police have adopted the same word twice over.

a punishment, perhaps, for an EXTORTIONIST who had 'twisted' money out of an innocent victim.

Other methods of inflicting pain or death still remembered in the language include 'hauling over coals', a favourite of the Church to obtain a confession of heresy (Roman Catholic inquisitors not being allowed to spill blood), and the Scottish 'iron maiden', a nasty piece of work whose spikes saw the end of many a politician with too much ambition. If a torture victim eventually confessed then the tormentor might be authorised to take pity and administer a quick end: being a stroke of mercy, it was a 'blow of grace' or as the French would have it, a COUP DE GRÂCE. As the law stood for centuries, the admission of guilt or return of a guilty verdict enabled the courts to seize the culprit's property. One who refused to plead at all could not be tried, so could not be convicted and could not, therefore, suffer confiscation of property as well as death. In order that one's family might benefit, it was possible to stand mute and subsequently suffer *peine forte et dure*, 'punishment, intense and severe'. An individual who refused to plead and so stood mute could quite literally come under pressure, for the punishment involved being laid down and pressed under heavy weights until a plea was obtained. Should death intervene then the property was safe. Nowadays the pressures of life are rather less onerous.

Echoes of the past abound everywhere. Once the CLINK was a specific prison named after an area in Southwark also called the Clink; in fact the site of the prison, which burned down in the eighteenth century, is still called Clink Street (London SE1). Now the word clink can be applied to any prison. During the American Civil War, a prisoner-of-war camp near Andersonville had a line marked within the perimeter fence, beyond which the prisoners were not permitted to go; anyone who crossed it would be shot dead, so prisoners were safer keeping to their DEADLINE than they were going over it.

As prisons have evolved, so also have the crimes which provided their inmates. The Latin verb, *facere*, to make, has provided us with the honest blacksmith's FORGE but also with the crime of FORGERY. One who 'makes known' or utters a story is usually harmless but one who circulates or utters counterfeit money commits a serious crime. More recent, but still more than three hundred years old, is the name of the practice of taking children or 'nabbing kids': KIDNAPPING. Once they were taken for sale to ships' captains but now it is more lucrative to sell them back to their parents. More recent still is SABOTAGE, named after the French word *sabot*, a shoe or clog, itself taken from a similar Turkish word SHABATA. How the word sabotage arose no one seems to know for certain: perhaps the underlying idea of encumbrance is exactly parallel to that possessed by the word 'clog', or perhaps the bad workmanship or clumsiness of peasants' shoes suggested the association; it may be that the connection is provided by peasants trampling down their master's crops, thus sabotaging the harvest; or perhaps the practice of removing *sabots* or railway 'shoes' which attach the line to the sleepers has produced the present meaning of the word. Yet another possibility is that recalcitrant workers, instead of 'throwing a spanner into the works' as they might do nowadays, would sabotage production by throwing a clog into the machinery. In any event the word sabotage is unrecorded in English until 1910.

What we lose on the swings, we gain on the roundabouts and there is at least one unpleasant crime which seems to have fallen by the wayside: the word MAYHEM, originally Old French, once denoted the crime of deliberately maiming or disabling in order to prevent retaliation. The crime is gone but the word MAYHEM still survives, along with its alternative form MAIM.

17

A legal tangle

To their eternal credit the Normans did not attempt to impose their own system of justice on the conquered Anglo-Saxons of eleventh-century England. Had they done so, the rigidly codified Roman legal system might well have formed the basis of almost all national law in the Western World. Whatever the other consequences of the Normans' decision, it is certain that English law would not have developed in the way that it has, and equally certain that the entire English-speaking world would have been the poorer. Of course there were some changes in the administration of justice following William's invasion: Canon Law was separated from the main body of law and its administration was taken over by the Church; the Common Law was gradually unified and refined by judges for the General Eyre, or circuit judges as their later counterparts were known; and a whole new legal vocabulary was introduced.

The few remnants of Anglo-Saxon legal vocabulary have tended to lose any connection with modern concepts of justice. The Anglo-Saxon word *doeman* meant 'to give judgement' but it has evolved into the less judicial modern term DEEM. Closely related is the word DOOM – the crack of doom is simply the day of judgement and the original form *dom* forms part of another word for a day of judgement: DOMESDAY, as in the Domesday Book. The idea that supernatural forces could be summed to give judgement resulted in the ancient practice of trial by ordeal. The Anglo-Saxon word *ordel*, which also meant simply 'judgement', was applied to a practice which took a number of forms. Ordeal of boiling water required the accused to immerse a hand in hot water. This was the usual ordeal for those of low birth; high-born persons were generally subjected to ordeal of fire, which involved either holding or walking over red-hot

iron; if no wound appeared after three days then the accused was deemed to be not guilty. Other ordeals were not so harsh on the genuinely innocent: ordeal of the bier, for example, required a suspected murderer to touch the corpse of his alleged victim; if the body bled then guilt was established, if not then the suspect went free.

Priests, of course, had an easy time of it in late Anglo-Saxon times; for them was reserved the ordeal of the Eucharist; if they were guilty then their subsequent partaking of the sacrament would be a sacrilege and divine punishment was supposed to ensue, so no human intervention was necessary. In other words they could do exactly as they pleased: and they did. Trials by ordeal were abolished in the early thirteenth century except for the two best-known varieties. Ordeal by cold water was employed in order to kill off suspected non-Christians throughout the Middle Ages: it involved tying up the victims and then throwing them into deep water. If they sank then they were innocent, but often drowned anyway; if guilty they floated and were subsequently hanged or, in Scotland, burned. Wager of battle was the last ordeal to become officially inoperative: the right to it was successfully claimed by an accused murderer in 1818 but immediately afterwards the practice was abolished by statute.

A RECREANT is now a coward, but originally he was the loser in a wager of battle. In Old French the verb *recroire* meant to yield in such a battle and, since the loser was necessarily guilty, the term acquired the pejorative flavour which its descendant still possesses. The word CHALLENGE, Old French *chalenge*, was originally applied to an accusation and thus a summons to trial by combat. Ultimately it comes from the Latin *calumnia* meaning false accusation, as does the modern English word CALUMNY which retains the original meaning more closely. Spoken calumny is SLANDER, a close relation of SCANDAL, the common ancestor of these English words being the Old French *esclandre*. When written, calumny is known as LIBEL; this word comes from *libellus*, a term for a little book, the connection being provided by pamphlets which were used to spread scandal in

Elizabethan times. *Libellus* is a diminutive form of the Latin *liber*, a book, which also gives us the modern term for a collection of books, LIBRARY. Originally the word *liber* had meant 'tree bark', a material used for writing upon in earlier times, but it also meant 'free'. From this latter sense of the word come such terms as LIBERTY, LIBERATE, LIBERAL and LIBERTINE.

Trials by ordeal were not fair, in so far as the outcome did not necessarily determine true guilt or innocence. Modern concepts of justice and equity are traceable directly to ancient Rome. The word EQUITY itself comes from *aequus*, fair, and JUSTICE from *justus*, fair dealing. The Latin root *jus*, meaning 'law' or 'right', has two stems *jud-* and *jur-*. From the verb *judicare*, meaning 'to proclaim the law', come JUDGE and JUDGEMENT, JUDICIAL, JUDICIOUS, JUDICATURE, PREJUDICE and ADJUDICATE; while from *jurare*, to swear, come JURY, JURISDICTION and JURISPRUDENCE as well as a host of derivatives such as PERJURE, to swear falsely; CONJURE, to swear together; and ABJURE, to renounce an oath. The Latin word *dictio*, meaning 'declaration', also occurs in numerous slightly different forms in English: as well as the word JURISDICTION we have DICTUM, EDICT, CONTRADICT and many others, most of them having at least some connection with the law or with government. A VERDICT is merely a 'true declaration', or should be; and to ADDICT originally meant, in Roman law, to bind over judicially. But to bind over to the custody of a friend of the accused is to BAIL – this word also comes from a Latin word: *bailare*, to carry, for the bailor takes upon himself the burden of responsibility for the bailee.

Other imports from Rome include ALIBI, originally meaning simply 'elsewhere'; SUBPOENA, under penalty; and ONUS, burden. The word IGNORAMUS, meaning literally 'we do not know', was once written by grand juries on the back of indictments for which there was insufficient evidence to warrant trial by *petit* or PETTY jury. Gradually the present meaning of the word developed, although it was earlier applied only to lawyers who did not know as much as they ought. As the word acquired its later connotations its original function was taken over by the phrase 'no true bill', presumably because members of grand juries did not relish their association with the original epithet and its new, extended meaning. From *evidentia*, clearness, comes the word EVIDENCE and from another Latin term *morare*, to delay, comes MORATORIUM, a word properly applied to legal permission to delay payment of an account. 'Hue and cry' was the native English expression for an outcry requiring others to join in the pursuit of a felon, the practice being familiar in medieval England and, in a similar form, in nineteenth and twentieth century America. In both places the people who were obliged to join in the hue and cry formed a posse. The word POSSE, a contraction of the Latin expression *posse comitatus*, literally 'the force of the country', is a compound of *potis*, powerful, and *esse*, to be. The same two Latin words have, incidentally, produced another English term: that which has the 'power to be' is said to be POSSIBLE.

When a contract between two Romans was completed a straw would be broken to demonstrate that agreement had been reached. From this practice, the Latin word for straw, *stipula*, has provided the term STIPULATE: although written English contracts when complete are traditionally 'signed, sealed and delivered'. When two written copies of a contract were required, an old practice was to write the terms of the contract in duplicate on the same piece of parchment or paper. The document was then divided by a zig-zag tear or cut, and the parties could each retain a copy. An indentured clerk was one who had entered into such a contract of service with his employer and the contract itself, an INDENTURE, takes its name from its indented or saw-tooth edge; after all a DENTURE is only a set of teeth. On the other hand a deed which has only one party does not need to be divided into two; the edges of the document are, therefore, 'polled' or straight and the instrument is thus a DEED POLL.

Contracts which are not written require each party to provide some consideration, however small. In this respect lawyers make a nice distinction: consideration must be sufficient, that is it must exist, but it need not be adequate; in other words it need

DEVICE FOR PRODUCING DIMPLES.

No. 560,351.   Patented May 19, 1896.

'When it is desired to use the device for the production of dimples, the knob or pearl *c* of the arm *a* must be set on the selected spot on the body, the extension *d*, together with the cylinder *f*, put in position, then while holding the knob *n* with one hand the brace *i* must be made to revolve on the axis *x*. The cylinder *f* serves to mass and make the skin surrounding the spot where the dimple is to be produced malleable . . .'

This patent from the United States Patent Office, like all patents, is open to public inspection. A letter patent is an open letter since the word PATENT, comes from the Latin *patere* meaning to lie open.

not have a value commensurate with that provided by the other party. Because of this, an almost worthless token, such as a peppercorn, is sufficient consideration to exchange for the extensive use of, say, land and buildings and this type of exchange has provided the expression 'peppercorn rent'.

Legal documents, like contracts and wills, are famous for their use of long words, convoluted phraseology and repetitive cross-referencing. This reputation has existed for a considerable time and in the days when Latin was the language used for legal work, the term *quibus*, 'to whom', must have been one of the most frequent offenders; from it comes the word QUIBBLE.

A WILL, Anglo-Saxon *willan*, is simply a wish, whether the word is used as a verb or a noun. If there are insufficient assets in a dead man's estate to satisfy all the terms of his will then special rules apply. The application of these rules can be rather messy and so, since the fifteenth century, the term HOTCH POTCH has been applied to the method of dividing up an estate in accordance with them. Once again the derivation is Old French: a *hochepot* was literally a shaken pot, a vivid analogy for a legal process by which assets are mixed up. One meaning of the word TAIL is an estate which can be bequeathed only to heirs of the body. This word, related also to TALLY, is derived from the Old French *taille*, a notch or cut. From this meaning of TAIL comes the verb to ENTAIL which originally meant to bestow property subject to restrictions limiting its subsequent inheritance.

Legal parlance has provided the language with several phrases as well as numerous words. 'Time immemorial' is one such phrase with a rather more precise meaning than is generally recognised. Common Law originally developed from the unification of a large collection of local customs, but how long must a practice have been established before it becomes acceptable as a custom and thus acquires legal status? The Statute of Westminster tackled this problem in 1275 and decided that the appropriate period was that determined by living memory. The beginning of the reign of Richard I in AD 1189 was, as the authorities then said, 'the time when the memory of man runneth not to the contrary.' It is still possible to establish custom as a source of law if the custom has existed since time immemorial but it is usually difficult to establish that a custom has existed since AD 1189, so a convention has arisen which eases the burden of proof: if one party can establish that the custom has existed throughout living memory then it is up to the other party to prove that it has not existed since 1189. Another arbitrary legal period is a year and a day: this length of time was once used for many legal purposes and some of them still find applications in the modern world. For example, a killer whose victim dies after more than a year and a day following the attack cannot be tried for murder.

WITNESS is one of the few surviving legal terms from Anglo-Saxon times when it was spelt *witnes*. The Latin equivalent *testis* has provided ATTEST, to bear witness; CONTEST, to witness against; PROTEST, to witness forth, in dissent; and DETEST, originally to call down the gods to bear witness against; as well as TESTATE, INTESTATE, TESTATOR and TESTAMENT. Another word from *testis* is TESTICLE which is what used to be held while swearing an oath – before the Bible was employed for that purpose. The Bible itself refers to the ancient practice rather coyly as 'hand under thigh'. The word TEST, on the other hand comes from the Latin *testa*, a brick or piece of pottery; it arrived via the Old French *test*, whose modern equivalent *tête* has come to mean 'head' because of the resemblance of the skull to a potsherd. The use of the word TEST to mean an examination or trial seems to have resulted from the medieval practice of investigating a metal's purity by melting it in a pot. The development of the word seems unusually circuitous but an unusual history is at least preferable to an unknown one: TRY and thence TRIAL, for example, are related to the Old French *trier*, the ultimate origin of which is one of the many mysteries of the law.

Trials to which the public are not admitted are said to be held IN CAMERA. This phrase comes directly from the Latin and means 'in (the judge's private) chambers'. A *camera* is simply a vault or room and is related to the older Greek word *kamara* which could be applied to anything with an arched cover. The

Eighteenth Century bigwigs from an engraving by Hogarth

In criminal trials the monarch is represented in court by a senior judge who, for this reason, wears court dress. Being an important person he wears a full-bottomed wig and is thus called a BIG WIG. In full dress, judges also wear black hats and in the past such hats were also worn when passing sentence: from this practice (which, incidentally, theoretically continues for the few remaining capital sentences possible in the British Isles) comes the phrase 'to put on one's thinking cap'.

French judges also wear hats, and their custom of raising them to signify assent has provided the phrase 'to cap to' meaning to agree with.

modern photographic CAMERA is really a *camera obscura*, a hidden room, a smaller version of the judge's private room. Usually trials are held in open court to which the public and the press are admitted, but these courts are not as open as they once were. A COURT was originally an enclosure for sheep or cattle, known to the Romans as a *cohors*. It could be used to quarter a COHORT, a tenth of a Roman legion. The English word COURT came to be applied to any sort of farm enclosure, then to enclosures in other buildings. These enclosures would now usually be called courtyards, but in Cambridge the word court is still used to denote what in Oxford would be called a quadrangle. *Royal* or REAL tennis was originally played in courtyards and real tennis COURTS are still designed like medieval courtyards; lawn tennis, a relatively recent game, borrowed its terminology from the much older one. Sovereigns owned a particularly splendid enclosure which came to be called the Royal Court and the enclosures in which the sovereign's justice was dispensed were courts of law. Incidentally, there are a number of derivatives of the name of the Royal Court in English: indulging in COURTLY behaviour we might find COURTIERS and even COURTESANS although the latter term is now generally applied to common prostitutes rather than court strumpets. As a COURTESY they would enact a little ritual upon greeting each other, but now only women perform this CURTSY.

Immediately after qualifying, members of the bar are 'utter' or 'outer' barristers, but when they become Queen's Counsel, they are called within the bar and thenceforth wear silk gowns: thus they are said to TAKE SILK. On the other hand, if they are disqualified from practising then they are said to be DISBARRED. Prominent barristers are LEADING COUNSEL and important precedents are LEADING CASES. But LEADING QUESTIONS are ones which suggest the required answer and thus lead a witness on. Barristers may plead in any court but solicitors may only appear in the lower ones. Their name comes from the Latin verb *sollicitare*, meaning 'to plead, ask or invite', as does that of the other type of professional solicitor. Legal solicitors were, until 1873, involved only with matters of Equity; their counterparts who dealt only with the Common Law were called ATTORNEYS from the French *à*, to, and *tourner*, to turn. An attorney was someone to turn to for legal representation. In the USA attorneys have usurped the functions of both solicitors and barristers but in England such attorneys are extinct; even the Attorney General is not a true one, although he does enjoy a general 'power of attorney', in so far as he is empowered to act on behalf of another, in this case the Crown.

On the other side of justice is the CULPRIT whose name is a corruption of '*cul. pret*'. This in turn is a contraction of '*culpable: prest*' which was the phrase once uttered by the court prosecutor immediately after a plea of not guilty had been entered; derived ultimately from the Latin it was a short way of saying 'the accused is guilty, and I am ready to prove it'. The prosecutor is so-called because prosecuting involves following on behalf of the Crown. The Latin verb *sequire*, to follow, is thinly disguised in the word PROSECUTE and also in PERSECUTE, which means to follow with enmity. Similarly a series of events which follow one another are said to form a SEQUENCE and they often come together in a CONSEQUENCE. On the other hand a conclusion which does not follow from the previous argument is a NON SEQUITUR.

18

The natural order of things

Parliament is supreme. In other words it may validly pass any act that it wants to. Its actions may not be questioned by the courts, or by the Government of the day. This underlying constitutional principle has remained unchanged for centuries, although the balance of power has shifted considerably between the three parties which together make up parliament. Now the House of Commons is dominant, having broken the historical power of the Lords only in this century. Earlier both Houses had been engaged in a protracted battle with the Crown, each House jealously guarding its own historical rights while trying to wrest additional power from the King. For the moment at least the struggle for power is over and the House of Commons stands victorious. Nevertheless, the old order is still reflected in the British parliamentary system, having developed as it has since Anglo-Saxon times. Then there were three estates: the first was the Church; the second, the Nobility (including the Monarch); and the third was made up of the rest of society, mostly agricultural workers, the ones who did the work. Now the three estates are represented in parliament by the Lords spiritual, the Lords temporal and members of the House of Commons; and another powerful entity, a relative newcomer, the Press, has taken to styling itself the fourth estate.

Never was the pyramidic aspect of power more obvious than in feudal times: at the top of the heap, in theory at least, was the Pope; under him were emperors and kings; below them the great nobles; then the lesser nobles; then freemen and, at the bottom of the stack, serfs. Members of each stratum, except the very highest and lowest, held land as tenants of their immediate superiors. All were vassals of their overlords and therefore, to a greater or lesser extent, subordinate. As a result the word vassal has acquired connotations of inferiority and the diminutive version *vassalet* has deteriorated to become VALET and, worse still, VARLET. This downward social trend has affected a number of titles applicable to the lower orders. Also suffering from it is the VILLAIN who used to be a VILLEIN, a servant in a Roman farm or VILLA (several of which, incidentally, formed a VILLAGE). Other degenerates include the Anglo-Saxon *ceorl* who has become a CHURL and is therefore supposed to be CHURLISH, the Anglo-French menial, the English henchman, and the later *black guard* who has become a BLACKGUARD. Similarly a knave was at one time merely a boy, as indeed his German counterpart, a *knabe*, still is. The English word was transferred to servants and subsequently to rascals: the same old story. It is not uncommon for words meaning male-child to be transferred to assistants or servants, since youths often fulfilled these roles. As well as to the word knave, this has happened to the terms YEOMAN (literally '*youngman*'), GROOM, PAGE, GILLIE and JOCKEY. The same tendency can still be observed in action today: the term 'stable lad' for example, may be applied to men of any age, and 'boy', as used in South Africa and the Southern states of America, carries definite overtones of inferiority not usually found in England. Slaves and servants were not necessarily mere juniors, however; in the distant past they were often captive slaves, having been defeated in battle by their captors. The idea is reflected by a descendant of the Old Norse word *thraell*, meaning runner or servant: to '*en-thrall*' should literally be to capture and take into service, but now to ENTHRALL means to captivate only metaphorically.

Above the Anglo-Saxon churl was the freeman known as a *thegn*, or now as a THANE. He has also started off as a boy but, unlike most others, became socially mobile upwards. After the Conquest, English thanes were replaced by knights and barons, but over the border they continued their social climb so that Shakespeare had one, Macbeth, ascending to the Scottish throne. A KNIGHT, Anglo-Saxon *cniht*, was also no more than a boy originally; and a BARON, late Latin *baro*, was just a man. Because he was a king's man, the humble baron became a member of parliament and subsequently a lord. For this reason barons still sit in the House of Lords, but knights who started out in a similar way later found themselves in the House of Commons and, with the advent of democracy, eventually lost their representation altogether except as ordinary citizens. In this respect they resemble lesser barons or BARONETS who were first created by James I in order to raise money, although their title had existed, more or less informally, long before that.

In Anglo-Saxon times the next highest rank above a thane's was that of a nobleman. In contrast to the lowly *ceorl* such a one was an *eorl*, or as we now have it, an EARL, possibly a relation of the similarly powerful '*elder-man*' or ALDERMAN. Both titles were once applied to men who administered a part of a kingdom, such an area being to the Anglo-Saxon a *scir*, now a SHIRE. After the Norman invasion shires became known as COUNTIES; each was the domain of a COUNT whose title comes from the Latin *comitatus*, itself formed from the word *comes* meaning a 'companion'. Despite vigorous efforts to promote it the title of count never caught on in England. The native English preferred their earls. They were, however, prepared to accept, eventually, that the domain of an earl should be called a COUNTY, that his wife should be a COUNTESS, and that his immediate junior in the peerage should be a VISCOUNT. Literally a '*vice-count*', the first VISCOUNT was created in 1440. Much older was another representative of the royal authority in each shire; being an official now known as a reeve he was a '*shire reeve*' and has survived into modern times as a SHERIFF.

Originally the great nobles were all ranked the same and so were equals or PEERS, in other words, they were on a PAR, *par* being a Latin word for 'equal'. Now there are five different ranks within the peerage; in ascending order they are baron, viscount, earl, marquis (or marquess) and duke; their female counterpart titles being baroness, viscountess, countess, marchioness and duchess respectively. The feminine form of the second highest title suggests the original significance of its masculine equivalent, for the first marquises were noblemen who were responsible for the marches, or frontiers, of the kingdom. DUKES also had military responsibilities; their title, like that of the Venetian DOGE, is derived from the Latin verb *ducere*, to lead, for the first dukes were leaders of military troops. Also with Latin derivations are the titles of PRINCE, *princeps* a chief or leader, and of the SOVEREIGN. The latter term is ultimately derived from the word *super*, meaning 'above', but has acquired an ending which falsely suggests a connection with the word 'reign'. This title of sovereign may still be applied to rulers of either sex, but princes are now specifically male, their female counterparts having adopted the usual feminine suffix to become PRINCESSES.

There is a close relationship between the concepts of straightness and government, or at least there was in times gone by. Derived from the same root as CANE, the word CANNON was first applied to a straight tube and subsequently to large guns of the same shape, while the term CANYON is properly applied specifically to straight ravines; but also with the same ultimate ancestor is the word CANON meaning rule, law or decree. The Old English *canon*, Greek *kanon*, may all be derived from the Hebrew *qaneh*, the word for a cane or straight reed. Straightness is also analogous with honesty as the word 'true' demonstrates: a 'true' line is a straight one, while a 'true' judge is an honest and impartial one. Also interwoven with the connecting threads of government, honesty and straightness are further ones concerning royalty, leadership, goodness and direct movement. It seems that, thousands of years ago, our distant ancestors associated good leadership with the ability to guide well: the one who led the tribe during long migrations was also the one responsible for other types of guidance. Making decisions, administering justice, settling disputes and planning the next move were all responsibilities of the tribal leader.

As the migrating tribes, sharing a common language, spread across the continents of Asia and Europe different dialects developed and, in the course of time, these dialects became so dissimilar that they could be regarded as separate languages. Some of them are shown in Appendix A. It is certain, however, that some words are related to others in now distant languages. The Latin *rect-*, German *recht* and English RIGHT (Anglo-Saxon *riht*), for example, are essentially the same word, and so for that matter are the Latin *reg* and English RAJ (Sanskrit *rajan*).

Apparently the ancient Indo-Europeans had a word which meant something like 'movement in a straight line'. There is no physical record of such a word, only circumstantial evidence from derivative languages. Nevertheless this evidence is compelling, as the following collection of English words shows. Apparently akin to a similar Greek word, the Latin verb *regere* meant 'to guide straight' and was closely related to *rectus*, meaning simply 'straight'. From the Latin forms, either directly or through Old French, English has acquired the terms eRECT, diRECT, corRECT and RECTify (to set straight) along with the word RECTUM, denoting the straight section of intestine or *rectum intestinum*. To mathematicians a RECTangle is a RECTilinear, or straight-sided, figure with four right angles; to governors, an old administrative area with straight boundaries was a REGion. A governor, now usually only an ecclesiastical one, is a RECtor. More powerful rulers REGulate REGimes, impose REGimens on REGiments and publish rule books known as diRECTories.

Both ROYAL and REGAL have come into English via Old French from the Latin *regalis*, a word with almost exactly the same meaning as the modern English ones. A number of other terms associated with royalty have followed more or less the same trail from ancient Rome: between one REIGN and another comes a period known as an interREGNUM; a monarch who rules in his or her own right, like Elizabeth REGina, is REGnant; one who rules in place of a king or queen is a REGent; a university professor whose chair is of royal foundation is a REGius professor; one who kills a monarch is a REGicide; and a kingdom is a REALM. Royal equipment is REGalia; to treat royally is to REGale; and royal coins (whose names have lost their central 'g' sound) include the obsolete English RYAL, Spanish REAL, Portuguese REIS and still extant Brazilian milREIS, originally worth a thousandth of a reis.

The English language has adopted other distantly related words from less familiar Indo-European languages: for example, the terms RAJ, as in the 'Indian RAJ'; RAJA, meaning ruler; mahaRAJA, literally 'great ruler', having evolved from the Sanskrit word *rajan*, itself almost certainly derived from the original, unrecorded Indo-European version. Returning to Western Europe, the German word *reich*, which denotes an area governed by a single ruler, has a counterpart in English: RICH, Anglo-Saxon *rice*; those who rule tend to be, or to grow, wealthy. The word has thus acquired a new association; but an echo of the Anglo-Saxon form and meaning remains in the suffix -*ric*, a bishopRIC, for example, being the province under the control of a bishop. Etymologically *ric* is the same word as *reich* and, for that matter, the word *raj* and the name REG. As a name REG is short for REGINALD, Anglo-Saxon *regenweald*, the name of a powerful ruler. Even the word RULE, indirectly derived from the Latin word with identical meaning, *regula*, has this inbuilt connection of themes: to rule is to govern or to draw a straight line; a ruler does the first and helps with the second. The native English word which also combines these themes is RIGHT, directly derived from the Anglo-Saxon *riht*, a cousin of the Latin *rectus* and the modern German *recht*. To be RIGHT is to be straight and true, and to enjoy a RIGHT is to benefit from one's acknowledged status. Matching the Latin derivatives 'rectitude' and 'correct' we have the English RIGHTeousness and upRIGHT. By way of contrast that which is not straight is dishonest, false, unreliable and evil: it is, in other words, bent, twisted, warped, devious or snake-like, anything but straight. The connections between straight and 'good', and between crooked and 'bad' are very ancient.

Also dating from ancient times is the association of RIGHT with one, usually the stronger, side of the body. The name of the other side, the LEFT, is derived from a word meaning weak or worthless. Right is good, left is bad: that is the natural conclusion, not only in English but in other languages too. In Latin the words for right and left are DEXTER and SINISTER: both are used in the vocabulary of heraldry in this sense, but otherwise the connotations are generally good or bad respectively. One who is DEXTEROUS is capable (doubly so if ambi-DEXTROUS), while one who is SINISTER is evil. Those who are not capable are said to be GAUCHE, this description being borrowed from the French in whose language *gauche* also means 'left'. Furthermore a gauche person might be said to be MALADROIT, having a 'bad right' hand, while a dexterous one is literally ADROIT. The French term from which these English words are formed, *le droit*, means not only 'the right' but also 'the law', an association which is by now familiar.

Many words have developed in parallel within different languages, having started off in prehistoric times from the same single origin. On the other hand a word which has flourished in one language may never have existed in another or, altern-atively, may have died out at some stage. To fill the gap at a later time it may be convenient to borrow a word from another language. Thus the Romans, who turned the name *caesar* into a title, lent their new word to other nations as a title for an emperor. So it is that the Germans made their king into a KAISER and the Russians made theirs into a CZAR or TSAR. Far older is the title of a KING who to the Anglo-Saxons was a *cyning*, a 'son of the kin' or 'son of the tribe', a man of royal birth. His title, which has parallel forms in Icelandic, Danish, Swedish, Ger-man and Dutch, is based on the Anglo-Saxon word *cyn* meaning tribe or race, now more familiar as the term KIN. From it are also derived the words KIND (the way to behave to one's KIND or

KINDRED) and KINDLE (still used in some parts of the country with the meaning 'to bear young'); English has lost its word for a child which is represented in German by *kind*, but it has been reabsorbed in the word KINDERGARTEN, literally a 'children's garden'. The Anglo-Saxon word *cwen* meaning a woman also has similar forms in other Indo-European languages. The title could be applied to a woman of any class and has retained its social neutrality in the term for certain female animals: a she-cat, for example, is known as a QUEEN. But the word has also gone up in the world to become the more familiar QUEEN while, with a different spelling *cwene*, it has also descended to become QUEAN: a word applied to women of ill-repute, but now used only in dialect and by scrabble players. Queens of the raving variety have, in name at least, developed only recently.

19

Being a good sport

Governing the masses is a tiresome business, so the rulers of old were obliged to find a number of ways to entertain themselves. Better still they could employ others to entertain them: musicians, singers, dancers and actors all found ready sponsors amongst the great nobles. The best-loved entertainers were usually the court fools; often dwarves, sometimes politically powerful and occasionally female, court fools were invariably versatile; they played and sang, juggled, played tricks, dressed up, hit their audiences with bladders on the end of sticks, told jokes, and amused the assembly with their controlled flatulence. In the mid-thirteenth century, for example, Rolland le Pettour appeared before the king each Christmas Day in order to perform '*unum saltum et unum siffletum et unum bumbulum*' – a jump, a whistle and a fart; not perhaps the most sophisticated entertainment, but far preferable to the nauseous shallow mush that passes for entertainment nowadays at Christmas-time.

The inflated bladder, or wind-bag, tied to the end of a fool's wand was in Latin called a *follis*. From that word comes the French *fol* (feminine, *fou*) meaning jester, which incidentally is the title of a French chess piece corresponding to an English bishop. From the French word come the English terms FOLLY and FOOL which, because of their derivation, remind us of the entertainment value of 'raspberries' long before the introduction of new-fangled whoopee cushions. They also demonstrate how corresponding words acquire similar connotations in different languages, for the word BLADDER, Anglo-Saxon *blaedre*, is a close relative of the words BLATHER, BLETHER and BLITHER. A fool is a wind-bag, a BLITHERING idiot or alternatively a BLATHERSKITE, a bag full of something less pleasant.

Returning to the noise of a bellows or wind-bag, it is easy to

THE FOOL

see that the words BELLY, BELLOW and BELCH might be related, and that the verb BELL, meaning 'to roar', might be closely connected to BELLOW. Less obvious is the extension of the idea to include the sound of clanging metal but nevertheless this seems to be the origin of the more familiar meaning of the word BELL. The connection extends to fools because, as well as carrying bladders, they also wore bells sewn onto their caps and clothing. Their distinctive cap and bells provided their insignia as professional fools. Cromwell, according to legend, had the royal arms replaced by the fool's insignia as a water mark, so giving a name to a size of paper – FOOLSCAP. He had as little respect for the authority of parliament when he referred to a 'bauble' in the House of Commons. He was speaking, at the time, of the ornate mace which symbolises the authority of the House. Originally a 'pretty-pretty', or in Old French a *belbel*, such an article was a child's plaything: later a *babel*, it became an English BAUBLE, a baton of the court fool which provided Cromwell with his metaphor.

To the Romans a game was a *jocus*, to us it is a JOKE and the intention behind it is JOCULAR. A JOKER was a *joculator* who became known, in Old French, as a *jogleur*. Such an entertainer might be primarily a minstrel, a JONGLEUR, or perhaps a thrower and catcher, a JUGGLER. Actually a minstrel might be called upon to perform in a number of ways: like a MINISTER he was a junior with set duties to perform; the common predecessor of both MINISTER and MINSTREL was the Roman *ministerialis* who had also had assorted minor duties.

The Italian word for a fool was *pazzo*. It may well have provided English with one of its many terms for a jester, PATCH, but whether it did or not the English word has become well established since Sexton, Cardinal Wolsey's fool, acquired it as a nickname. Now it is little used except in the compound form CROSSPATCH and as a dog's name. Another possible explanation for the word is that, like piebald dogs, jesters had particoloured, apparently patched, coats. This dress was distinctive in a number of ways: for one thing it was often made of calf skin and buttoned down the back, for another it was generally coloured yellow and red. For these reasons the suggestion that someone should wear a CALF SKIN really implies foolishness, and the word GULL, which like 'gall' can mean 'yellow', has secondary meanings 'to dupe' and 'a dupe'; and of course a dupe is said to be gullible. Another term for a fool's particoloured dress is motley, from which word we have expressions such as MOTLEY CREW, meaning 'a gang of fools', and derivative words such as MOTTLED, meaning 'patchy' or 'spotted'. The Pied Piper of Hamelin is often depicted in motley dress but his outfit should really be black and white in order to be consistent with his name. The words 'pie' and 'pied' were originally associated with these colours as the terms PIEBALD, PIED wagtail and MAGPIE confirm, each being applied specifically to black and white animals or birds.

A fool's costume had further oddities which have left their mark on the language. The cock's comb which had formed part of his headgear produced an alternative title for the already many-styled fool, namely COXCOMB, and his single sleeve may well account for the expression SLEEVELESS ERRAND. As in days gone by it is still customary to send apprentices on sleeveless or fool's errands during the first of April, a day known as All Fool's Day. Even now a new trainee may be sent to the local ironmonger's for a 'long weight', but the ironmonger having heard it before knows that what he is expected to provide is a long wait. Some time later the youngster realises what day it is and feels rather foolish, as intended all along. Alternatively the trainee might be sent for a tin of elbow grease, for a rick mould to shape hay ricks, or for half a dozen peacock's eggs. Incidentally the countryman's contempt for the town dweller's gullibility and ignorance has resulted in Londoners being called 'cock's eggs'; the Anglo-Saxon form *coken-ey* is clearly recognisable as the ancestor of the modern COCKNEY.

There is an alternative explanation for the expression 'sleeveless errand'. Knights would, when possible, carry a token of a lady's favour; and since sleeves, being detachable, could easily serve as such tokens it is suggested that a sleeveless errand was one undertaken by a knight who had no lady's cause to champion and thus no lady's sleeve to sport. As a lady would pin a token to her champion's arm so it is now the practice, metaphorically, to pin one's faith to someone's sleeve, in other words to follow faithfully, because the giving and receiving of the token symbolised a pledge of faith. For his part the knight would show the feelings of his heart by wearing the token: he would wear his heart on his sleeve. As the lady's token hung from the knight's sleeve so she might depend upon him; figuratively, she could be said to hang on his sleeve; or perhaps she was hiding her mirth all the while by laughing up her sleeve. Another useful article of clothing was the glove or gauntlet which could be used by one knight to challenge another: the first would throw down the gauntlet and, taking up the challenge, the other would pick it up.

Knights, usually having a Norman ancestry, tended to use words derived from Old French. The words TOURNAMENT and TOURNEY have both developed from the word *tourner*, an Old French term which comes from the Latin and ultimately from the Greek; the underlying idea is of turning, which is exactly what lance-bearing combatants did after each run – until one of them was unseated. The idea of turning is also inherent in another French word for a similar sort of tournament, a *carrousel*, the predecessor of the modern fairground CAROUSEL. The winner in the field of battle was called the CHAMPION, a title derived via Old French from the Latin *campus*, literally meaning 'a field'; from an Old French word meaning vanquished, *cravant*, comes the modern English CRAVEN, and from another meaning 'admitting defeat' we have RECREANT. Matching the word JOUST, Old French *jouste*, however, is a native English term, TILT, Anglo-Saxon *tealt* which reflects the inherent unsteadiness of riding around while carrying shield and lance. Tilting may be a thing of the past but we still talk about GOING FULL TILT when charging onwards.

The Anglo-Saxon *hors* has outlived its partner *hengest*, the first word having become the modern HORSE and the second, with the same meaning, being preserved in the name HENGEST; two of the most famous early Saxon invaders were called

Hengist and Horsa. The French word *cheval* did not dislodge the native English terms for horses, presumably because the English words were in such common use throughout the country. Other terms associated with knighthood, however, were specifically used by the dominant Normans; indeed, many words related to horsemanship have been adapted from the French *cheval*. CAVALRY is the name given to mounted troops and a CAVALCADE is a procession on horseback; a French knight, a *chevalier*, is roughly comparable to an English CAVALIER, but a cavalier attitude is hardly consistent with the idea of CHIVALRY. A junior who followed the banner of a senior knight was a *bas chevalier*, which is one of several conceivable derivations of the word BACHELOR as once applied to aspiring knights and preserved in the expression 'Knight Bachelor'.

Another word for a horse was the Anglo-Saxon *mearh* from which comes the name of a female horse, MARE. Similar forms of the word existed throughout Europe and, combined with another widespread term, *scealc*, servant, they produced compound words for horse-servants. From the Old French version *mareschal* we have the modern English MARSHAL. Similarly the head, or 'count', of a stable was called, in Late Latin, a *comes stabuli*; again through Old French it has developed into an English word and is now spelt CONSTABLE. Owning and riding horses provided extensive scope for showing one's status. A well-turned-out horse conveyed the same message that the latest Rolls Royce does now. Not only did the owner and rider gain prestige, so also through the ages did the servants in charge of their stables. Not knowing that a HENCHMAN was really a '*hengest-man*' or horse attendant (because the word henchman had already dropped out of general use), Sir Walter Scott made the word popular again with the meaning of 'haunch man' or servant who stays at his master's side. For this reason the term henchman is now used as though meaning 'menial but loyal follower' whereas, until it started to fall out of use, the word had been gaining in status, as its partners 'marshal' and 'constable' have continued to do. Most titles applicable to servants have suffered from diminishing status, notable exceptions being

A knight's training in the use of a lance included practice with a device called a QUINTAIN. The name is derived from the Latin quintus, fifth, apparently because Roman soldiers used the area near to the camp of the fifth division of the legion for military exercise.

There is still a quintain in at least one English village (Offham, Kent) which has survived to this day. Failure to strike the target squarely results in the tilter being smacked in the back by the weight attached to the opposite end of the rotating arm.

Mr A has just started his training: B, Esq., has graduated to sitting on a wooden horse: Sir C is demonstrating how it ought to be done.

provided by the ones connected with horses which have almost always increased their standing. But the pig-keeper did not do too badly either: once a 'sty-ward', he is now a STEWARD, possibly a high officer of state. It is quite likely however that at least some stewards were originally in charge of important households, which were in ancient times also called '*stys*'; after all a pig-sty is only a pig-house. Robert the Steward, whose family provided the stewards to the Scottish Royal Household, ascended to the Scottish throne himself in 1158 and so provided the name of the royal house of Stuart. The Lord High Constable ranks immediately above the Earl Marshal who in turn ranks immediately above the Lord Steward of the (Royal) Household. Slightly lower in the order of precedence is the Master of the Horse, who nevertheless outranks any ordinary duke.

When not amusing themselves by fighting each other, members of the court could always entertain themselves by hunting. Long before it became fashionable for gentlemen to shoot with guns, they were achieving the same ends with other weapons, and a knowledge of hunting lore has always been an important sign of good breeding. As well as assorted weaponry, other animals could also be used to assist the hunter: in addition to the ever-important horse for transport, there were, for example, hounds for chasing land animals and hawks for catching airborne ones. Horses and hounds are still common enough and the hunting cry for foxes, 'tally-ho!', is still familiar though its origins are lost in the fog of time. On the other hand the cry 'so-ho!', which is recorded much earlier, is now less well-known as a hunting cry. It was used to direct attention to the object of the chase, usually a hare, and has left an echo of itself as the name of the old hare-coursing fields in London: now the area is built up, but it is still known as SOHO. The ideas of chasing and catching have tended to become confused in some ways: indeed the words CHASE, CATCH and CAPTURE are all derived, via Norman French, from the Latin *captare*, meaning 'to try to catch', and both CHASE and CATCH originally meant the same thing. The object of the chase has a name which also reflects this association of ideas. It is now known as the quarry but the word quarry was originally applied to the least appealing parts of the dead animal which were fed to the hounds once the chase was over. Having found a new use for the word we have adopted another one for the unappetising parts of a carcase. Since they tend to fall out when the animal is cut up they are known as the '*off-fall*' or OFFAL.

Many hunting terms also double as expressions with technical meanings in falconry. Both 'quarry' and 'leash' were borrowed by the latter from the former, but the word LURE has travelled in the opposite direction. In Old French it was spelt *luere* and was applied to a crude model of a bird containing raw meat which, when swung around, would recall a trained hawk. Its purpose has apparently been misunderstood, for the word LURE has extended its meaning and, as a verb, is used to mean not only 'to attract' but also 'to entrap'; and a lure itself is now no more than a bait or trap. Another expression which has been adopted into general speech from the world of falconry is the phrase 'to turn tail' meaning to turn and flee; yet others have lost their original senses altogether. A well-bred bird of prey is a hawk 'of good nest' or, as the French say, *de bon aire*, and a human being of good family is, therefore by analogy, said to be DEBONAIR.

Having changed its meaning more than most is the word MEWS, which is ultimately derived from the Latin *mutare*, to change, via Old French *muer*, to change or moult. When a hawk moulted it was put in a cage or MEW, so the word MEW came to mean cage or barred prison. Later the royal stables were built on a site previously used for keeping hawks' cages and so rows of stables also became known as MEWS. Now the stables at the back of rows of large terraced houses have been converted into garages or small houses, and the access roads to such places are thus also called MEWS.

20

Fair game

Falconry, huntin' and shootin' as pastimes of the ruling classes have survived to the present day. By contrast the equally cruel entertainments of the masses have been stopped, at least officially, since the last century. In less hypocritical times the infliction of pain and suffering was recognised as an acceptable source of entertainment for all, except perhaps the victim. Whether human or animal, blood and death could be relied upon to draw the crowds: public executions, bull and bear baiting, dog and cock fighting, and a selection of other such spectacles once provided fun for all the family. Among the linguistic remnants of various kinds of baiting are terms such as BEAR GARDEN and BULL DOG. A BEAR GARDEN is now any rowdy place, but originally it was one where bears were baited; in Southwark (London SE1) there is a place still called Bear Gardens which occupies the site of an old bear baiting ring. BULL DOGS were bred specifically for baiting animals, especially as their name suggests, bulls; as a place name, the word BULLRING survives in many towns, the best known probably being Birmingham. There is another animal which has been so badly treated that it has given its name to the language as a virtual synonym for the verb to bait: to harry unmercifully is to BADGER.

The most popular blood sport of old has left more evidence of its popularity. Officially ended in 1849, cockfighting now takes place in secret and also continues to retain a prominent place in the national memory. In London alone there are at least two sites which have kept their names: Cockpit Yard (WC1) and Cockpit Steps (SE1), this latter being the site of the royal cockpit. Since the beginning of this century there have been two battles royal in the so-called 'cockpit' of Europe; those who fought were said to be 'game' while those who refused were given white feathers. Either way the men involved were likened to cocks, for the best fighting cocks are known as gamecocks; and those birds, if properly bred, have not a single white feather in their entire plumage. Being good fighters such birds might have the misfortune to be entered in a 'battle royal' of four, eight or sixteen pairs, the winners of each round going on to the next until only one bird remained. However many contestants, the area for fighting was a cockpit, just as historically, on a large scale, Belgium has been the cockpit for fights amongst the nations of Europe. But the smaller area is reminiscent of the enclosed spaces in sailing ships and in aeroplanes which are, therefore, called cockpits. In contrast to aggressive gamecocks young chickens are extremely timid; and as a result of their well-known cowardice expressions like 'chicken hearted' and 'chicken livered' have arisen. But the phrase to 'chicken out' might have a different origin: the Romans, who incidentally first brought cockfighting to England, saw no point in joining battle unless the omens were right. In order to predict the outcome of a possible engagement, close watch would be kept on the grain-eating activities of cocks. If the omens were not propitious then the army might very wisely decide to chicken out.

Individual animal fights designed for human pleasure may have been officially restricted, but consenting adults are still permitted to provide public entertainment by setting about each other. At the beginning of boxing matches, or rather bare knuckle fights, the contestants started each round facing each other, with their left feet touching a scratched line on the ground. To start with they would both be keen to COME UP TO SCRATCH but soon one of them might regret having to TOE THE LINE in this way. Now boxers start in opposite corners and wear gloves, so it is left to others to fight with the GLOVES OFF. A loser might still be DOWN AND OUT. Another possibility is that his second might THROW IN THE TOWEL to signal acceptance of defeat; yet another is that the fighter might, having accepted a bribe to take a 'fall', fail to try his best, take a beating and thus become a FALL GUY.

More vicious, though less violent than any physical competition, are a vast range of activities which are known as games. What these activities have in common is the participation of more than one player, a feature which is reflected in the word GAME, being as it is a descendant of the Anglo-Saxon *gamen*; *ga* meant together, so the word really means something like 'men together'. People who gathered together to amuse themselves often bet upon the outcome of games and this close connection has provided the words for the activities of GAMING and GAMBLING. The old *gamen* form has survived more recognisably in GAMMON, a term used in the game of BACKGAMMON. Swapping the backgammon board around will result in a losing position becoming a winning one, and players who get away with this obvious form of cheating will have TURNED THE TABLES on their opponents.

Cheating, as every player knows, is an integral part of most games. For this reason the verb 'to gammon' has acquired a secondary meaning of cheating or duping, and wise players ensure that their opponents keep their hands ABOVE BOARD. This precaution is less important for backgammon players than for card players because these latter are well known for sharp practice. Before gamblers started to take money from each other using card decks of clubs, diamonds, hearts and spades, fortune tellers were already using suits of clubs, money, cups and swords to relieve customers of their silver. The first card decks appeared in Italy in the fourteenth century; from them come the fortune teller's tarot cards and later the modern conventional playing cards. Different countries, however, have developed the packs in different ways: Italian ones retain the original suits while, for various reasons, other nations have altered them; for example, the Spanish *espada* meaning 'a sword' has been changed to the more familiar word 'spade' in England, and the corresponding symbol has been altered accordingly. As well as changing the names of the suits, the number of cards has been reduced. By discarding the knights who originally ranked between the queens and the knaves, the number of court cards in each suit has been cut to three (king,

THE WHEEL OF FORTUNE

queen and jack) from the original four: king, queen, knight and knave. Jack and knave, of course, are alternative names for the same card which, depicting as it does a servant, hardly warrants the title court card. The misnomer is explained by the fact that COURT CARD is really a corrupted form of the earlier *coat card*, an expression which accurately describes the knave as well as the king and queen. Though not displaying coats themselves, the other cards are still identified by their suits. In the original packs there were a further twenty-two cards not belonging to any of the four suits. Of these, twenty-one have been abandoned, the only survivor being the fool, now usually called the joker.

One of the oldest card games known in England is CRIBBAGE. Its name is derived from the word CRIB which in Anglo-Saxon times meant 'manger', as indeed it still does. Later the word was applied to other box-like constructions used for storage and, in particular, to the store of cards acquired by the dealer of each cribbage hand; that collection of cards is now more usually referred to as the 'box'. Towards the end of a game it may be important to prevent the dealer from getting a good box; more important perhaps than obtaining a high score oneself. Playing in such an obstructive way is known as BILKING or BALKING one's opponent; the term is derived from the Anglo-Saxon word *balca*, which was first applied to a ridge, then to any other such obstacle and finally to anything which checked or obstructed freedom of movement. The BALK lines on snooker tables are so named for similar reasons. Returning to the game of cribbage, players PEG AWAY by moving wooden pegs along a block of wood in order to keep the score. The expression may have been borrowed from Saxon drinkers who marked the level of liquid in their shared bowls with similar pegs in order to ensure that everyone got a fair share; but the winner of a cribbage game is solely responsible for the phrase to peg out. If one circuit of the board is to determine the winner, the players will PEG OUT when their wooden scoring pins have moved over the course of 60 holes and finished up at the sixty-first. Other players who have failed to get their pegs half way round by then still have them stuck in part of the wooden block called the lurch. Such losers are said to have been LEFT IN THE LURCH.

Another early card game, first recorded in the sixteenth century, was called TRIUMPH. The word was already an English one, having been borrowed from the Old French *triumphe* which, in turn, came from the Latin *triumphus*, itself adapted from the Greek word *thriambos* meaning a hymn to Dionysus. The name of the card game changed from TRIUMPH to TRUMP and subsequently to RUFF; this last title is derived from the same ultimate root, but developed through Italian *trionfo*, *ronfa* and then Old French *ronfle* and *roffle*. Having diverged on the way out of Rome, the verbal paths crossed in the late sixteenth century and have since converged on the bridge table where the terms ruff and trump are now interchangeable. The game of ruff developed and acquired new names: 'honours', referring to 'court' or honour cards; 'whisk', perhaps a description of the way that tricks are removed from the table; and 'slam'. By the second half of the seventeenth century *whisk* had become WHIST but it was over two hundred years later that *biritch*, a game similar to Dummy Whist, first surfaced. The origin of the word is a mystery but its subsequent evolution is well known, for it is now familiar as BRIDGE, the name of a game in which the terms 'slam' and 'honours', as well as 'ruff' and 'trump', are still thriving.

Like the word bridge, PONTOON sounds as though it refers to a method of crossing rivers; in fact neither game has any such connection and the latter name is simply a corrupted form of its French title, *vingt-un* or *vingt-et-un*, meaning twenty-one, this number being the maximum permitted score of a hand. Other card games have more obvious names: NAP is just a contraction of the name of the Emperor *Napoleon*; SOLO is a game in which one player competes solo against the others; and BRAG is a game in which the players bluff and brag about their hands during the course of the betting. One form of brag, however, has a more obscurely evolved name, possibly associated with a container used for keeping the kitty separate: POKER seems to be named after the word 'poke' which, as in the phrase 'a pig in a poke', means bag. When the poke, or buck as it was also called, was transferred to the next player, so relieving the present one of betting responsibilities, then the old incumbent had PASSED THE BUCK and it was no longer up to him to put chips into the kitty; it was the next player's turn to CHIP IN.

The element of betting in card games appealed to the second Earl of Yarborough who found a way to dispense with the tedious business of actually playing. He would bet, at odds of 1,000 to 1, against a hand of thirteen cards having none higher than a nine; the true odds are nearer to 2,000 to 1 and so in the long term he could expect to make a reasonable profit. A bridge hand with no card higher than a nine is still called a YARBOR-OUGH, but another gaming earl has left a greater impression upon the language: eating snacks while still at the gambling table he provided a now widely used term for such a snack. He was the Earl of SANDWICH. As well as providing new words, gambling noblemen have been productive in other ways: it was only when influential gamblers discovered apparent inconsistencies in the workings of chance that mathematicians became interested and developed the probability theory – the basis of the science of statistics.

Dice, as well as cards, are often used to introduce probability theory at an elementary level. Indeed mathematicians are almost the sole guardians of the singular form of the word 'dice'. One is a DIE, two or more are DICE; the terms follow the Middle English forms: one *dee*, two *dees*, which are in turn similar to the Old French forms *de* and *des*. Ultimately the source is the Latin verb *dare*, meaning 'to give' or, as in this case, 'to play'. Playing with dice is an ancient and widespread pastime. The North African Arabs certainly used dice; their term for chance, and for a die, was *al-zahr* which to the Spanish became *azar*. As a name of a dice game this became the English word HAZARD which has since acquired a suggestion of danger, a result of the uncertainty involved in games of chance. A similar development has affected the word JEOPARDY which comes from the Old French *iu parti*, a term applied to an even match the eventual outcome of which remained uncertain. This parallels a medieval Latin

A sixteenth century print illustrating the evils of overeating and drinking. It seems that these sins were associated with bad breath and with gambling – as witnessed by the playing cards set in this glutton's cap.

phrase *jocus partitus*, meaning a divided game or wager. The idea is that of a draw, the stake money being divided up and returned since no one had won. Winning at the game of hazard might depend upon a second throw, a 'chance', after the first or main one: thus a player might well have an eye to the MAIN CHANCE.

Depending upon the game being played, an ACE may be a good or a bad throw. Its name comes from a Latin word for a unit, *as*, and has since been borrowed by card and domino players. None of these activities was approved of by the Church but nevertheless monks are usually credited with giving the game of DOMINOES its name. The story is that, having won a game, a monk would pull up his hood (winter hoods were called dominoes) and say *faire domino* to indicate that the game was over. Indeed many players still say 'domino' upon laying down their last card. Though, like dice, dominoes were often made of bone they are still referred to as cards; derived like the words CHART and CHARTER from the Latin *charta*, a papyrus leaf, the term CARD was first used in English in connection with what are now called more specifically playing cards.

Indirectly associated with the deuce of gambling games is the DEUCE of tennis players; in both the underlying meaning is 'two'. The word as used in tennis comes from the French phrase *à deux le jeu* meaning 'two (points) to play'. The game itself has two main forms: the recent lawn tennis and the much older, indoor version now known as real tennis. Modern real tennis courts still resemble medieval courtyards where the game was originally played, and where the players might run literally from post to pillar; now we move from PILLAR TO POST in other circumstances. The name of the game itself has an uncertain origin; it may be from the Old French *tenies*, denoting the string, now a net, over which the ball must pass; or it may be from *tenez*, a word used to warn that a ball was to be served; or it may even be derived from *Tinnis*, the name of an Egyptian city from where the linen for tennis balls came. Like many terms associated with tennis, the word LOVE, meaning nil, has a French origin. It is really *l'oeuf*, 'the egg', a pun on the resemblance between the shape of an egg and that of the symbol for zero. Similar examples of wit have proved the American term GOOSE EGG (also meaning zero) and the English cricketing expression 'out for a duck egg', now usually abbreviated to 'out for a duck'. The games of cricket and tennis also share an official known as an UMPIRE. Earlier a *numpire*, such a person was in Old French a *nonper*, literally ' *'non-pair'*, an odd-man-out who, belonging to neither side, could be relied upon to give impartial judgements. Umpires were also called sticklers but the word 'stickler' has now attached itself to others who are responsible for applying rules; a stickler is one who keeps strictly to the rules: perhaps too strictly. From cricket also comes the expression HAT TRICK which originally denoted the taking of three wickets in three balls, the customary reward for which was a new hat. CRICKET itself may be named from the Anglo-Saxon word *cryc*, a stick or staff, which is not so dissimilar from the modern CROOK. Similarly the word *hock*, meaning a stick curved at one end, is closely related to HOOK and the game played with it, HOCKEY. Another word for the game is 'bandy' and the implement used in it is also a bandy. This usage agrees with the word as employed in the phrase BANDY-LEGGED; but 'bandying words' seems to be a reference to the earlier meaning of the word which was 'to hit back and forth'. It was used specifically in this way in the game of tennis before being taken over by hockey in the seventeenth century.

Like the necks of those inverted flamingoes used by croquet players in Lewis Carroll's *Alice in Wonderland*, early implements for playing the game were also curved; indeed a French word for a hook, *croc*, has provided the very title of the game, CROQUET. An earlier version was known to Charles II who enjoyed playing it in St James's Park, the game being already popular in a nearby alley leading from Catherine Street. The game was called PALL-MALL from the Italian *palla*, a ball, and *maglio*, a wooden hammer, the two pieces of equipment necessary to play it. The wooden hammer was known in English as a MALL, a name which is related to another term for a hammer, MAUL. A small mall is, of course, a MALLET. The title of the game was sometimes spelt PELL MELL, partly no doubt because of the confusion with the unrelated French expression *pêle-mêle*. The place where the game was first played, Catherine Street, has been renamed PALL MALL, still occasionally pronounced as though spelt Pell Mell. On the other hand, the King's favourite site is now called the MALL, pronounced as though it were the Maul.

Elsewhere in England the game of skittles was popular although, like similar forms of enjoyment, it was disapproved of by the Church. Religious fanatics in America went as far as making the game, also called ninepins, illegal in some states; as a result resourceful players invented a new game by adding an extra skittle, and so provided the world with tenpin bowling. In the original game of ninepins the front pin or skittle, being the most important, was the KINGPIN. Certain arrangements of

'Boyes – Sport', a seventeenth century illustration showing some popular boys sports. Amongst them are bowls, ninepin bowling, golf, shooting and stilt-walking.

The boy in the middle is spinning a top. When tops are spinning so fast that they appear stationary they are said to sleep; hence the unlikely phrase to SLEEP LIKE A TOP.

Golf is a very old game and has provided the language with a number of terms including 'stymie', the word for a ball lying between one's own ball and the hole. 'To stymie' is to block or obstruct.

skittles were also sufficiently important to warrant individual titles. One such arrangement, with skittles remaining only at the corners, was called a cocked hat and it is this arrangement which is referred to in the phrase to knock into a COCKED HAT. Bowling competitions of various kinds were very popular in the Middle Ages and are still frequently found at fairs, fêtes and galas. The winning prize was invariably a young pig, so the victor would quite literally 'BRING HOME THE BACON'.

All games involve an element of competition; without it there would be little point in playing. Indeed more competitive games tend to be the most popular and enduring. Often they simulate more serious contests and this is well illustrated by the game of chess which unashamedly imitates a good old-fashioned war. The name of the game, CHESS, is ultimately derived from a Persian word for a king which in modern English is usually rendered as SHAH. As well as kings, queens, bishops and knights, the chessboard combatants include the curiously-named rooks and pawns. By way of Spain and France the ROOK has travelled with his king from Persia; unrelated to the bird of the same name, he is really a *rukh* or warrior, although the piece is usually represented as a castle in modern sets. A PAWN is a *peon* or foot soldier whose name comes ultimately from the Latin word *pedo*, meaning foot. His modern counterpart is a PIONEER; still a real foot soldier, he precedes the rest of a marching army just as his name precedes the names of his comrades in the next chapter.

21

A war of words

The social pressures of overpopulation and advancing technology have conspired to make modern warfare more dangerous than ever before, and the removal of the supreme commanders to a safe distance from the field of battle has made military decisions more dangerously cavalier than ever. Nevertheless modern armies still employ strategies which are well tested in the animal world. Governments, individuals and many other living creatures employ techniques such as threatening, bluffing and tactically withdrawing when necessary. If successful such strategies will avoid a physical conflict altogether; if not then they will merely precede one. Snarls and threats are diplomatic negotiations designed to minimise the risk of physical conflict. Methods used by primitive animals and modern diplomats are the same; only the language is different. The close association between the threat of violence and the violence itself is reflected in a family of English words which have a single ancient ancestor: to threaten is to 'shout', to fight is to 'shoot' and to run away is to 'scoot'.

Historically the English have been almost permanently at war with one or another European nation, often with the French. As a result of this, and of the introduction of Norman French after the Conquest, many words with warlike connotations have been acquired, directly or indirectly, from Old French. Like all good conquerors William Duke of Normandy, or William the Bastard as he was better known, introduced a nightly curfew. The English adopted the French term for the signal which gave the instruction to put out the fires and retire for the night. The signal was a ringing bell and the Old French expression for it was *covre-feu*, literally 'cover-fire', which accounts for the word CURFEW with its military connotations. Curfew bells are still rung at the end of each day in a number of ancient English cities even though the curfew, military or otherwise, has long ceased to be enforced.

Mixed with the many French words adopted by English are others from elsewhere in Europe: for example, the Teutonic *werra* is related to the Norman French *werre* and the Old French *guerre*, the switch between the initial 'w' and 'g' being quite common in these languages. The 'u' serves simply as an indicator that the 'g' is hard. In English both forms flourish to give pairs of words such as ward and guard, warden and guardian, warranty and guarantee, wage and gage (as in 'engage' and 'mortgage'), and warn and garnish. Most of these pairs, or doublets as they are called, still have similar meanings to each other. The Teutonic *werre* has a descendant in English, WAR; but the French form of the word never caught on. Even the French phrase *nom de guerre*, meaning pseudonym or literally 'name of war', becomes in England *nom de plume* or 'pen name'. Matching the native warrior is the less honourable foreign guerrilla; but the word GUERRILLA, or GUERRILLERO, is not taken from the French. The name comes from Spanish in which language *guerra* means 'war', *guerrilla* means 'little war', and the word *guerrillero* denotes a fighter in such a war. Back in France and England the soldiers who were positioned at the front of the army were the 'forward guard' or *avant garde*. Now the leaders of artistic fashion are said to be AVANT GARDE and the front of an army is called the vanguard, in contrast to the back, the rearguard. Those who preceded an army on the move through woodlands would often mark their path by hacking bark from tree trunks on the way. These marks were, like white flashes on horses' noses, called blazes and the action of making them upon tree trunks was that of BLAZING A TRAIL.

The Gaelic *sluagh*, host, and *gairm*, shout, produced a word for the shouts of an army, *sluaghgairm*. From it comes the modern SLOGAN which, in the hands of advertising agents, is far more dreadful than its ancient ancestor. From the same source comes the word SLUG-HORN. Introduced in the eighteenth century by a writer who misunderstood the original Gaelic term it is used as a synonym for 'trumpet', and also as an excellent example of a ghost-word, i.e. one invented by error on the false assumption that it already exists.

Like Gaelic words, those from ancient Greece have little application to modern concepts of war. Nevertheless some Greek ones have survived by assuming new figurative uses: an AEGIS is still a protective shield and the word PHALANX continues to be applied to united, well-organised bodies, whether armed or not. With a name derived from the Greek word *trophe*, turning, a TROPHY was originally a war memorial constructed on the battlefield, specifically one at the turning point where the enemy was put to flight. The Greek word for forgetfulness, *amnesia*, produced both AMNESIA, also meaning forgetfulness, and AMNESTY, the name of an agreement by which differences are forgotten.

Roman words have also tended to lose their military connotations, and for similar reasons. The triangular military formation called an ECHELON is no longer used, so the word has adopted new figurative meanings. Related to the French *échelon* meaning 'a rung of a ladder', its ultimate source is the Latin *scala*, a ladder; from the same root comes the rung-like SCALE of a ruler and the action of SCALING a ladder. Also with new meanings are the words CENTURY and DECIMATE. In Latin a *centum* was a hundred and a *centuria* was a body of a hundred men. From the latter, by way of France, comes CENTURY, a word which in English is restricted in general use to certain measures of a hundred; obvious examples are provided by hundreds of years and scores of a hundred runs in cricket. The Latin verb *decimare* meant to select one in every ten for punishment as, for example, recaptured army deserters might be selected for execution. Thus in English to DECIMATE is to destroy a tenth part. To be under the yoke of an oppressor, or to pass under such a yoke, is to suffer subjugation: made from the Latin *sub*, under, and *jugum*, a yoke, the word SUBJUGATE was originally applied to a Roman practice obliging defeated foes to pass under a construction of three spears arranged to resemble a yoke.

Being near to home, frequent and not so remote in time, the European wars of the Middle Ages have provided many words, some of which have kept their military associations. From the armouries in use at various times we still have terms such as MACE, describing a weapon now used only for ceremonial purposes; FREELANCE, meaning free to sell services – as of a knight for hire; LAUNCH, meaning the action of throwing a lance; PANOPLY, a word of Greek origin which refers to a full set of armour; PUMMEL, the action of hitting with a pommel, an apple-shaped object such as the one found on the hilt of many swords; and BATTLEAXE then, as now, a fearsome creation. By error the vicious sixteen-foot long pike lives on as the PIKESTAFF but the expression in which it is commonly used should really be 'as plain as a packstaff': the phrase refers to the smoothness of a pedlar's staff and not to the visible impact of a pike.

English longbowmen were for a long time the envy of Europe: their range might not have matched that of Genoese crossbowmen but their speed and accuracy were phenomenal. For many years Englishmen were obliged by law to practise their bowmanship each Sunday and such practice was indeed necessary: few men today would have the strength to draw a full-sized longbow. For practice a small round shield or *targe* was often employed; the word is hardly ever used now but its diminutive form, TARGET, lives on. If the target is distant then the archer must aim above the bull's-eye in order to hit it, but if the target is sufficiently near then it is possible to point the arrow directly at the centre. Because French bull's-eyes are traditionally white such shots could be called *point blanc* and this almost certainly accounts for the English expression POINT BLANK range. A shot taken without any aim at all is known as a SNAPSHOT, a term which has found an appropriate new function in amateur photography. One aspect of an archer's skill was the speed with which he could rearm, but another was his accuracy over different distances. In order to improve accuracy over a variable range a common practice was to aim for one of a number of objects positioned at different distances from the archer. To do this was to rove; later the word was applied figuratively to random utterances which might or might not hit the mark, and now it is applied to various forms of movement back and forth. When attempting a 'long shot' one is still likely to either 'overshoot' or 'fall short' of the target. Other words

Two types of battering ram. Type A, the *ares simplex* or 'simple ram' has its business end fashioned like a ram's head because rams are renowned for their butting proclivities. Type B, a composite ram, looks more practical.

A. *Aries Simplex* .   B. *Aries Compositus*

which have lost their strong association with bowmanship include artillery, whine, and toxin. At one time the word 'ARTILLERY', now applied to gunnery, was used in connection with longbowmen and crossbowmen; and WHINE, Anglo-Saxon *hwinan*, was a description of the noise made by flying arrows. The word TOXIN is now applied to poisons but the Greek *toxin* was a word for a bow (and arrow). The connection is provided by the phrase *toxikon pharmakon* meaning something like 'arrow-poison', a reference to the poison once used to smear arrow heads. Modern archers are known as TOXOPHILITES or 'bow lovers', the ancient title of archer no longer being grand enough for longbowmen: even the chess piece once known as the archer has been renamed, and refashioned, as a bishop.

Related to the French word for war, *guerre*, is the Old French word for a watch tower, *guérite*. From it comes the modern English GARRET, a word which is still used to describe a small room at the top of a building. Those who manned such garrets were said by the Italians to be *all'erta*, literally 'at the look-out'. In French the corresponding term was *à l'airte* and later, as *alerte*, the expression became the English word ALERT. Following the same route came the Shakespearean ALARUM and modern ALARM: originally the Italian phrase was *all'armi* which means 'to arms!' but in time the English word for the instruction transferred itself to the corresponding state of mind. Lookout posts on the ground have provided the words SENTRY and SENTINEL, for both are related to the Old French *sentinelle* which meant 'sentry-box'. But the original Italian word *sentina* was used for two distinct constructions: as well as referring to a field latrine the term was also applied to the hold of a ship where bilge water accumulates. The first sentinels were the unlucky sailors whose job it was to monitor the level of bilge water.

Back on dry land the guards who were posted away from the camp acquired their titles from the outer defences where they were stationed. These defences were pointed stakes driven into the ground and directed towards potential attackers. Such a stake in French was a *piquet*, a word which the English adopted in two forms, the original PIQUET and the anglicised PICKET.

With this split personality the word now serves for military and naval guards (piquets) and for the trade union guards (pickets).

Towers were not only used for lookout posts. While besieging a castle, movable constructions could be employed to enable the attackers to get up to the battlements and then into the fortifications. Derived from the Old French *berfroi*, the word for such a tower was BELFRY; the term had no connection with bells and acquired its modern meaning of bell-tower in the fifteenth century. Besieging a castle often took a long time and the attackers might well have had to sit around waiting for months or even years on end. From the Latin word *obsidere* which means 'to sit down before' comes the term OBSESS, the earliest meaning of which was to besiege; the modern meaning has arrived by analogy for the mind can be thought of as a fortress which is liable to be besieged or obsessed by evil spirits. In a similar way the word SIEGE, which in Old French meant 'seat', acquired its more familiar meaning in English; in modern French however *siège* still means seat. Having time on their side attackers often tunnelled under the foundations of the besieged castle. In this way it was possible to gain access directly or indirectly by destabilising the walls. Such tunnels were simply mines, and the foundations would thus be UNDERMINED. After the introduction of gunpowder it was possible to speed up the process by the judicious use of explosives, a practice which has resulted in the name of the modern military LAND MINE.

22

Word War II

Without supplies a besieged army could not last; fresh provisions from outside were needed and these were likely to be waylaid by the attackers. A French word which meant 'to hide in bushes', *embusher*, has given us the modern AMBUSH; but the practice was not the most honourable of techniques, as witnessed by a descendant of the Latin equivalent, *insidiae*: the English word INSIDIOUS. Often, of course, the site of a battle was far removed from the nearest stronghold and temporary accommodation would be required. Such accommodation for a Teutonic *hari*, or army, was provided by a HARBOUR, merely a place of shelter, and the soldier sent ahead to arrange it was a HARBINGER. Now only a forerunner, the military harbinger has been replaced by the modern quartermaster whose task it is to provide more sophisticated accommodation. Other English words which retain the otherwise disused *hari* include HARRY and HARRIER: to HARRY was originally 'to lay waste' as a conquering army would, and a HARRIER is a bird which harries its prey. The word HERRIOT was once applied to army equipment and now survives as a surname, just as HERMAN, 'army man', survives as a forename. A number of old army routes still have names like the HARE WAY and of course the shallow of the river where the army crossed is called HEREFORD. Probably related to the same root is the word HARLOT. Originally a harlot was anyone, usually a man, who made his living by following an army; but human nature being what it is women could generally make a better living as camp-followers, and the meaning of the word has changed accordingly. Also changed is the word CAMP which was originally used for a battle and later for a battle site. It is related to the German *kampf*, a word which has retained its earlier meaning so that, for example, Adolf Hitler's infamous book *Mein Kampf* translates as 'My Battle' or 'My Struggle'. The English term is more closely related to Latin words which have also provided the English CAMPUS and CAMPAIGN as well as the French region called *CHAMPAGNE* where many battles have been fought. Also related is the cowardly SCAMP who 'de-camps' or deserts during a battle; his name comes, via the French, from the Latin *ex campo*. A more recent form of cowardice which requires an element of forethought is the wearing of an outfit which can be turned inside-out to reveal the enemy's colours. If the battle is going badly then the clothes are taken off, turned inside-out and put on again; a soldier who does this is a TURNCOAT. Invading forces have been known to set fire to their sailing vessels after disembarking in order to rule out the possibility of retreat: a practice which is remembered in the phrase TO BURN ONE'S BOATS.

Once the advancing troops were sufficiently certain of victory the order 'havoc' would be given; this signalled that the battle was done and that the looting could begin. We still 'cry havoc', but not in quite the same circumstances. The commanders of the losing side would often be held for ransom and would sometimes be required to sign a blank document to which the victor could later add whatever surrender terms he desired. In French a blank sheet of paper could be called a CARTE BLANCHE and, although the surrender document was not completely blank because of the signature, this term has been adopted to describe unlimited powers similar to those conferred by such a document.

Until relatively recently armies had much in common with those of the Middle Ages and even earlier, but modern technology has changed military techniques beyond recognition. Private armies (with the exception of the Atholl Highlanders) are now illegal and despite a constitutional technicality which disallows such things the British army is, to all intents and purposes, a standing one; that is, it is in continuous existence even during peace-time. In the past regiments were raised and used by anyone with sufficient influence. Command structures and uniforms are now standardised whereas they were once ill-defined or non-existent. The titles of the various army ranks continue to reflect two thousand years of history. A private is a private soldier analogous to Roman private citizens who were so-called because they held no office and took no part in public life. The CORPORAL's title come from an Italian word *caporale*, meaning 'head man' or 'chief', but a SERGEANT was originally only a '*servant*'. As his sibling, the legal SERJEANT, rose in status so also did the military SERGEANT MAJOR whose rank once corresponded approximately to what would now be a Lieutenant Colonel. A LIEUTENANT is just what he appears to be, a *lieu tenant* or one who stands in place of another. The Latin equivalent of the French term is *locum tenens*, a phrase which has been contracted to LOCUM in order to provide the name given to one medical practitioner who stands in for another.

The military lieutenant stands in place of a CAPTAIN, an officer whose title, derived from the Old French *capitaine*, like that of the more humble corporal, means 'head man'. CHIEF-TAIN is just another form of CAPTAIN and there are still some Scottish clans whose chiefs are properly addressed as 'Captain'. MAJORS and MAYORS both derive their titles from the Latin *maior* which means 'a superior', and the status of an army major is a reminder of the older position of Sergeant Major. A Lieutenant Colonel is an officer who stands in for his immediate superior, a COLONEL. The spelling of this word corresponds to the Latin *colonna*, a column (in this case of soldiers), but the pronunciation still reflects the early English form of the word *coronel*. From *brigare*, an Italian word for a quarrel, comes the title of a

BRIGADIER as well as that of the body which he commands – a BRIGADE. The less respectable BRIGAND is also related.

Military GENERALS take their titles from the word general as used as an adjective, so that, for example, a Major General is really a 'general Major'. To complicate matters, though, the major referred to is really a Sergeant Major and thus the rank was originally that of Sergeant Major General. Next comes the Lieutenant General, and after that the Captain General. Except for members of the Royal Family, the rank of Captain General no longer exists; the modern rank is the General. He ranks immediately below the highest officer who, since 1736, has been called a Field Marshal. Ironically the illustrious marshal and the lowly batman were originally both servants in charge of horses; the marshal lost his association with horses long ago but the batman lost his only during World War I when irregular soldiers misunderstood his function. The BAT of BATMAN holds an unlikely surprise. English BAT, French *bât* and Old French *bast*, are all closely related words for a pack-saddle; pack-saddles served as beds for old campaigners whose activities in them resulted in illegitimate offspring or BASTARDS, the military counterparts of the naval 'sons of guns'.

Most of the large European wars have seen the introduction of new weaponry with words to match. Two unlikely ones from World War I are TANK and BLIMP; TANK was the code name used on the packing cases in which the new machines were shipped to mainland Europe. Originally used to conceal the true nature of the shipments from the enemy, the word caught on and was accepted into general use. BLIMP, on the other hand, was deliberately invented: the unsuccessful prototype limp balloon was an *A-limp* and the next, successful model was a *B-limp*. World War II saw the introduction of the BREN gun, the name of which comes from the two places where it was first manufactured, *Br*no in Czechoslovakia and *En*field in England. During the same conflict, American servicemen first called themselves GIs, because all their American military equipment bore those initials; the letters stand for Government Issue. British TOMMIES acquired their name from the fictitious Tommy

SALUTING DEVIOE.

No. 556,248.   Patented Mar. 10, 1896.

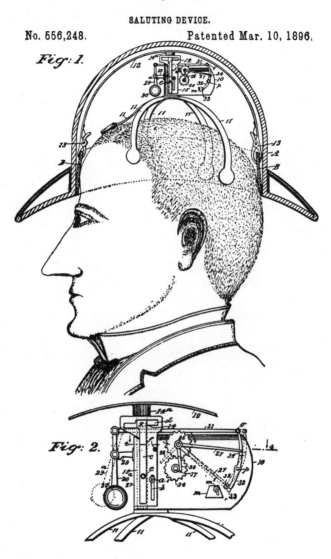

Fig: 1.

Fig: 2.

This saluting device raises the hat and rotates it when the owner's head is bowed. The idea never really caught on.

Military salutes are designed partially to show that the right hand is weaponless, partly to demonstrate that the junior needs to shade his eyes in the presence of a figuratively brilliant superior. The word SALUTE comes from the Latin verb *salutare*, meaning 'to greet' or 'wish good health to'.

Atkins, who used to feature in sample documents designed to help servicemen when filling in their own forms.

Most specialised army units derive their names from their functions or from their specialised armaments. In particular the development of explosives and firearms has impressed itself upon military vocabulary. Since early bombs were shaped like pomegranates, the French called such a weapon a *pomegranade* and the English turned this into GRENADE. The troops responsible for these bombs, GRENADIERS, became redundant in the eighteenth century; but the title has continued, even though the new type of grenade, in use only since World War I, is now widely used by other troops. Originally with a similar function were the BOMBARDIERS who dealt with BOMBS, both of these words being derived from the Greek term for a humming noise, *bombos*.

Ancient guns have provided the names for the FUSILIERS and DRAGOONS, a *fusil* being a flintlock gun named after its firing mechanism and a *dragoon* being a musket which, like a dragon, breathed fire. The firing mechanism of a flintlock involved a spark igniting gunpowder in a flashpan attached to the gun. If the gun did not fire properly then there would be only a FLASH IN THE PAN. The lock as in 'flintlock' is now remembered in a phrase which is used to indicate all of the constituent parts: the parts of an old gun were the LOCK, STOCK AND BARREL. Occasionally the names of people are transferred to large guns. In recent times, the most famous example is the German piece of ordnance called BIG BERTHA after *Frau Bertha Krupp* whose family firm was mistakenly thought to have manufactured it. In a similar way the very first GUN in England seems to have been named after another woman with war-like associations; 'Lady Gunnhildr' was the name of a weapon listed in the Exchequer accounts of 1330 but it may not have been named after a specific person since in Icelandic *gunnr* means 'war' and *hildr* means 'battle'.

Early guns were little more than hollow tubes which were sufficiently strong to withstand an explosion at one end. The basic shape resembles a cane and it is no surprise to find that the words CANE and CANON both derive from the Greek *kanna* which means 'reed'; earlier related forms are the Hebrew *qaneh* and the Arabic *qanet*. The words ARSENAL and MAGAZINE also come indirectly from Arabic: an ARSENAL was originally a workshop, then a work place, then a dock, and finally, since ammunition was stored in the Venetian arsenal, any store of munitions. We have the word in its present form from Italian, in which language *arzana* means 'arsenal' and *darsena* means 'wet-dock'. Similarly a MAGAZINE is so-called from the Italian word *magazzino*: it was originally a storehouse and later became a specialised storehouse for ammunition; from there the word also became attached to small stores of ammunition such as the magazine of a hand-gun, and, at first metaphorically, to a store of written information.

A medieval mortar used to attack castles. Notice that one of the grenades (shaped like a pomegranate with spikes) appears to be designed to fragment upon impact. What is now called shrapnel was anticipated by early military scientists including Leonardo da Vinci. General Henry Shrapnel gave his name to SHRAPNEL during the Peninsular War in the early nineteenth century.

Some of the words in this chapter have acquired wider meanings, having once been military jargon, but most have become military words as warfare has developed and new terms have been required. Because these developments have taken place over thousands of years, and in many different countries, the modern vocabulary of warfare represents a patchwork of different languages. Amongst the military words still in common use are those derived from ancient languages such as Hebrew, Greek and Latin, from Arabic and Icelandic, from Celtic, Anglo-Saxon and French, more recently from other European languages and more recently still from the speech of other nations throughout the world. We even have a number of expressions from the North American Indians. It was, for example, they who originally smoked the peace pipe, and they who would literally bury the hatchet. War has always been a grim business but those who engage in it have managed to preserve a sense of humour. The Americans who called themselves GIs are not so very different from their sixteenth century European ancestors who called their new war machine a *petard*. The PETARD was a bell-shaped engine, half-way between a bomb and a canon, which was used to blow in castle gates during sieges. Since these machines were likely to explode at any time, the soldiers who worked on them were liable to be HOIST WITH THEIR OWN PETARD. The danger seems to have been taken lightly since, as the dictionaries delicately put it, a French *pétard* was one who 'breaks wind', just like Rolland le Pettour from Chapter 10.

23

A sailor's yarn

The term Anglo-Saxon is applied to the English Saxons and, by extension, to the Germanic though not necessarily Saxon inhabitants of England before the Conquest. Like the old Saxons of mainland Europe, the Anglo-Saxons were always willing to fight when they had to, and were often quite happy to join battle even when it was not strictly necessary. The name SAXON is derived from *seax*, an old word for a long knife, just as the equally warlike FRANKS were named after their favourite weapon, a *franka* or javelin. The English no longer think of themselves as Saxons but the Highland Scots continue to use that title, or at least the Gaelic rendering of it, SASSENACH. In order to win new territories, and in particular to win England from the resident Celts, the Anglo-Saxons had to excel in battle. But first they had to get to the shores of Britain: not too great a problem because the coastal Germanic peoples were also excellent seamen. Their extensive sailing vocabulary matched their skill, and the skill of English sailors throughout the centuries, as two different meanings of the word 'craft' seem to confirm: craft is skill but a craft is a sailing vessel.

As the naval words developed in England so also did the parallel forms of another great seafaring nation, the Dutch. The centuries of rivalry are now passed and Dutch ships no longer carry a broom on their masts to show that they 'sweep the seas'; but neither does the Royal Navy insist that Dutch ships dip their top sails in salute when passing a British one, in order to acknowledge that Britannia rules the waves. Nevertheless the two nations still possess vast and similar stores of words relating to the sea. The English language also remembers old rivalries: we continue to refer, for example, to DUTCH COURAGE, meaning artificial courage induced by drink; DUTCH COMFORT, no comfort at all; DUTCH NIGHTINGALES, frogs; DUTCH TREATS, arrangements by which parties GO DUTCH or pay for themselves; DUTCH WIVES, bolsters; and DOUBLE DUTCH, incomprehensible speech.

A DUTCHMAN'S LOG is a piece of wood thrown into the sea ahead of the ship; as the vessel moves on, a note is made of the time taken for it to pass between two fixed points on the moving ship, thus enabling the speed of the vessel to be estimated. The method is the opposite of the usual one for measuring speed through the water, which is exactly why it is called Dutch: the more usual method is to tie a rope to a log and drop it over the stern, keeping hold of the rope and paying it out as necessary without dragging the log. Again the operation could be timed and the length of rope employed could be used to calculate the ship's speed. Such details could be recorded in the ship's book which thus became known as a LOG BOOK and the action of recording became known as LOGGING. The rope had knots tied in it at regular intervals in order that the distance could be measured easily, so a ship's speed could be measured in KNOTS.

To find the depth of water a lead weight on the end of a line could be lowered overboard until the bottom was reached. Having a relatively easy task the man who did this was said to SWING THE LEAD. The instrument used for this purpose was a PLUMBLINE, so-named from the Latin word *plumbum*, lead, and the weight itself was a PLUMMET. One who fashioned such weights, as well as other leaden items, was a PLUMBER, and the action of using plumblines was known as PLUMBING THE

DEPTHS. Being measured in fathoms, the depth would then be fathomed and we still talking about fathoming out a difficult matter when trying to get to the bottom of it. The word FATHOM, incidentally, denoting a length of six feet, comes from the Anglo-Saxon word *fæthm* meaning 'outstretched arms', the span of which formed the original measure. On the river boats of North America in the last century, plumblines were used to find the depth at various parts of the river. When the two-fathom mark on the line was reached the fact would be shouted to the pilot. The cry used provided a pen-name for a writer who was interested in such matters, MARK TWAIN.

Navigating at sea was a more difficult business, especially in bad weather and over large distances when the curvature of the Earth becomes an important consideration. Sometimes a ship's position could be decided only by estimating the directions of motion and distances moved since leaving some point with known latitude and longitude. This method was known as *decided reckoning*, which seems to account for the term *de'd reckoning* and thus the more usual DEAD RECKONING. On the other hand, navigation is relatively simple in good weather over a short distance: then the Earth's curvature can be ignored and it is all *plane sailing* or, as we unknowing land-lubbers prefer it, PLAIN SAILING.

In rough weather a sailing ship might be in danger of being driven aground and, being unable to control its course, the master might, as a last resort, drop (or slam on) the anchors. The starboard one is the 'best bower' and the port the 'small bower' but for centuries they have kept their old names – despite being of identical size. If they failed there might be a special emergency anchor specifically for this purpose, a 'sheet anchor'; its name is now used to describe anything for additional safety. Some ships had twenty or so anchors for various purposes, the main ones being attached to the large posts or 'bits': the anchor cable could, therefore, extend only as far as the BITTER END – when the ship might be BROUGHT UP SHORT. Rather than go through the noisy and conspicuous business of raising an anchor it might be more discreet in certain circumstances to GIVE THE SLIP by slipping or detaching the anchor; if it was to be recovered later it could be buoyed, but if the sole object was to get away as quickly as possible then the cable would be chopped through and left. To do this, as many ships of the Spanish Armada did when threatened by English fire-ships, was to CUT AND RUN: and to make a quick get-away it was usual to RUN BEFORE THE WIND, which is why, presumably, a considerable part of the Spanish fleet headed north and was subsequently wrecked off the Scottish coast.

In order to avoid unnecessary injuries it was important to CLEAR THE DECKS for action before engaging the enemy and, since time was often short, speed was important. A drum was used to convey orders in the past and the practice was to BEAT TO QUARTERS, or action stations, in double time, i.e. AT THE DOUBLE. British warships were recognised in action by a large red flag flown from a mast and each ship's position in the order of battle could be identified from the colour of another flag. This continued until 1864, when the old Red, White and Blue Ensigns started being used for their present purposes. Before then the front squadron, commanded by an Admiral of the White or Vice-Admiral, had flown a White Ensign; the middle squadron, commanded by an Admiral of the Red had flown a red one; and the *rear* squadron, under a REAR ADMIRAL, or Admiral of the Blue, had flown a blue one. To signal that no quarter would be given a black flag would be flown, and to signal defeat a white one. Another way to convey an intention to surrender was to lower one's flag or STRIKE ONE'S COLOURS, and a captain who ruled out the possibility of such a thing would literally NAIL HIS COLOURS TO THE MAST. Less honourable commanders, like pirates of popular myth, would reveal their true colours only when it was too late to retaliate; otherwise they sailed UNDER FALSE COLOURS.

Other naval flags which have become well known include the Union Jack, the Blue Peter and the quarantine flag. The National flag or Jack flown from the jackstaff at the front of the vessel while at anchor provides the more widely used title of the UNION JACK. A BLUE PETER is really a blue repeater, a flag to request that a signal be repeated, while the yellow flag known loosely as a quarantine flag would be flown when disease was suspected on board ship. The usual period of isolation required for vessels flying such a flag was forty days, the same period that a widow was allowed to remain in her husband's house after his death. The same name was used for the former interval as for the latter: QUARANTINE, from the Italian *quarantina* meaning 'a period of forty days'; *quaranta* being Italian for forty.

Originally an admiral was a military commander known to the Arabs as an *'amir*, but perhaps because of some admirable quality the word has acquired a superfluous 'd' in becoming ADMIRAL. The French have retained the earlier form *amiral* without the additional letter and neither has it intruded into the title of the land-based foreign prince, or EMIR. Much more junior is the trainee officer who was stationed amidships when on duty. He has become a MIDSHIPMAN but is also known as a snotty, perhaps because of a youthful habit now prevented by the distinctive buttons on his cuffs. No longer are ordinary citizens 'pressed' into naval service: in fact they never officially were, for PRESS in the expression PRESS GANG is from the Old French word *prest* meaning loan or advance, a usage preserved in the accountants' term IMPREST which is applied to a method of running petty cash systems. Drinkers might unsuspectingly accept an advance payment by drinking beer into which prest-money had been put: by using glass bottoms in their metal tankards drinking men could see any coins in the bottom and avoid the danger of unwittingly taking the KING'S SHILLING, the statutory amount of money advanced to new recruits.

Naval discipline was, it seems now, unreasonably harsh; miscreants who were hanged from the yardarm got off relatively lightly in some respects; at least death was relatively quick from strangulation, if not quicker from a broken neck. An alternative punishment was flogging: 'to be flogged around the fleet' was to be lashed severely on each of the ships then in port; the fewer the ships, the more likely the chances of survival. A cat-o'-nine-tails was the instrument used until the practice of flogging was abolished by the Royal Navy in 1879. It was administered on the open deck rather than below decks, where there was literally not enough room to 'swing a cat' round. Another unpleasant fate was provided by the practice of keelhauling: a rope was strung under the keel from one yard arm to the opposite one and the unfortunate seaman was then hauled under the ship with it. If he was dragged too slowly then he would drown; too fast and he would be cut to shreds by the encrusted underside of the ship. If he survived he could have another go.

Life at sea was not all bad. Until this century women were generally allowed on board ship and this practice has resulted in at least one common phrase. Inevitably these women frequently became pregnant and, since voyages often took several years, they were obliged to give birth on board ship. In order to obtain some degree of privacy the births often took place on deck, behind a canvas screen near to the midship gun; if, as was often the case, paternity was in doubt, the baby would be entered in the ship's records as a SON OF A GUN.

The wavy surface of the sea has provided many words for the English language. In various guises the Latin word *unda*, denoting water in motion, appears in a number of terms, many of which carry suggestions of excess or overflow: water which flows in INUNDATES, the excess is REDUNDANT and the whole mass ABUNDANT. Sea water ABOUNDS over the planet's surface and those in it are SURROUNDED, this last word being derived from the Latin *super* and *undare*; again the underlying idea is one of overflow just as it is in the term SUPERABUNDANCE. The word UNDULATE, also derived from the verb *undare*, means to move in waves and so it is almost interchangeable with the word FLUCTUATE, which comes from the Latin word *fluere*, to flow. An inflow of power leads to INFLUENCE and of money to AFFLUENCE, and an outflow of more earthy substances is EFFLUENT. FLUIDS which flow together meet at a CONFLUENCE, and an excess is SUPERFLUOUS.

When the waves grow violent, a ship in distress may throw cargo overboard in order to maintain control. Such goods, being '*jettisoned*', are called JETSAM but it may subsequently be difficult to distinguish them from other '*floating*' wreckage, or

FLOTSAM. Before moving on to another collection of maritime words it may be worth noting how the meaning of a phrase can be changed, and sometimes even enhanced, when a word in it falls out of use. Usually a similar looking or sounding word fills in the gap or, even better, the same word with a different meaning can be used: the phrase will still make some sort of sense although the apparent meaning may be radically altered. Everyone knows what the word monkey means, but not that it was once also applied to a type of gun trolley. Sometimes such trollies were constructed from materials other than iron, the metal from which cannon balls were made. In cold weather the different materials would contract at different rates and as a result the pile of cannon balls stacked on the monkey could become destabilised. All this has passed into history yet when the weather is sufficiently icy we still talk about it being cold enough to FREEZE THE BALLS OFF A BRASS MONKEY.

24

I must go down to the sea again

Every profession has its own vocabulary of technical words. Specialised terms which belong to such jargons occasionally find themselves let loose in the outside world and may consequently suffer an identity crisis. The word 'exocet' has, since the Falklands conflict of 1982, passed from a very small circle of users into the public domain. Whether or not it will survive in this new environment only time will tell. If it does then the precedents suggest that its personality will change to some extent. If a vogue word does not find a safe niche in this competitive world then the chances are that it will perish; but the exocet has existed in myth for over two thousand years already. A 'cete' was a whale or sea-monster so an 'exocete' might be thought to be a monster which leaves the water. In fact the word EXOCET is formed from the Greek *exokoitos*, the name of a fish which slept out of the water. The name literally means something like 'sleep-out' and was presumably applied to some sort of sea mammal, such as a seal, which enjoys sunbathing during the day. Nowadays most sea mammals are known to be harmless and the real monsters are recognised to be the two-

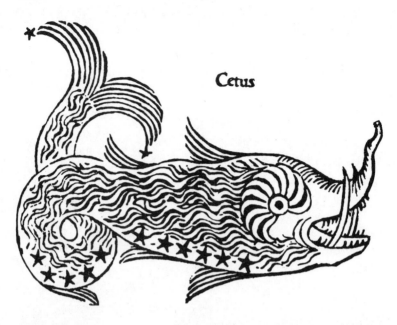

The constellation of Cetus the whale as pictured in a Fifteenth Century work on astronomy. The word CETE and its derivative CETACIOUS, along with the name of CETUS, is taken from the Greek term for a whale or sea monster *kete*.

legged kind who manufacture exocet weapons. A fish which really does leave the water, the so-called flying-fish, is scientifically known as *exocoetus volitans*.

The seas, or more correctly the men who sail on them, have produced an astonishing number of technical terms to describe their very specialised activities. Over the last few hundred years some of these terms have become vogue words and phrases. Passing inland, and spending so much time there, they have lost their sea legs. VOGUE itself was once such a word. It is now a respectable land-lubber meaning little more than fashion, but the ideas of drifting with the tide or sailing with the wind are reminiscent of its earlier meanings, 'to sway', 'to make progress' and, originally, 'to row'. Its ancestor, the Italian *voga*, was applied to the stroke of an oar in water. Other AWOL maritime terms which have found new identities on land are CHOCK-A-BLOCK, AI, SPIN A YARN and DEVIL TO PAY. CHOCK-A-

BLOCK is a term now usually used to describe a state of being completely full. A chock is really a wedge and a block is part of a pulley system: when tightened sufficiently two blocks will eventually meet and further tightening will be impossible; when the block and tackle is in this state it is truly chock-a-block. The phrase CHOCK-FULL, a variation of *choke-full*, seems to have influenced its more recent meaning. Incidentally the word 'overhaul' originally meant to relax the tension in such a block and tackle system. AI is now used to describe the quality of almost anything, but the letter A originally referred to the state of a ship's hull and the number I to the state of its stores. SPINNING A YARN was what sailors did while telling unlikely stories; the two activities must have been so regularly carried out together that one acquired the name of the other. A ROGUE'S YARN is a strand, usually of jute, inlaid into a rope. Its colour denotes important details such as the strength of the rope, but originally its purpose was to deter rogues from stealing naval property since the coloured strands would immediately identify the true owner; the Royal Navy used yellow yarn for Chatham, blue for Portsmouth and red for Devonport. The devil is a seam on the side of a wooden vessel near to the water line; such seams need to be caulked or payed with pitch in order to keep them watertight, and thus the phrase THE DEVIL TO PAY has a completely different meaning from that usually intended. In fact the original was 'the devil to pay and no pitch hot'. Because of its position, the devil was notoriously difficult to pay and those who had to do it were literally BETWEEN THE DEVIL AND THE DEEP BLUE SEA.

On land tar was used in small amounts to protect animal sores. A dialect pronunciation for a sheep, 'ship', has been confused with the more usual type of ship and hence the proverb about 'spoiling the ship for a ha'porth of tar'. The first recorded use of the phrase refers to the danger of losing a hog for a halfpenny worth of tar.

Other phrases with an unexpected maritime history are SPICK AND SPAN, SWEET FA and ROUND ROBIN. *Spick* is just another form of the word spike and *span* meant chip; the words were used to describe a brand new ship which would presumably still sport shiny metal nail heads and fresh wood chips on its virgin decks. The German and Dutch languages both have similar, and older, expressions. A far more recent phrase is SWEET FA; abbreviated from *sweet Francis Adams* it was first applied to tinned meat and then later to things of little or no value. Fanny Adams, in 1867, was brutally murdered and her body dismembered at the same time that tinned mutton was introduced into the Royal Navy galleys. The coincidence was clearly too much for the ratings to accept. For similar reasons the merchant service referred to their tinned meat as Harriet Lane. A ROUND ROBIN is not a robin at all but rather a French *ruban rond*, a round ribbon. The man whose name appeared first on a written petition to the captain stood a fair chance of being severely punished; it was safer to arrange for all the names to appear in a circle so that none could be identified as the ring leader: the names were, therefore, written on a round ribbon, a ROUND ROBIN.

Other words and phrases have passed into common speech without losing the salty flavour of the sea. SPLICING THE MAIN-BRACE is an obvious example: its literal meaning is clear enough but its present meaning of having a drink seems to be derived from the custom of issuing extra rum rations after the especially difficult splicing job had been completed. Wind and sails have obviously been important to sailors since ancient times. It is no surprise, therefore, that so many sailing terms in general use should reflect their importance. One does not need to be a mariner to SAIL CLOSE TO THE WIND or BEFORE THE WIND, nor to TRIM ONE'S SAILS. If something is missing one can always WHISTLE FOR IT, much as the becalmed sea-farers of old would employ sympathetic magic by whistling for the wind. To aim for an objective is to 'SET ONE'S GYB (sail)' at it. And we still talk of skyscrapers although we rarely mean by the word what was originally meant: triangular sky-sails set at the very top of the mast.

The phrase to CLUE UP is very recent and seems to be based upon the old naval term to 'clew up' which means to draw the lower ends of sails towards the yards; there is also a corresponding phrase to *clew down*. CLUE is merely a variation of the older form CLEW which comes from the Anglo-Saxon *cleowen* and originally meant a ball of thread such as that used by Theseus to escape from the Minotaur's labyrinth. The ropes at the lower edges of a sail used for regulating its tension are properly called sheets; a sail with all three sheets in the wind would be out of control and by analogy a drunken man is said to have THREE SHEETS IN THE WIND. A sheet bend is a knot which is used to tie a sheet to another rope of different thickness. Two ropes of equal thickness, such as reef points, are joined with a reef knot. A reefer was one who tied up the sails when they were not required. As well as tying reef knots he wore a REEFING JACKET; from the appearance of his reefed sails probably comes the now rather quaint term REEFER meaning a marijuana cigarette.

Sailing close to the wind is rather dangerous because a change in the wind's direction may cause the ship to be TAKEN ABACK. In order to avoid this danger the helmsman would not sail as close as possible (close-hauled) but he would leave a safety margin. This was known as sailing 'by and large' – a phrase which still retains a suggestion of inexactitude. In practice being taken aback was more likely to happen as a result of deliberate manoeuvre than by accident. A sailing ship could be stopped relatively quickly by turning her into the wind and thus having her taken aback, but this was generally unlikely to occur by mischance. A more common danger when sailing close to the wind was to have the wind taken out of the sails – in which case they would be luff, that is, they would shake impotently in the breeze. Sailing 'by and large' would ensure that the vessel remained *aluff* or, as the modern version has it, ALOOF. HARD UP is yet another nautical term: when a ship could not make headway because of foul weather, her helm would be put hard up and she would have to weather the storm. If, however, she was driven ashore then it might be found to be impossible subsequently to shift her: she would be said to be HARD AND FAST.

The names of many sailing vessels reflect their original

function. Sometimes the connection is obvious, sometimes disguised. A COLLIER is simply a ship which carries coal and a PACKET, originally a *packet boat*, was merely one which carried mail and goods between two ports. A TUG is literally just a *tug boat* and a TENDER is really an *attender*, a ship which attends or acts under the orders of another. An INDIAMAN was a ship which traded with India or with the Indies, an East Indiaman with the East and a West Indiaman with the West, but despite their names they were, like men o' war and all other ships, invariably referred to as 'she' rather than 'he' when a pronoun was needed. A CLIPPER is named from the Old Norse word *clippa* because it clips the waves with its raking bows and a CUTTER may possibly be named for similar reasons. As the English could cross the sea so the Dutch would *kruis* it; adopting the word gave the term CRUISE and hence CRUISER. The Dutch word *jagten*, to speed or hunt, is the root of the English YACHT which helps to explain its unlikely pronunciation. Amongst the many other Dutch terms for sailing vessels which have been borrowed from Holland is the name of the SLOOP which in Dutch was *sloep*. From a Spanish word by way of France and Holland we have GALLEON, the Old French *galie* having already provided us with the word GALLEY. The Middle Dutch word *treghelen*, to drag, has provided the word TRAWLER as the name of a boat which drags fishing nets and, more recently, *lichter* seems to account for the name of the LIGHTER, the original use of such vessels being to lighten or unload larger vessels which were themselves unable to be wharfed because of shallow water. The modern word SHIP comes from the Anglo-Saxon *scip* which is closely related to other Teutonic forms. The Dutch equivalent is *schip* and the German *schiff*; the former is obviously related to the English SKIPPER (the master of a ship) and the latter to SKIFF (a rowing boat). The very first vessels were simply hollowed out logs: a fact which is reflected in the similarity between the word SHIP and the ancient Greek word *skaphein*, to hollow. The word vessel retains a similar duality: it can be used equally well to describe a ship or any other hollow object such as a vase.

The Greek *argos* meaning swift provided the name of Jason's

Nave Admospherica.

An Eighteenth Century design for an 'air-ship'

The Greek word for a ship was *naus*. From it comes NAUTICAL, NAUTILUS, NAUSEA (sea sickness) and apparently from the sufferings of the nauseous NOISE. Passing into Latin, *naus* became *navis* and has subsequently provided the words NAVY, NAVIGATE and NAVVY, a navvy being originally a navigator who helped to build the English canal system. Churches were likened to ships, a fact which accounts for the name of the NAVE. There is an oddly proportioned church in Brighton, St. Martin's, which has dimensions equal to those of Noah's ark.

ship, the *Argo*, and of his crew, the Argonauts, but surprisingly it is not related to ARGOSY, the name of a large merchant vessel. This word comes from *Ragusa*, a port on the Adriatic coast which is now called Dubrovnik. Other naval words which have come from around the world include LAUNCH, ultimately from the Malay *lanchar*, quick; CATAMARAN, from a Tamil word *kattamaram*, 'tied tree'; and JUNK which is from Portuguese and perhaps ultimately from the Javanese *djong*. The Anglo-Saxon *bat* developed into the modern BOAT; it was commanded by the BOATSWAIN whose title is now generally contracted to BO'S'N. The ship's boat was in the past called the cock boat and its commander was the COCKSWAIN. Another Dutch interloper, the so-called jolly boat, has replaced the cock boat but the cock-swain or coxswain retains his ancient function, sometimes under the guise of a COX. Naval terms are often contracted and thus become difficult for the uninitiated to understand. Thus the FO'C'S'LE is really a FORECASTLE: it was once a castle-like structure at the front of a ship. At the other end was the after castle but this term was superseded by 'quarter deck'. This area was the officers' preserve; they lived aft while the hands lived forward; thus to SERVE BEFORE THE MAST is to serve as a common sailor.

The Anglo-Saxon word *boga* could be applied to anything bent. From it is derived the word BOW: as well as being the curved front of a ship it is also a curved weapon, a knot with loops, and (with a different spelling) a curved branch; as a verb it also retains its implication of bending. At the other end of the ship is the STERN; its similarity to the word STEER is no coincidence since the steering equipment, the rudder, is located at the stern. A Latin word meaning to steer, *gubernare*, itself borrowed from Greek, acquired a secondary meaning which is better-known in its English descendant, the verb to GOVERN. Sticking more closely to the original form is the word GUBER-NATORIAL which means 'pertaining to a governor or to govern-ment'. Steering equipment has not always been placed at the back of a vessel. A common practice in early times was to use an oar or board on one side in order to influence a boat's direction. It was customary to use the same side consistently so that that side became known as the STARBOARD, literally '*steerboard*'. The word BOARD is a descendant of a common Germanic one which is represented in Anglo-Saxon by *bord*. The term was originally applied to planks and thus to the sides of wooden vessels; indeed a BOARD is still a piece of wood and a BORDER is still a side or an edge. To be on board is to be within the sides of a ship and to go overboard is to find oneself on the other side, in the water.

To board is to embark and thus get oneself within the ship's sides; and motors are of two kinds, in-board and out-board, depending upon which side of the stern board they reside. Anything which floats by, such as a Dutch log, will simply GO BY THE BOARD. On the other side of the boat opposite to the starboard was the LARBOARD, but it is not clear whether this term was originally *laddeborde*, 'lading-side' or *leereborde*, 'empty-side'. The words starboard and larboard are very old but, because they were apt to be misheard and thus confused, the term larboard was abandoned (officially by the Royal Navy only in 1844) in favour of the word 'port'. The Latin *portus*, a gate, gave the Old English *port*, a harbour, a gateway to the country. Since the lading side, traditionally the larboard, was also the port side the use of PORT for 'larboard' was a natural progression. The original meaning of *portus*, a gate, has also produced the words PORTAL, PORTHOLE and PORTCULLIS as well as indirect derivatives including IMPORT, EXPORT, PORTER, OPPORTUNE and IMPORTUNE which had, at one time, an association with ports or harbours. To import was to bring into the country through a port and to export was to take away from the country through a port. A porter was one who carried goods around the port. The conditions which allowed a ship to make port easily, such as close proximity and a following wind, were opportune, while unfavourable conditions were inopportune or importune.

25

Travelling through time

Sails no longer feature on most working ships although the ships themselves are still said to sail. Similarly we talk about riding a bicycle as though it were a horse and we still drive cars, even though there is no longer an animal to drive. Much of the language of transport is taken from the past; sometimes old words are resurrected and new life breathed into them, sometimes existing ones are simply allocated new meanings. Very occasionally a deliberately invented or artificially introduced word survives; but most such interlopers are doomed to pine away and die, giving way to democratically-elected replacements from the well-tried past. The titles of the Royal Automobile Club and the Automobile Association are reminders that, in the early days of motor transport, horseless carriages were christened automobiles. Originally used in France and based on the Greek *automatos* the word AUTOMOBILE means literally 'self-moving': it was accepted well enough in America, but in Britain the public preferred a name which was suggested in a daily newspaper during 1895, and so it is that English automobiles are usually called motor cars or simply cars.

The word CAR has long been used in England, as has its diminutive form CART. Both are derived, via Old Norman French, from the Latin word *carrus* which denoted a wheeled vehicle, a CHARIOT. Also related is the word CHARGE, to load, and which may also be applied to loads like those of gunpowder which are needed to refill a gun. A load is a burden so that it is possible to be charged with a duty or a crime, or even to be charged a fee. Similarly a horse loaded up ready for battle is called a CHARGER. To charge is also to career, to gallop forward, though possibly moving from side to side. Originally a CAREER was a race-track along which horses and chariots charged but now the word denotes a course chosen to compete in the rat-race

of life. Again it is derived ultimately from *carrus*, the Latin word which has produced so many English ones. Also from this source is the name of a ship's load, CARGO, and from a related verb meaning to load we have the word CARICATURE. It seems that the first caricatures were exaggerated pictures or images of people loaded on to and carried around in carts for public approval or ridicule. On the continent peasants still adore caricatures of saints as they are carted around, but in England the only popular remnant of this practice is the making of effigies of Guy Fawkes which are then dragged around on trollies for public entertainment. These trollies are sometimes called go-carts although the original go-carts, in use centuries ago, were frameworks on castors which were used to help babies to learn to walk.

The French word corresponding to the English CAR is *char*, and a 'car with seats' is thus a *CHAR-A-BANCS* or, as the English preferred, a CHARABANC. Actually the English did not like the word much anyway, so it was superseded by another good old-fashioned term coach, or more specifically motor coach. The French had, in fact, already exported the name of the horse-drawn COACH some three hundred years earlier, having themselves borrowed their version, *coche*, from the name of a town in Hungary called *Kocs*; the original name for the vehicle was *Kocsi szeker* which means simply 'Koc's cart'. A coach which takes passengers from one *stage* of their journey to the next is a STAGE COACH and, figuratively, a tutor who helps a student along an academic journey is also called a COACH. Carriages with hoods in two independently movable parts are named after another European town, LANDAU in Bavaria, where such carriages were first made in the eighteenth century.

By a rather indirect route the name of the HACKNEY CARRIAGE may be derived from that of the London borough of Hackney. Horses were once bred there for sale at Smithfield Market; in the Middle Ages such horses may well have been called after the place from which they came and this would explain why the word HACKNEY came to denote a particular type of horse. At first a HACKNEY was a medium-sized horse such as might be used for riding; then, since such horses were often hired out and subjected to tiring, repetitive dull work, the word HACKNEY used as a verb, came to mean the same as 'overwork' and an overworked horse, or now anything else which is overworked, can be said to be HACKNEYED. By extension, literary drudges are known as HACKNEYS or HACKS. Various early horse-related meanings still endure however: for example a tired horse can still be called a HACK and certain types of riding are referred to as HACKING. A carriage let out to hire is a HACKNEY CARRIAGE, although the immediate connection is provided by the fact that the vehicle is available for public hire, rather than that it is pulled by a hackney, or even that it comes from Hackney. Incidentally, just as a hack becomes hackneyed so another horse, a *jade*, becomes JADED.

Hackney carriages are now usually called TAXIS. This name comes from the term TAXIMETER CAB which, to take things one stage further, is really TAXIMETER CABRIOLET. A TAXIMETER is a device which automatically measures the tax or charge to the passenger, its name being borrowed indirectly from the Germans who had formed it from Greek elements which literally mean 'charge-measure'. A CABRIOLET is just a little *cabriole*, a two-wheeled carriage which, because of its relative lightness, was likely to leap into the air when moving over uneven surfaces. The word comes from the Italian *capriolare* which means 'to leap into the air like a young goat', the Latin word for a goat being *caper*. So also a CAPER is a playful leap, the isle of goats is called CAPRI, one whose mind jumps around is said to be CAPRICIOUS and the sign of the zodiac represented by a goat's horn is called CAPRICORN. To sum up: a taxi is a carriage which jumps like a young goat and which is fitted with a device for measuring the charge to be paid by passengers. The charge may depend upon a number of factors, only one of which is the distance travelled. A PERAMBULATOR however is, or rather was, a wheeled machine used specifically for measuring distances; derived from the Latin words *per*, through and *ambulare*, to walk, the word has transferred itself to another wheeled machine and has contracted to become the now familiar PRAM.

Words which have been pressed into service as names of motor vehicles have sources which are many and varied. The Persian *karwan*, for example, has become the English word CARAVAN: originally denoting a group of travellers such as might band together to cross a dangerous desert, the word has been transferred to covered carriages like those used by gypsies or now by holidaymakers; and the shorter form, VAN, has now become standard for smaller covered vehicles. Further east, in India, there once existed a huge vehicle designed to carry an idol of the god Krishna. Devotees of the god sacrificed themselves under its enormous wheels and the vehicle itself became known by one of the titles of Krishna, *Jagannath*, from the Sanskrit words *jagat*, world, and *nathas*, a lord or protector. The god may have been the protector of the world but his anglicised namesake can hardly be said to warrant the title, for the word JUGGERNAUT is now applied to vehicles whose sacrificial victims are not so keen to meet their fate as their religious predecessors were. Nearer to home the French people of the province known as *Limousin* were fond of wearing hooded cloaks, which accounts for the fact that early motor cars with closed bodies and separate hoods for the driver became known as LIMOUSINES. A driver of early steam engined vehicles would usually stoke the engine himself so he became known as a CHAUFFEUR after his Old French counterpart the *chaufer* or 'stoker' whose name is ultimately derived from the Latin word meaning 'to make hot'. Motor vehicles with a single enclosed compartment, in which the driver as well as the passengers sat, became known as SEDANS after the earlier non-motorised sedan chair. Originally the name had been given to a box furnished with a seat for one person and carried by two others by means of poles attached to each side, and is probably derived from the Latin word for a seat *sedes*. From that same Latin source come words such as SEDENTARY (sitting), SEDATE (settled), and SEDATIVE (that which helps one become sedate). As one sat in a sedan so one originally lay in a LITTER, for the word meant the same as the modern French *lit*, simply a bed. Being carried around, the bed gave its name to a vehicle similar to a sedan but larger. Since straw and rushes made up the bedding and gave an untidy appearance, the word LITTER came to denote a state of disorder and then simply rubbish lying around in such a state. This last meaning arose only in the eighteenth century, over two hundred years after the messy state had suggested LITTER as a word to describe a confusion of newly-born animals.

English LORRIES seem to have been named after someone in the last century whose name was *Laurie* but the American TRUCK has a longer and slightly more certain history. Related in origin to the name of the TRUCKLE bed which, being fitted with castors, can be rolled out of sight under a larger bed, the word can be traced back to Rome and thence to ancient Greece where

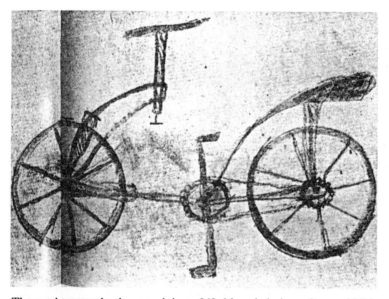

The word BICYCLE has been used since 1868 although the invention to which it is applied dates from earlier in the same century. The name is derived from the Latin elements *bi*, two, and *cyclus*, wheel.

As usual Leonardo da Vinci was there long before everyone else. The above drawing was made by him or one of his students hundreds of years before the first known bicycle was made. It was accompanied by entertaining doodles of ambulatory male genitalia and lay hidden for centuries until recently when it was discovered in an album, the page having been glued in with the opposite side showing.

trochos meant a runner or wheel. The name of the TRAM CAR comes from an Old Dutch word *trame*, a baulk or beam; in English the word tram has been used for hundreds of years to denote vehicles which were led by long side-handles or shafts, also known as trams. More recently, in the last century, the French called their public vehicles *voitures omnibus*, literally 'carriages for all'; the 'for all' part caught on in England and public vehicles became known as OMNIBUSES, but as usual a shorter form was preferred so we now refer to them as BUSES. The USA has also had a hand in naming new vehicles for it was only as recently as World War II that the Americans developed a General Purpose vehicle the initials of which, GP, suggested the word JEEP.

There are a number of words of classical origin which have established themselves, despite the popular dislike of learned names. VEHICLE, for example, is derived from the Latin word *vehiculum*, itself related to the verb *vehere*, to carry, and the familiar BICYCLE is named after its two wheels in the same way that a TRICYCLE is named after its three. The word BIKE, a corrupted form of BICYCLE, is well on the way to establishing itself as the words bus and pram have already been established. Another Latin word TANDEM meaning 'at length' seems to be securely entrenched within the language since it is now used for many types of connected pairs. Also well established are the terms TRACTOR and TRACTION engine, these names being derived from the Latin word *tractus* which is connected to the verb *trahere*, to draw or pull. This last word has also given to the English language the word TRAIN, generally used to denote an object which is, or a sequence of objects which are, drawn along behind others; common examples are the trailing part of a gown or robe, the trailing entourage of a professor and the trailing carriages of a railway engine. The leader of the educational train is one who TRAINS others; and the leader of a series of railway carriages is also called a TRAIN.

Most railway vocabulary is taken straight from the days of the horse-drawn carriage, a habit which is exactly paralleled by the North American Indians who spoke of the railway engine as an 'iron horse'. We do not go quite that far but we do talk about the railWAY, and in America the corresponding term is the rail-ROAD. Passengers travel in CARRIAGES or COACHES; at the front is a DRIVER and at the rear is a GUARD, as though the days of highway robbery were still with us, as indeed they are at least metaphorically. Fortunately we are somehow able to distinguish new meanings from old and it makes perfect sense to talk about driving cattle or trains, riding horses or bicycles, and sailing with or without sails. We can even fly without using wings.

26

Jack of all trades

Historically wood has been the main material from which vehicles and sailing vessels have been made; and since the title WRIGHT, Anglo-Saxon *wryhta*, is applied to woodworkers, it is hardly surprising that a joiner or carpenter who specialised in a specific type of work should become known as a wheelwright, cartwright, ploughwright or shipwright. These job descriptions have, like many others, provided surnames for families which have lost any association with the trade in question long ago. Waggons are no longer called *wains* yet there are many people who bear the name Wainwright; with two notable exceptions (Noah's Ark and the *Ark Royal*) ships are no longer called arks, yet the name Arkwright is still familiar. Similarly one who builds a wooden *mill* is a millwright and those who build plays have become known as playwrights – although the product of their labours is not always so wooden. This last job description has not yet been crystallised as a specific family name since it was first used only in the seventeenth century.

An ancient word meaning to strike, cut or hew developed in a similar way in many North European countries; in England it is represented by a word for one who smites, SMITH, and is exactly the same now as it was in Anglo-Saxon times. It has, of course, also provided the name SMITH but since it was applied to metal workers and since metals were known by their colours, specialist smiths became known as blacksmiths if they worked with iron, whitesmiths if they worked with tin, brownsmiths if with copper, greensmiths if with (tarnished) brass and greysmiths (or plumbers) if they specialised in lead. Silversmith and Goldsmith are less ambiguous names since the name of the metal is the same as that of the colour, although it seems that at least one goldsmith has been called by the name Redesmith. Those who worked with alloys also had names which used the word for the metals rather than their colours, but the name of the *'alloy-smith'* has now been corrupted to LEYSMITH. The name Touchstone is derived from that of a type of jasper once used by goldsmiths to assess the quality of a piece of gold. The gold would be rubbed against the touchstone and the mark left would reveal to the expert eye its purity. In England the Goldsmiths' Livery Company assays the coin of the realm and any gold article sent for testing. If the gold content is inadequate the item will be broken up, otherwise it will be stamped or marked. Because this testing and stamping was done in the Goldsmiths' Hall, the stamp became known as a HALLMARK. Now anything which comes up to the mark is said to bear the HALLMARK OF QUALITY; although the phrase to COME UP TO THE MARK has been confused with a similar expression, to come up to scratch, from the world of boxing.

As a blacksmith is one who works with iron, so an iron-monger is one who deals in articles made from that metal: the word MONGER being derived from the Old English *mangere* itself ultimately from the Latin word *mango*, a dealer or trader. The name of the mango fruit is unrelated, having been imported from the Far East. The name of another fruit, a type of apple, arrived on these shores several centuries before that of the mango; the name, applied to a particular type of ribbed apple, was costard. It had first been used fairly soon after the Conquest, although it was some time before a dealer in *costards* came to be called a COSTERMONGER, the earlier term being, reasonably enough, COSTARD-MONGER. Costards are rarely heard of nowadays but we still have costermongers who deal in other types of apple and in fruit generally. Similarly a dealer in fish is a FISHMONGER, a dealer in cheese is a CHEESEMONGER, a dealer in war is a WARMONGER, a dealer in scandal is a SCANDALMONGER and a dealer in scares is a SCAREMONGER.

An alternative name for a dealer or trader has been provided by a derivative of the Latin word *merx* which denoted wares for sale. The derivative *mercari* is related to the name of the Roman god of commerce, MERCURY, and by way of Old French to the name MARCHANT. This is just an old form of the word MER-CHANT and is also related to other words concerned with trade. Trade itself is called COMMERCE, an area set aside for trade is a MARKET, one who trades for money is MERCENARY; and such a one may even be called a MERCENARY if the trade in question is military. A merchant who deals in large or gross quantities has become known as a '*grosser*' or GROCER although the title has now been transferred from wholesale spice dealers to more general traders. Dealing directly with the public, retailers tend to sell smaller quantities: because small transactions were recorded by use of *tally* sticks, or because goods sold were 'cut up' into smaller parts, shop-keepers came to be called RE-TAILERS, the name being taken from the Old French word *retaille*, meaning a 'piece cut off'; small pieces or matters are known as DETAILS for similar reasons. Furthermore, people who make a living by cutting up cloth have come to be known as TAILORS.

Before cloth was ready for the tailor, it had to be woven and properly prepared. A piece of cloth when newly-woven was known to the Anglo-Saxons as a WEB; the word is still used in this sense although it is more familiar now as the name of the spider's woven gossamer. The surnames WEBB and WEBSTER are reminders of the original use of the word, the suffix *-ster* being at one time attached to the names of women workers. (Similarly the name BAXTER is just a variation of the earlier Bakester, the feminine form of the word baker, and the name BREWSTER is the feminine equivalent of the male brewer.) Having been woven, the cloth would need to be washed and trampled, then stretched and dried: trampling the material in order to clean and thicken it is known as fulling, so people whose occupation this was came to be known as FULLERS, and one of the chemicals they used has acquired the name FULLER'S EARTH. In this sense the name FULLER, from Old English *fullere*, ultimately has a Latin origin, the native Anglo-Saxon equivalent being WALKER. This name is also derived from the description of the occupation, for the word has developed from the Anglo-Saxon verb *wealcan* which meant 'to roll'. In some parts of the country the name Fuller is more common, in others Walker. When fulled, cloth would be stretched or tucked, the word TUCK having come from the Anglo-Saxon word *tucian*, to tug, pull or stretch. A TUCKER would stretch the cloth on a frame known as a tenter, the cloth being attached to the sides of the frame by means of hooks. So the subject of prolonged tension is said to be ON TENTERHOOKS. A tenter ground in the east end of London has long since been built over, but roads in the area still bear names like Tenter Ground and Tent Street. A TENT, Latin *tentorium*, is of course just a length of cloth stretched over a framework.

A milliner now sells hats but the original MILLINERS of the sixteenth century were really *millaners*: traders who imported fancy goods, especially clothing, from Milan. It is not uncommon for place names to be transferred in this way to famous cloths or materials produced there. Thus, for example, JERSEYS were originally made in Jersey, and WORSTED first came from Worsted in Norfolk. Cloth from Nîmes in France was cloth *de Nîmes* or as we now say DENIM; from it we make JEANS although they properly belong to a place called Gênes, better known in England as Genoa. GAUZE came originally from Gaza in Palestine, DAMASK from Damascus, CASHMIR from Kashmir and CALICO from Calicut. The name TWEED first came about as an error, for the cloth was just twill: a shipment from Scotland was labelled *tweel* (i.e. twill) but the word was misread as TWEED and so a new meaning was born. By contrast the name of a striped material from *Attabi* has now almost fallen into disuse, although

This eighteenth century etching by William Hogarth is supposed to illustrate the evils of gin drinking. Traders in Gin Lane can be identified by their shop signs: three golden balls are still displayed outside the pawnbroker's shop and a red and white striped pole still denotes a barber's.

Barbers used to be barber-surgeons, a fact which is reflected in the use of a pole, representing the staff once held by patients during blood letting. Its spiral pattern imitates blood and bandages, and the brass knob on the end is a vestigial brass bowl; such bowls were used to collect the blood and were sometimes suspended from the end of barbers' poles.

The tankards and coffin show that gin sellers and an undertaker operated here. The practice of displaying such signs seems to have provided a phrase for the English language for, when traders lived above their places of work, it would make perfect sense to talk about where one HANGS OUT, i.e. where one hangs out one's sign.

a variation of it is preserved in the title of the familiar TABBY cat. The quarter of Baghdad from which striped silk taffeta came had been named *Attaby* after a prince called '*attab*, so by a circuitous route the TABBY cat is really named after a man. Usually it is the other way about, for many names applied to human beings derive from ones belonging to animals; obvious examples of this process are provided by the surnames Bull, Hogg, Fox, Kidd, Steed, Deer, Wolfe, Lyon and Hare. Although old spellings are sometimes preserved in them the reference is still obvious enough: sometimes it is to physical characteristics, sometimes to moral ones supposedly possessed by the animal. Keepers of animals also have titles which incorporate the names of their charges; thus a '*sheep-herd*' becomes known as SHEPHERD; a '*ewe-herd*' becomes EWART or occasionally HOWARD; a '*lamb-herd*' becomes LAMBERT; and a '*wether-herd*' becomes known as WEATHERHEAD, although alternatively this name may represent the less than complimentary '*wether-head*' the suggestion being that the possessor of it has a head like a wether or ram. A pig-keeper may become known as a 'hog-herd', HOGGARD, or '*swine-herd*', SWINARD; while a '*cow-herd*' comes to be called COWARD and a '*calf-herd*', CALVERT or CALVARD. Similarly keepers of goats, colts and geese may have acquired the names GOTHARD, COLTARD and GOSSARD respectively.

Many names are thinly disguised descriptions of their original possessor and very often the description refers to the trade pursued. Thus a falconer's descendants became known as FAULKNER or perhaps FAULKS; those of a forester, FORSTER; of a wood-cutter, SAWYER; of a candle-maker, CHANDLER; of a pilot or *steersman*, STURMAN, and one who fashioned goods out of horn might easily acquire the name HORNER. The first BROKERS were people who BROACHED casks of wine, the name of the occupation and the practice deriving from the Latin *broccare* which meant specifically 'to tap a cask'. Arrowsmiths and Fletchers made arrows. The origin of the name ARROWSMITH is straightforward enough, but the origins of FLETCHER and the synonymous FLECKER are not so obvious. They are derived from the Anglo-Saxon word *flycge* which has itself developed into FLEDGE; a fully-fledged bird, arrow or anything else being one which is fully feathered. One who cuts or trims beards is a BARBER, the title of whom comes from the Latin word *barba*, beard. So also the BARB of the arrowsmith's arrow is a sort of beard in that it projects down from the head and tapers to a point.

Other common surnames derive from physical characteristics and again the inherent reference may be more or less obvious. Thus the names LONG, SHORT, LARGE and STRONG are clearly references to physical characteristics although our ancestors were not as sensitive as we are; they certainly seem to have had few qualms about giving names to people who might not necessarily be proud of the particular personal characteristic chosen to provide those names. Crookshank, for example, means literally 'crooked-leg'; Ballard means 'bald-head'; Puddifoot means 'stumpy-foot'; Bossey is a reference to a boss or protuberance such as a hump-back; and with Celtic meanings, Cambel is really 'crooked-mouth' and Kennedy 'ugly head'. The other two most common sources of family names are place names and parental forenames. Quite often this second type of name is formed by adding to the name of the individual's father a word which means 'son of'. English parallels the Scandinavian languages in possessing a class of names which end in '-son'. In Scotland the usual equivalent is the prefix 'Mac-' which corresponds to the Irish 'Mc', although each of these forms does occur in both countries. Furthermore the Irish have another prefix 'O'-', meaning 'of', to serve the same purpose. The Normans introduced into England their equivalent prefix *fis* which has developed into the English 'FITZ-' and corresponds to the modern French word *fils*. So the son of Hugh might be called HUGHSON, MCHUGH, MACHUGH, O'HUGH or FITZHUGH. Furthermore the Welsh have their own equivalent which, although less well known in England, occurs in some common names: *ap Hugh* is just another son of Hugh, now more familiar as PUGH.

In Hebrew the term for 'son of' is *ben*, and even this word from distant lands has found a place in English for it occurs in the name BENJAMIN. Applied to a favourite son and meaning literally 'son of my right hand' it was, like other biblical names, introduced to England in the train of Christianity. Another biblical name which has found favour in many European languages is *Jochanan* literally meaning 'the Lord is gracious': in Latin it is rendered *Johannes*, a name which the Germans shortened to *Johann* or to the familiar *Hans*; in Italian the name is *Giovanni*, in Spanish it is *Juan*, in Czech, Polish and Dutch *Jan* and in modern Greek *Zan* or *Yani*. The Russian form is *Ivan* and the French is *Jean*. In England it is JOHN, in Wales EVAN, in Scotland IAIN and in Ireland SEAN or SHAWN. Feminine forms include JANE, JANET, JANICE, JENNIE, JEANETTE, JUANITA, JEAN, JOAN and JOANNA, this latter name being the nearest to the original Hebrew still preserved in English. *Johannes Factotem* is a Latin expression which translates as 'John do-everything', for the word FACTOTUM is formed from the Latin words *facere*, to make, and *totum*, everything. In English the corresponding phrase is, of course, 'Jack of all trades', although the name Jack is really from the Hebrew JACOB by way of the Latin name *Jacobus*. This name also has derivatives throughout Europe, for example, the French *Jacques*, Gaelic HAMISH, Irish SEUMAS or SHAMUS and English JAMES. The Italian form is *Iago* and the Spanish one is *Diego*, which accounts for the name of the place dedicated to St James, SANTIAGO, and for the term DAGO as sometimes applied to Spaniards.

It is often the case that things which appear to have been brought under the control of the Christians have, in reality, retained their old ways. So it is that we call forenames Christian names, even though they often refer to the pre-Christian beliefs of the Indo-European peoples. Those with access to the old ways might bear names like ALFREDA or ALFRED, both meaning literally 'elf-counsel', for the Anglo-Saxon word *rede* meant council (thus Ethelred the Unready bears a curious title: he was named Ethelred, 'noble-counsel', but was called *unrede* because of the bad counsel on which he acted). Place names also recall the old ways for many still retain their ancient names, sometimes in a corrupted form. Thus WANSDYKE is 'Woden's dyke',

WOODNESBOROUGH is 'Woden's Borough' or 'Woden's fortress' and WORMSHILL is 'Woden's hill'. FREEFOLK, FROYLE, FRYUP, FRIDAYTHORPE and FROGBURY are all named after the goddess Freya and there are numerous other examples throughout the country. Returning to so-called Christian names we have THORA, the title of one devoted to the god Thor, and ARTHUR, the name of one who is an 'eagle of Thor'.

From ancient Greece comes DIONYSUS, the name of a god whose interest was generally focused on important matters such as revelry and drinking wine. He has left many lasting impressions on the English language in a number of different ways; he is, for example, remembered in the names DION, DENISE and DENIS. But more than this, he is indirectly responsible for the wonders and horrors of showbusiness, and this topic needs a chapter to itself.

27

Thank you; next please

Our so-called permissive society is only permissive in comparison with Puritan and Victorian morality. In comparison with
the diversions enjoyed in England in earlier times it is immediately apparent that the range of acceptable entertainment has
been restricted, not enhanced. Public singing and dancing has
to be licensed; British drinking restrictions provide the rest
of the world with incredulous amusement; promiscuity is
regarded as immoral; sadism is vicariously transferred to the
cinema screen; and the practice of taking drugs has suddenly
become, after thousands of innocent years, illegal. Between
them the Government and the Church have endeavoured to
restrict or wipe out almost every kind of public entertainment
available to the masses: in their stead we are left with suitably
censored pap, the fare of modern television.

Everything was different before Saturnalia became Christmas and the Spring fertility rites became Easter. In those days
the equivalent of a vicar's tea party was called an *agape*, after a
Greek word meaning love. These agapes, or Christian love
feasts, featured most, if not all, of the sinful activities men-

tioned above and were, to all intents and purposes, updated dionysian or bacchanalian revels. Originally devoted to the worship of the Greek god Dionysus, the counterpart of the Roman god Bacchus, such festivities were known as *orgia*, but whether devoted to Greek, Roman or Christian gods they would now be called ORGIES. Incidentally the word Bacchanalia may just conceivably have been corrupted to provide a well-known public house name, 'The Bag O' Nails'. There are still echoes of early Dionysian or Bacchic rites in the languages and traditions of Western culture. In particular the acting profession has benefited from the fun and games, for without the worship of Dionysus and its associated play-acting, 'The Theatre' as we know it might never have come into existence.

The Greek word *theoria*, which meant 'a viewing', is the origin of the English THEATRE, which people look at, and also of THEOREM and THEORY which are what mathematicians and scientists look into. The action depicted in the early theatre became highly stylised and invariably followed a fixed pattern. It may seem odd that anyone should want to watch a play the plot of which would be well known, yet this is a feature which has always remained closely attached throughout the development of drama. In this respect the Roman theatre was similar to the Greek; and over a thousand years later the Italian *commedia dell'arte* was still stylised, as were the traditional Mystery plays and the performances of the Mummers in England. Even today the ballet, opera and pantomime follow these ancient traditions, and the same could be said of Shakespeare's plays.

A Greek called Thespis is generally recognised as the first true actor. He lived in the sixth century BC and gave his name to the word THESPIAN, an alternative term for an actor. Amongst other innovations, he is credited with the idea of introducing an antagonist who struggles against the main character, the protagonist. The PROTAGONIST acquired his name from the Greek words *protos*, first, and *agonistes*, a contender, because he was indeed the first contender. The ANTAGONIST gets his name similarly: *anti* means against so he was literally one in contention with the protagonist, and thus ANTAGONISED him. An *agon* was an assembly, such as those present at an athletic or dramatic contest. From this association came the word *agonia*, a struggle, as did the word *agonistes*, but from the idea of an inner moral struggle came the word AGONY. Once this word was applied only to mental pain but now it has widened its meaning to include any acute suffering. Another character was the *hypokrites* or HYPOCRITE whose original failing was merely that he answered back, and yet another was *Eiron*, an underdog who eventually came out on top. His tricks involved the pretence of ignorance and were called *eironeia*, from which comes the modern version IRONY. In particular, dramatic and tragic irony are technical terms applied to a special theatrical device by which the audience understands the full meaning of an actor's words, while some or all of those on stage supposedly fail to comprehend their full implications.

The term applied to the actor's device of addressing the audience, supposedly without other actors being able to hear, is apostrophe. This meaning is nearer to that of the Greek word than is the other one associated with punctuation: APOSTROPHE is related to *apo*, off, and *strophein*, to turn, and indeed the actor does turn off from this stage dialogue in order to address the audience. In the earliest theatres, movements were divided into three distinct phases, two of which, the *strophe* and *antistrophe*, involved turning movements. The other phase was the *epode*, or after-song, during which the chorus remained stationary. Another sort of turn occurred when things started to go wrong for the protagonist. Here the action turned against him and this point was thus called a CATASTROPHE, a word derived from the Greek elements *cata*, down or against, and the familiar *strophe*. The *epode* is obsolete but there is still the simpler ODE. Now a poem, it was originally a song like the ones sung by the chorus. The members of the CHORUS, or *choros*, were dancers and singers which accounts for the seeming inconsistency between the terms CHORAL, 'pertaining to a choir', and CHOREOGRAPHY, the written instructions for ballet steps and thus the design of a dance. The area across which the original Greek chorus progressed and turned was the ORCHESTRA. Related to the word *orcheistai*, to dance, it was the first place where the chorus danced, but later the Romans used this area for seating; thus the floor of a theatre is called the orchestra and further, since the musicians used to sit on the front rows of these seats, the word is applied to them as well.

The origins of both COMEDY and TRAGEDY lie in the ancient Greek village revels. The former comes from *komos*, revel, which is in turn related to *kome* or village, and the latter from *tragos*, a goat-song. Why tragedy should be associated with goat-song is not known for certain: one possibility is that a goat was the prize in early Dionysian singing contests, another is that the first tragedies were songs to be sung during the ritual sacrifice of a goat. In Shakespeare's day there were three basic types of play: comedies, tragedies and histories. A history depicts supposedly factual events and takes its name from Latin. In this language a *histrion* was a performer in a play, and from him also comes the word HISTRIONIC, an epithet which is now also applied to non-theatrical actors.

From ancient Greece come the words CINEMA and ODEON. The cinema is, of course, a very recent invention and so the Greeks had no word for it. They did, however, have words for movement, *kinema*, and for a picture or drawing, *graphikos*, and from these words the film pioneers created CINEMATOGRAPH, now abbreviated to CINEMA just as the expression 'moving pictures' has been abbreviated to MOVIES. On the other hand the *odeon* would be as familiar to an ancient Greek as to the modern movie-goer: to the Greeks it was a building designed for musical performances and the singing of odes. Before buildings were specifically designed for the performing arts, a covered place had been used and in the very earliest times performances had been given in the open air. A covered place, or specifically a stage cover, was a *skene*, the ancestor of the modern SCENE and SCENERY. The theatre has changed a lot since ancient times but there are still echoes of the early stylised performances. Stage plays other than musicals do not generally feature singing but we still refer to a MELODRAMA, a word derived from *melos*, a song, and DRAMA, both elements being Greek in origin. In the eighteenth century few theatres were licensed to stage plays but all were able to put on musical evenings with songs, recitations and dressing up. These events developed into the nineteenth century music hall while the word melodrama attached itself to another form of entertainment: the sensational and overdone drama so beloved of the Victorians.

When only one actor speaks, the piece is a MONOLOGUE but when more do so they engage in DIALOGUE. Similarly a speech made before the start of a play is a PROLOGUE and one after it is an EPILOGUE. These words are all Greek but the Romans were later responsible for quite a few theatrical terms, although some of them, like PERSON, PRETEXT and EXPLODE, have lost their associations. The word PERSON has developed from the Latin *persona*, a player in a drama. The player was so-called because of the mask which he wore in order to exaggerate his facial expressions. These masks not only enabled the audience to see the actors' emotions better, they also acted like megaphones which amplified the actors' voices. In fact it was this second feature which was responsible for the name of the mask and hence of the player; *persona* comes from *per*, through, and *sonare*, to sound. These actors, the *dramatis personae*, IMPERSONATED others and one group of people, which was a particular favourite for this treatment, was the *praetexta*, a class of Roman citizens who acquired their name from their distinctive clothing. Because the front was embroidered it was literally *praetexta*, 'woven in front'. The actors imitating the people who wore this distinctive clothing were called *praetextatae*; since they dressed up as important people, which they were not, they provided the modern PRETEXT, a word which also describes something which is other than it appears.

At the end of the play the audience would EXPLODE. That is, they would clap, for in Latin *explodere* meant 'to break into clapping'. This would occur in response to the instruction PLAUDIT which would be given by the actors at the end of the play. APPLAUSE has taken over from the word explode which has now been applied to louder and more sudden noises. Something deserving of applause was PLAUSIBLE but this term has evolved differently: it came to mean fair-spoken and later acquired its current meaning of seemingly reasonable or believable. Spontaneous and prolonged applause is now called an OVATION from the Latin *ovare*, to exult. In Roman times an ovation was an enthusiastic reception given to popular figures returning to Rome, but it was less impressive than the more ceremonious *triumphus* or TRIUMPH, which incidentally takes its name from a Greek word for a hymn to Dionysus, *trionphos*. Those who do the applauding are the AUDIENCE for they are the ones who have listened to the performance. Related to the Latin *audire*, to hear, the AUDIENCE is made up of listeners, or AUDITORS, who sit in the AUDITORIUM. On the stage are the actors who have passed an AUDITION and so confirmed, amongst other things, that they will be AUDIBLE.

In the sixteenth century, more than a thousand years after the Roman Empire started to crumble, the Italians were still performing stylised dramas. The most famous of these is undoubtedly the *commedia dell'arte* which featured a number of characters whose names live on in English. The main characters were Harlequin and his sweetheart Columbine, the daughter of the old dotard called Pantaloon. Pantaloon wore loose baggy trousers which, until the nineteenth century, were regarded as particularly funny. When this attire did eventually become fashionable it took its name from the old fool who had worn it for centuries; thus trousers or PANTALOONS, or later PANTS, became respectable, although alternative early names were 'unmentionables' and 'inexcusables'. More than a hundred years later, PANTIES were the new unmentionables. The original Pantaloon, San Pantaleone, an obscure saint who lived in Roman times, would probably have been dismayed had he had reason to imagine that his name would develop as it has.

Another character was Zanni from whom comes the word ZANY; the Italian name is another form of Giovanni, which corresponds to the English name John, and the performer was a secondary clown whose function was to mimic the chief one. For this reason the word zany is now applied to certain kinds of humour – usually to the type not really understood by the user of the word. The original type of humour engaged in by Zanni was literally slapstick. Clowns would carry two or more straight sticks of wood which were held together: when another performer was hit by this SLAPSTICK there would be a resounding crack as the sticks slapped together – but it would appear to the audience that the sound resulted from the actor being struck. This it seems was regarded as extremely funny, but it was not the only source of humour. Equally amusing was Scaramouch, a braggart who started fights but who was really a coward. From his name, or at least from the same source as his name, come the English SKIRMISH, SCRUMMAGE and SCRIMMAGE, in which he might easily have become involved.

This sort of slapstick entertainment found its way to England in the early eighteenth century as pantomime, literally 'an imitation of all things', which the Romans and Greeks would have called simply *mimos* or MIME. Even today there are many similarities between the Italian *commedia dell'arte* and the British pantomime. There is an element of stage magic, stock characters and a predictable story, there are funny costumes and the same old slapstick humour: the only thing to have changed is the plot, and that is largely irrelevant anyway. This sort of comedy is not to be taken seriously as the names of its near relations show: FARCE takes its name from the Latin *farcire*, to stuff, because the first farces were stuffed into the interludes between the serious acts of a play. The Latin word for mockery was *burla* from *burra*, a puff of wool, and thus, figuratively, nonsense. Adopted by the later Italians, *burla* became *burlesco* and hence the English BURLESQUE. VAUDEVILLE is simply *vau de ville* although when it originated in Normandy it was more accurately known as *Vau de Vire*, from the valley of the Vire.

Slapstick comedy is looked down upon by the serious actor, but it is sometimes necessary to compromise. In order to survive it may be necessary for the struggling artist to turn his hand to popular entertainment. In general this sort of work is called catchpenny but when the audience is lead specifically to an easy laugh it is CLAPTRAP. These words have relatively recent origins as do some other familiar terms. The SPOTLIGHT which really does create a spot of light is very recent; before its introduction the thing to be in was the LIMELIGHT, the stage lighting used before the advent of electricity and generated by burning lime. This form of lighting caused considerable glare so that the actors liked their off-stage room to be painted in a rather dull colour. The traditional colour chosen was green and the room was, therefore, called the GREENROOM, a name which, despite redecoration, it still retains. An unlikely refugee from the theatre is the word PARQUET. Originally it meant a small part of a 'park'; then a courtyard and later the wooden floor of such a courtyard; next it was applied to the wooden floor of a theatre, since early theatres were just courtyards; and finally it has come to mean any wooden floor set in a particular pattern.

Some words assume several identities and occasionally manage to sustain these separate personalities without undue confusion. Soon after the introduction of printing in the fifteenth century the earliest catchword appeared. Originally it was a word at the bottom of a page which duplicated the first one of the next. This catchword enabled the reader to achieve a greater degree of fluency than would otherwise have been possible. Later the term acquired a theatrical meaning analogous to its printing one; the last word or words of one actor formed the cue for another and so formed an oral catchword or catchphrase. Now, entertainers have extended the meaning, and a comedian's catchphrases have become little more than cues for the audience to respond to, usually by laughing. These different meanings of the word are all similar enough, and yet sufficiently easy to distinguish, in order to enable them to coexist happily.

Like actors, words constantly jostle for new parts to play. Some will be auditioning for the first time, but many will have had successful roles before. If they perform well then they might be asked to stay; otherwise it's a case of 'don't call us, we'll call you'.

28

The family pedigree

In many respects words are like living creatures. They are born, they grow old and eventually they die. Some are still-born, some die in infancy, and some die of old age; yet others live on and on like primitive organisms slowly changing and developing in shape and form. During their long lifetimes such words generally bear offspring themselves. As in any family group relationships become complicated after a few generations and ancestries will be lost for ever unless detailed records are kept. Only in the last few hundred years have we started to investigate the family relationships between words, but since the beginning of recorded history we have taken great care to remember the names of and relationships between our ancestors. Genealogical charts help to show complicated interrelationships and a few simple conventions help to explain clearly who is related to whom. Drawing lines from parent to offspring, genealogists fancied that their marks resembled crane's feet; and a simple drawing of a crane's foot (人) came to indicate direct descent. In the variety of French used in England in the fifteenth century a 'foot of crane' was a *pee de grue*, a description which has been turned into the word PEDIGREE.

The words mother, father, son, daughter, brother and sister are all very old and all have parallel forms in other Indo-European languages. An English MOTHER is just an up-dated Anglo-Saxon *moder*, herself not so very different from a Dutch *moeder*, an Icelandic *moðir*, a German *mutter*, a Danish or Swedish *moder*, an Irish or Gaelic *mathair*, a Persian *madar*, a Russian *mat*, a Greek *mater*, and a French *mère*. In Sanskrit the corresponding form of the word is *matr* and in Latin it is *mater* which gives us a word for a womb, MATRIX; for a married woman, MATRON; for marriage itself, MATRIMONY and for that which is motherly, MATERNAL.

A FATHER was to the Anglo-Saxons a *fæder*. To the Dutch he is *vader*, to Icelanders he is *faðir*, to Germans he is *vater*, and to Danes and Swedes he is *fader*; in Persian he is known as *pidar*, in Sanskrit *pidr*, in French *père*, and in Greek and Latin a *pater*. PATERNITY is really the same as fatherhood and PATRIOTISM is a love of one's father-land.

The words 'brother' and 'sister' are also represented in most of the Indo-European languages as to a lesser extent are 'son' and 'daughter'.

The words mamma, dadda, pappa and babba, or ones very similar to them, occur all over the world. These sounds are to be found not only in Indo-European languages but also in remote and unrelated tongues from every continent. The words are the first understandable noises that an infant makes, and their meanings are generally attributed to the mother, father and baby itself, although not necessarily in that order. It is only a matter of convention that English children are encouraged to call their mother *mamma*, MAMMY, MOMMY or MUMMY, their father *pappa*, *dadda* or DADDY, and themselves *babba* or BABY. Other permutations serve just as well in other parts of the world. In a sense babies cease to be infants as soon as they start to talk because the word INFANT, derived from the Latin *infans*, means literally 'one who cannot speak'. Another word for a baby or foetus later came to mean a baby girl but is now usually used of older girls and boys indiscriminately. The word, CHILD, is derived from an ancient term for a womb; a connection which

A pair of physically connected twins, called Chang and Eng, were born in 1811 and shown as freaks throughout Europe and America. They were born in Thailand, then called Siam, and were the original SIAMESE TWINS. This picture shows them with some of their 22 children.

The word TWIN is closely related to the words TWAIN, TWICE and TWO, the underlying idea being that of 'two-ness'. Other related words include twine and twill (both suggesting two threads) and twig (where a branch splits into two).

is remembered when we speak of childbirth, rather than 'baby-birth', and childbed, rather than 'babybed'. The Romans had a poor opinion of those who did not speak Greek or Latin or any of the other languages regarded as cultured. Like the Greeks before them, they fancied that other languages consisted of child-like babbling, and the *ba-ba* sound which they thought they heard provided a convenient name for those uncultured foreigners, now known as BARBARIANS.

The Latin word for ancestor, *avus*, was applied specifically to a grandfather and its diminutive form *avunculus* to a mother's brother. Travelling into English via Old French this latter word contracted in length and generalised its meaning to give the word UNCLE; in a similar way the Latin term for a father's sister has provided the Old French *ante* and thus the modern English AUNT, as well as the modern French *tante*. One who behaves like an *avus*, or uncle, is said to be AVUNCULAR; while one who resembles a distant ancestor, such as a Roman *atavus* or great-great-grandfather, is said to be ATAVISTIC. Just as *avus* originally meant ancestor so *nepos* meant a descendant and in particular a grandson; the female equivalent was *neptis*. Again via the French these words have given to the English language the titles NEPHEW and NIECE, as well as the term NEPOTISM. The title COUSIN is another traveller from ancient Rome. Derived from a word denoting a cousin on the mother's side, it has been generalised to provide its present meaning. During its history as part of the English language it has been more general still; Shakespeare used it to indicate almost any degree of kinship; and even today the monarch addresses peers of the realm and European monarchs as 'Cousin', even if they are not.

A grandparent is literally a 'great parent', which is reasonable enough, but it is more difficult to justify a grandchild being a 'great child'. The French are more reasonable in this respect and call a grandfather a *grandpère* and a grandmother a *grand-mère* while a grandson is a *petit fils*, a 'small son', and a granddaughter is a *petite fille*, a 'small daughter'. In the past the title grandfather became contracted to GRANFER and then to GAFFER. This contracted form has stayed in the language but its meaning has gradually changed so that it now means a boss or a foreman. Grandmothers acquired similar familiar forms of their title such as GRANNAM, GRANNY and GAMMER. Unlike gaffer, the term gammer has dropped out of the language, although it appears now and then in odd places: for example, an early English comedy entitled *Gammer Gurton's Nedle* which deals with Granny Gurton's lost needle is still occasionally performed. Another term for grandmother was BELDAME. *Belle dame*, literally 'beautiful lady', was at one time a polite form of address but came to be used ironically and was applied specifically to older women who were no longer especially beautiful. The title DAME is derived from the Latin word for a lady, *domina*, and so the forms of address MADAM, and MA'AM, mean simply 'my lady'. A small lady is a diminutive dame or DAMSEL but her title is rarely used now, except when she is in distress. Where the word damsel might once have been used, we now use the term girl. In the Middle Ages, however, a girl might have been either male or female since the word could be used of either sex. In order to be specific it might be necessary to talk, for example, of a knave-girl, meaning a boy. The word WENCH was originally neuter as well, so a boy could also be called by that title. Its Anglo-Saxon ancestor *wencel* had meant simply 'weak' but since women are supposed to be the weaker members of the family they eventually monopolised the word.

The word FAMILY is adopted from the Latin word for a household, *familia*. Members of a household are FAMILIAR with each other, and the witches' FAMILIAR is a reminder that the word is also related to the Latin *famulus*, servant. In Anglo-Saxon times the head of a household was called a *hlafweard*, a *'loaf ward'* or bread-keeper; and his title was contracted to *hlaford* and then to LORD. His female counterpart was a bread-kneader, a *hlafdige* or later a *laefdi*, what we now call a LADY. The word *hlaef* has become LOAF and *dige* represents a word which we now use for the material kneaded rather than the action of kneading: DOUGH. In a similar way a servant was a *hlafaeta*, a *'loaf-eater'*, which just might account for the name of the modern LOAFER; but this is only speculation since there is no documentary link between the Anglo-Saxon and the modern English words. Eating together has always been an important ritual between friends and family, a fact which is also reflected in the words COMPANION, Old French *compain*, and COMPANY, Old French *companie*, both of which mean something like 'bread-together'. Nowadays we call the head of a household the bread-winner, presumably because we usually buy bread rather than bake it at home as our ancestors did.

As lords and ladies were gradually elevated they were replaced by their Latin counterparts. The head of the household was the MASTER, from *magister*, a word which also gave the titles MAGISTRATE, MISTER and indirectly the feminine form MISTRESS. The style 'Mistress' was often abbreviated to Mis and only in the eighteenth century did the pattern of calling unmarried women Miss and married ones Mrs become standard. Just as the senior woman in the household had been a lady or bread-kneader, so her juniors had titles which reflected their ancient functions. The word daughter, for example, is descended from an ancient word which meant 'to milk'. A WIFE was a woman who acquired her title from her practice of weaving: the Anglo-Saxon word for joining or weaving was *wifan* while that for woman was *wif*. From the word *wif* and the equally old *mann* came the word *wifman*, later WOMAN, which probably refers to the idea of female mankind rather than any suggestion of women belonging to men. The implication of marriage did not attach itself to the word wife until it was already well established. Indeed, in some uses of the word, it still retains its original sense: fishwife, alewife, housewife and midwife ('with-woman') are examples of the word used in its earlier sense, and AN OLD WIVES' TALE is really just an old women's tale. The present meaning of the word wife started to develop over a thousand years ago when men talked about their wives or their old wives just as today men talk of their women or old women, meaning their spouses. A SPINSTER, like a SPIDER, is simply one who spins. Spinning is the traditional occupation of women, especially young ones, so that during the seventeenth century it became customary to affix the word spinster to unmarried women's names. From there the title has come to indicate an old maid. Part of the equipment needed for spinning is called a DISTAFF. This word has changed little from Anglo-Saxon times when it was written *distaef*; *diesse* being a term for a bunch of flax and *staef* simply a STAFF. Because women spun while the men got on with the serious business of killing each other, the wife's side of the family came to be known as the distaff side while the husband's came to be known as the spear side.

The Anglo-Saxon *cniht* was originally no more than a youth.

Later he became a servant and then specifically a nobleman's servant. Eventually such servants acquired fighting prowess and prestige of their own, and thus became the KNIGHTS of the Middle Ages. As knights became elevated in rank, they acquired servants of their own and just as their title changed in meaning so too did their subordinates. The Romans had called a shield-bearer a *scutarius*, a title which in Old French became *escuier* and thence the English ESQUIRE. In the Middle Ages the esquire was promoted from a shield bearer to a trainee fighter, and when he won his spurs he would himself become a knight. Since the age of chivalry the title has become more and more popular and now the abbreviation Esq. is almost as common as Mr. Clipping the initial 'e' from 'esquire' has produced the title SQUIRE, a style now used only by rustics, humorists and second-hand motor car dealers. The more usual form of address, SIR, is just a shorter form of SIRE, itself contracted from SENIOR, a word which in Latin meant 'older' and which has also provided the Spanish title SEÑOR. An elder is generally also a senior.

Words disappear from the language as mysteriously as they appear. Some, like *besaile*, an old word for a great-grandfather, vanish altogether, while others leave clues as to their former existence. When *sibb*, meaning race, was lost to the language the word SIBLING, meaning brother or sister, still remained. God-parents were *Godsibs* and, having much in common, would have had a lot to talk about. Indeed this is exactly how GOSSIPS got their title. Again, from the Old English *astieped*, meaning bereaved, all that is left is the prefix STEP – as in stepfather, one who replaces a dead father. Like most family pedigrees, that of the English language is complicated, convoluted and unlikely. Words are born when they are needed and die when they are not. Needs change with time and words develop to match those needs. Sometimes whole groups of words are rendered obsolete and perhaps it is only a matter of time before the age-old mother and father, brother and sister, and son and daughter are all replaced by the single word 'clone'. Originally mere twigs to the Greeks, clones may one day supplant whole family trees.

29

Tying knots

At first it may seem odd that modern English has few words of Anglo-Saxon origin which are associated with marriage. But given that marriage did not become a sacrament of the Church until the thirteenth century, this shortcoming is largely explained. Relationships before that, and for a long time afterwards, had been a great deal less rigorously permanent than they were to become by the early twentieth century. In England, informal marriages were stopped by an act of Parliament in 1753 but it was not until 1940 that such arrangements became invalid in Scotland. Nevertheless, it is the Victorian age which enjoys a reputation for enforcing moral constraint. The truth is that the Victorians played only a part in restricting the scope of what was acceptable and increasing the scope of what was not. Only now, after more than seven centuries, is the general tendency being reversed. As the tide of Christian influence has turned so the shore of English licence has again been revealed.

When Lord Hardwicke's Act was passed in 1753, it did away with many forms of marriage including Roman Catholic ones. Also stopped were the FLEET and MAYFAIR marriages, named from the places in London where they were performed. The only forms of marriage which remained valid were those of the Church of England, the Quakers and the Jews. In order to become legally married agnostics, atheists and members of other religions could always travel across the Scottish border, find two witnesses, and validly marry themselves by a simple declaration. Anyone could do this anywhere in Scotland but the popular image is of a young eloping couple being wed by the blacksmith at Gretna Green. Informal marriages in Scotland became subject to restrictions in 1856 and after 1940 the services of a priest became necessary; nevertheless, Scottish marriage law is still different from that of England. For example the minimum age at which marriage can be contracted is sixteen years in England; but in Scotland it is fourteen for boys, and for girls only twelve.

Whether recognised by the courts or not, so-called Common Law marriages are certainly recognised by the population at large. We still talk about TAKING THE JUMP or JUMPING OVER THE BROOMSTICK, sometimes not realising that such an action was once sufficient to seal a marriage contract. The usual version of the ceremony was to place a broomstick across the threshold of a house, and for the two people to jump over it. Getting a divorce was equally simple: one party needed only to replace the broomstick in the doorway and then jump back. Even today bridegrooms often perform a special ceremony at the threshold of the bride's new house: perhaps if the bride is carried in she will not have the right to jump back out. The broomstick itself is sometimes called a BESOM from the Anglo-Saxon word *besema* which meant a bundle of twigs. Now the word broom is more commonly used for this purpose, but the phrase 'TO JUMP THE BESOM' is still in use in places where the word besom has been transferred to the women who might have used such things. In North Wales the phrase may be applied to any sort of wedding, including a Church one, but in Yorkshire it can be insulting since it implies the absence of an acceptable ceremony.

Like informal marriages, trial ones are hardly recent inventions. The practice of HANDFASTING, 'hand-fastening' or joining hands to make a temporary marriage agreement is only one of many arrangements which have existed throughout the country. Now bundled together with the absurd title of 'living in sin' such trial partnerships are common again; only the formal agreements are no longer recognised because the accepted ceremonies have fallen into disuse. Like the modern shaking of hands, handfasting symbolises the sealing of a contract: the giving of one pledge and the acceptance of another. This idea of exchange, whether of promises or tokens which symbolise them, underlies much of the language of marriage and of a similar institution now known as engagement. Indeed, the distinction between being married and being engaged to be married has not always been as important as it is now. Legal marriage is of course a contract, but until recently an agreement to marry was also a contract, and failure to satisfy it might result in a civil action for breach of promise. What lawyers call 'intimacy' might not always have been condoned between the dates of engagement and marriage, but at least the security arrangements would usually be relaxed.

TO ENGAGE is to give a promise, for the word comes from the Old French *gage* which literally means 'pledge'. The Old French 'g' tended to become 'w' in Norman French, a fact which accounts for the English WAGE, also originally meaning no more than a pledge. The corresponding Anglo-Saxon word was *wedd*, which has now become WED, but another word, PLIGHT, Anglo-Saxon *pliht*, originally meaning 'risk', also came into Middle English to mean the same as pledge. To plight one's TROTH is merely to pledge one's *'truth'*, or good faith. Troths are plighted on the wedding day, but the parties involved may already be BETROTHED. On both engagement and wedding days, rings are given to symbolise the new bond; in fact there is more than symbolism here, for BOND is only a variation of the Old Norse word *band*. A BAND of gold BINDS the couple together like a knot or BEND. If this bondage proved too much, the fetter could always be removed: as the RING, Anglo-Saxon *hring*, was returned so the agreement was dissolved and an immediate divorce obtained. A common practice at one time was to

245245245

engrave a line of verse on the inside of golden rings and, because poetry was called *poesy*, such rings became POSY rings; furthermore, being accompanied by floral tributes, the flowers themselves became known as POSIES. The engraved rings are out of fashion but brides still carry posies.

To the Romans the word for a fiancé was *sponsus*, related to

An old view of Eros, the Greek god of EROTIC love, shooting his arrow at a likely looking couple.

The Victorians, who did not approve of such things, thought of sweethearts as forbidden delicacies or 'sweet-tarts'. The tone of disapproval is still present in the slang term for a woman of liberal affections, and the modern TART has lost her sweetness.

FIDO, a popular name for a faithful dog, is formed from the Latin word for trust, *fides*, which also accounts for the word FIDELITY meaning trustworthiness. From the Latin verb meaning 'to trust', *fidere*, the French created the word *fier* which blossoms to provide the titles of an engaged couple: she is a FIANCÉE, he a FIANCÉ.

the verb *spondere*, to speak or pledge. From the verb comes the English SPONSOR as well as a word for speaking back, RESPONDING, and for speaking-back-together, CORRESPONDING. Of more direct interest is the Old French derivative *spose* which meant 'spoken!' because from it we have the words ESPOUSE and SPOUSE. Again the underlying theme is the ubiquitous pledge: one who is engaged or married is spoken for. To the Anglo-Saxons one who was spoken for or betrothed was a *bryd*. From that word comes the modern BRIDE and from the *brydealu*, or later BRIDE-ALE, comes the word BRIDAL. Now it means only 'pertaining to a bride' but the original meaning was quite different. A bridal was a feast or celebration at which pledges were exchanged and at which the man and woman, along with the assembled witnesses, would share a drinking cup to symbolise the new union. The BRIDELOPE, *'bride-lope'* or bridal-run, a convention by which the bridegroom conducted his bride back to his house, is now obsolete. The late Anglo-Saxon form *brydlop* is the oldest known Teutonic word for a wedding, which suggests that taking members of the opposite sex home might once have had more significance than it does now. Either way, the man most involved was a *brydguma*; now a BRIDEGROOM, although the word *guma* meant only man and had nothing to do with the word groom.

As already mentioned in the previous chapter, the term 'wife' originally meant merely 'woman'. Similarly a HUSBAND was just a *husbonda*, a 'house-bondman' or bondman who owned property, what in more egalitarian times is called a householder. Remnants of his earlier bachelor days still exist, so that a HUSBANDMAN is one who may be interested in animal HUSBANDRY and may need to HUSBAND his (or her) resources. On the other hand, the house-woman or housewife has left little evidence of her maiden-hood, although she has given her name to a sewing bag, a HOUSEWIFE or HUSSIF, and also to the disreputable young HUSSY. As applied to women, the word MAID is now applied, except in dialect, only to servants. Earlier it was synonymous with virgin but before that it meant only girl or young woman; the first and third meanings are combined in compounds such as milk-maid, dairy-maid and barmaid. Nevertheless, it is the suggestion of virginity which has been transferred to compound words as maiden speech, maiden over and maiden voyage, and also to the less well known maiden assize (at which no cases were heard), maiden tide (during which no vessels dock) and maiden castle (one which has never fallen during a siege).

At the wedding itself, the functions of the bridesmaids (earlier bridemaids), who must themselves be unmarried, include dressing up in a costume similar to the bride's. This is done, or at least was in earlier times, to confuse evil spirits who might wish to cause trouble: not being able to identify the specially-dressed bride, they would be obliged to give up and go away. Many such ancient beliefs and customs survive in different ways; thus the shoes which once played an important part in Saxon ceremonies have now become boots tied to the back of the newly-weds' motor car; the corn which once conferred fertility has become rice or confetti, and the practice of DANCING ATTENDANCE, or dancing with each of the guests, is mirrored by the modern custom of exchanging kisses with them. Traditions linger on for a long time in one form or another, and so do the associated words. For example, the Latin verb *maritare*, to marry, has provided words such as MARRY, MARRIAGE and MARITAL. Wedding veils were used by the Romans, and indeed their word for a cloud or a veil, *nubes*, is still remembered in England. The wedding rites were *nuptiae* and are now NUPTIALS while one who is ready to marry is NUBILE, a fact which will doubtlessly disappoint many users of the word who seem to have developed other ideas about its meaning. More devastating still will be the news that a NYMPH, or at least a Greek *nymphe*, is after all only a bride. As well as being responsible for creating new members of the species the two parties to a marriage represent a bond between two families. In the past such bonds have cemented tribal agreements and forged new political alliances. To a greater or lesser extent they still do in various parts of the world. In England this facet has become of less importance and with it has declined the attendant commercial considerations. Dowries may now be uncommon but they are not unknown; from the Old French verb *doer*, to give (especially as a marriage portion) comes the English DOWRY as well as a collection of related words such as ENDOW and DOWAGER. Even WEDLOCK itself reflects the ancient practice of giving and receiving ceremonial gifts, since the LOCK here does not represent the Anglo-Saxon *loc* but rather the similar *lac* meaning gift. So WEDLOCK is really a pledge-gift not a marriage-lock. Good news to some perhaps. The word GIFT itself was used in Anglo-Saxon times to mean specifically a payment for a wife; and its plural form was used to mean 'marriage'.

Since the bride brought to her new husband's house her own possessions as well as her dowry, it was important to distinguish between the two. The Greek word for a dowry was *pherne* and for 'beyond' *para*; with a little help from Latin these elements became PARAPHERNALIA, a word once applied to the wife's goods held in her own name 'beyond the dowry'. The traffic in presents was not all one way: for one thing it was customary to give to a new wife a gift on the morning after the marriage. In German a morning-gift is called a *morgengabe*, a word which, after processing by the ever-busy Romans, became part of the expression *matrimonium ad morganaticam* meaning what is now referred to as 'MORGANATIC marriage'. Such a marriage occurred when a man of rank married a woman of low station: her children could not subsequently inherit from their father, but the new wife still got her morning-gift.

Our cynical forefathers thought that sweet love would be likely to wane like the moon after a month of marriage. So the newly-married couples enjoyed their HONEYMOON while they could. After all, those same cynics were right about many things. They knew, for example, that the one sure thing in life is death; and that death always lurks just around the next corner.

30

The end

As marriage ceremonies mark the transition from one state to another, so similar rites of passage mark other important changes during life's meandering course. Of the other rituals common to almost all societies and all ages, the most striking are those associated with death. Most ancient cultures held similar beliefs about the fundamental aspects of death: that it is not final; that some intangible essence continues to exist after physical life has ceased; and that this incorporeal essence must be prepared for a journey to another world. Also common is the association of death and mourning with specific colours. In most of Europe black is now used: the same colour as that employed by the Romans, Greeks and before them the Egyptians. But in other parts of the Middle East brown, blue, white and violet were commonly used and in the Far East white and yellow are more usual.

Most British funerary practices are, like the use of the colour black, borrowed from the Romans. Floral tributes, processions and feasts were all as common in ancient Rome as they are in modern Britain. Perhaps the feasts are less impressive now, in fact they are often little more than tea parties; nevertheless they fulfil the same function as the grander occasions of the past. Another tradition which is common in various cultures is the clanging of gongs or ringing of bells while someone is dying; the intention behind it is to scare away evil spirits which might otherwise waylay a newly released soul. In Christian countries, the PASSING bell is, or was, used for this purpose. During the burial service another bell or 'teller' was rung: three times for a child, six for a woman and nine for a man. Thus nine *tellers* signal the end of a man's life, or as the corrupted form has it NINE TAILORS MAKE A MAN. Some customs associated with the passing of the soul from this world to the next still endure in parts of the country. All knots must be loosened so that the disembodied spirit should not be bound, mirrors should be covered in order that it should not see itself and so become confused or frightened, and the doors should be left open to allow it free passage.

Because the soul may wait for several days before leaving, it is regarded as bad manners to leave the body alone until burial, and so during this time a body-watch or lich wake should be kept. The Anglo-Saxon word *lic*, meaning form, corpse or body, has almost fallen into disuse except in compounds such as LICH WAKE. Others survivors include the LICH-GATE, the churchyard gate where coffins rest temporarily; LICH-WAY, the path along which bodies should be taken for burial (often an ancient track otherwise fallen into disuse); LICH-OWL, the bird which traditionally warns of death; and, possibly, LICHFIELD, the field of the dead bodies. From the Anglo-Saxon words *liflic*, *deadlic* and *deathlic* come the modern forms LIVELY, DEADLY and DEATHLY and from a word meaning 'same-form', *gelic*, we have the modern LIKE as in LIFELIKE and DEATHLIKE. In Latin the equivalent of *lic* was *corpus*, meaning a body, dead or alive. The legal prerogative writ known as *habeas corpus* is used to prevent the false imprisonment of living bodies, but the term CORPSE is applied to dead ones. Small bodies are CORPUSCLES and large ones can be said to be CORPULENT but both, being solid bodies, may be said to be CORPOREAL; conceptual bodies include the

The orchestra of the dead as pictured in the fifteenth century. These revellers appear to have anticipated the invention of rock 'n' roll by several hundred years.

In Greek the word for 'body' was *soma* and for 'dried-up' *skeleton*, so a dried-up body was a *skeleton soma*: what we now know more simply as a SKELETON.

military CORPS and the legal CORPORATION. In the past a body was, and to poets sometimes still is, a CORSE; and less prosaically a close-fitting bodice is called a CORSET.

Those who have departed this life are said to have 'passed on' to the 'next world'. This idea of parting is reflected in the word LIFE which to the Anglo-Saxons was *lif*, related to the verb *lifan*, to remain, or to be LEFT behind. The departed leave behind the living who are now said to be BEREFT, but originally it was the dead who were BEREAVED since the Anglo-Saxon word *bereafian* meant 'to snatch away'. Now the dead are supposed to go up to heaven or down to hell but in earlier times they were thought to

GO WEST like the ephemeral sun. From mainland Europe it appeared that the dying sun descended upon the British Isles which were thus known as the Isles of the Dead. In Latin the verb 'to go' is *ire*; attached to *per* meaning 'through' or in this case 'thorough', and processed by the French, it gives the word PERISH. Thus to go entirely, is to perish and similarly 'going to meet' one's ancestors was, to the Romans, *obituarius*, hence the English OBITUARY. More recently pilots who, during World War II, ditched into the sea were said to go into the drink; and since Burton beer was a popular type of drink, the airmen who never returned had simply 'gone for a Burton'.

An Old Norse word *deyja* has developed into the modern English DIE, while related Anglo-Saxon words DEAD and DEATH are identical to their modern equivalents. A violent death was to the Anglo-Saxons *morthor*, a word which has developed into the modern term MURDER. A murderer was earlier known as a *bana*, a word which has developed into the modern BANE, and which came to be associated with poison: hence the names of the poisonous baneberry fruit and of plants such as henbane, dogbane, fleabane, ratsbane, wolfsbane and leopard's-bane. An Anglo-Saxon verb meaning to die was *steorfan*, a close relative of the modern German *sterben* which has exactly the same meaning. In English the word came to be associated with slow deaths such as those caused by disease, hunger or cold and this explains why the modern English form STARVE means both to die of hunger and, in Yorkshire at least, to die of cold. Another Anglo-Saxon verb, *sweltan*, meant to faint away, to languish, or to die of oppressive heat. The modern form of the word is the less serious SWELTER, and the conditions which cause sweltering are 'sweltery' or as we now say SULTRY.

TO KILL is merely to QUELL, both words having developed from the Anglo-Saxon *cwellan*, but to kill someone of import-ance is to assassinate them. The original ASSASSINS were Moslem fanatics who flourished in Persia in the twelfth and thirteenth centuries and who obtained their name, earlier *hashishin*, from that of the drug HASHISH (now often shortened to HASH) which they reputedly took before their frequent murdering sprees.

Back in England animals and humans, however important, were SLAIN; in Anglo-Saxon times the equivalent of our modern SLAY was *slean* and the even older Saxon form *slahan* has become SLAUGHTER. 'Slaughtering-on' through an enemy, for example, is an ONSLAUGHT and killing human beings is MANSLAUGHTER. But slaughtering animals is a more organised business; before cutting their throats they might be hung from a beam by their back legs. From the Old French *buquet*, meaning yolk or beam, comes the dialect word BUCKET meaning the wooden frame used for slaughter, which seems to account for the picturesque phrase TO KICK THE BUCKET, as a suspended animal might do in its death throes.

Killing human beings is called HOMICIDE, a word which in Latin was *homicidium* from *homo*, man, and *caedere*, to kill. The word can also be applied to the killer so that a HOMICIDE is one who kills a fellow human being. Similarly a FRATRICIDE is one who kills a brother; one who kills a king is a REGICIDE and one who kills a parent is a PARRICIDE. Specifically those who kill their father are PATRICIDES and those who kill their mother are MATRICIDES. A killer of a sister is a SORORICIDE and of an infant, an INFANTICIDE. The words came into use in English from the Middle Ages onwards, in the order in which they are listed; some were first applied to the crime, others to its perpetrator, but they each developed their dual personalities as noun and verb fairly quickly. There are many other less common combinations such as that for the killing of a tyrant, TYRANNICIDE; and in 1944 the term GENOCIDE was coined for use in the Nuremberg trials of the following year: the first part of the word is from the Greek *genos*, a race or nation.

Also from World War II comes the word KAMIKAZE borrowed from the Japanese *kami kaze* meaning divine wind. The reference is to a typhoon which once saved Japan from a Mongol invasion. But the Japanese had already pioneered a less pleasant method of self destruction. Often referred to as HARIKARI it is really *hara kiri*, a phrase meaning simply 'belly cut'.

Once dead, bodies may be taken to a MORGUE just as live French prisoners used to be taken to a *morgue* for identification.

Now the word is almost synonymous with MORTUARY which has an entirely different history. Derived from the Latin word *mors*, death, MORTUARY was originally a sort of wealth-tax by which, upon the owner's death, the second best chattel in the estate automatically went to the Church. Now the mortuary may be the scene of a *post mortem* or 'after-death' operation. Those subject to death are MORTAL while those immune from it are IMMORTAL, and those who are unduly interested in the subject are MORBID. Having lain in a morgue or mortuary American bodies may go to a MORTICIAN but English ones go to an UNDERTAKER, a person who now accepts specific assignments to dispose of bodies but who, in the past, might have accepted any undertaking. The undertaker will wash and embalm the body, and lay it in a COFFIN, a sort of basket which to the Greeks was a *kophinos*. Then it will be loaded into a HEARSE; now a motor vehicle, this was originally no more than a frame resembling the large rakes or harrows used by farmers. Furnished with candles, such frames became funeral canopies and later the name was applied to the biers and then to the more recent motor vehicles which replaced them; the older sense of the word is, however, preserved in the term REHEARSE which literally means 'to rake over again'. To the Anglo-Saxons a GRAVE was a *græf*, a word related to the verb *grafan*, to dig, from which we also have ENGRAVE and GROOVE. In many Indo-European languages there is a close relationship between the idea of swelling and the raised mound of earth over a grave which is reflected in a number of words. From the Greek *tumbos*, a mound or grave, comes the English TOMB while the Latin *tumulus* has been taken over without alteration. Related to the Latin word *funus*, burial ground, are the names of the FUNERAL itself, of the associated FUNERARY rites and of the general FUNEREAL atmosphere; but the burial ground is now a CEMETERY, a more permanent resting place than the original Greek *koimeterion* which was merely a dormitory. At one time the Greeks placed dead bodies in limestone coffins; this was done for the same reason that in England hanged criminals were buried in lime within the prison grounds, namely to speed the decomposition of the body.

Because the stone was thought by the Greeks to consume the body the stone container was named from the words *sarx*, flesh, and *phagein*, to eat: a SARCOPHAGUS is really a 'flesh-eater'.

In the fourth century BC a famous tomb was built for the King of Caria; he was named *Mausolus* and his last resting place, destroyed by an earthquake in 1375, was the original MAUSOLEUM. Now also well known is the CENOTAPH in Whitehall which, like other cenotaphs, is named from the Greek *kenos*, empty, and *taphos*, tomb. At the tomb was made a funeral oration which, because it was delivered over, *epi*, the *taphos*, became known to the Romans as an *epitaphum*. Now committed to writing, it is an EPITAPH. From the Latin *postumus* meaning the very last, comes the English POSTHUMOUS which has acquired an 'h' by error. The word is often used as though derived from *post*, after, and *humus* earth, so that it seems to suggest 'after burial' and therefore 'after death'. Since only death can ensure that the birth of a child or the award of an honour will be the 'very last', the changed meaning is not too drastic and indeed the new one is probably more useful. By contrast the word *humus* really does appear in the English term meaning to take out of the ground – EXHUME. Exhumation is now generally carried out for justifiable reasons but it was not so long ago that the aptly-named resurrectionists were disinterring bodies for medical research. When dead bodies ran short it was always possible to create some more, and this is exactly what William Burke did by smothering innocent victims in order to supply an eminent Edinburgh surgeon. Burke was hanged for his crimes in 1829 but his name lives on: to BURKE still means to smother.

Genuine bodily resurrection was believed in by members of many cultures and it was commonly thought to be important to preserve the body, or at least the bones. Because of this the Egyptians mummified their dead and the North American Indians required their scalps; for without their hair to grasp the Great Spirit in the Sky could not hoist them aloft to the Happy Hunting Ground. Apart from special cases such as the supposed bodily Assumption of Mary into heaven, this sort of belief is

becoming less and less common as primitive ideas are dis-
credited. Now we all know what really happens to bodies once
they are cosily tucked away underground: they are kept busy
pushing up the daisies.

—— Appendix A ——

The Indo-European family tree – edited highlights

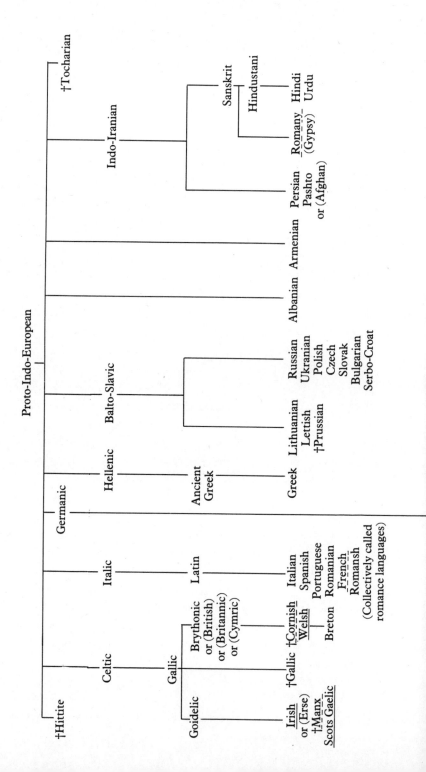

Proto-Indo-European

†Hittite

Celtic
Goidelic
Irish or (Erse)
†Manx
Scots Gaelic
Gallic
†Gallic †Cornish Welsh Breton
Brythonic or (British) or (Britannic) or (Cymric)

Italic
Latin
Italian Spanish Portuguese Romanian French Romansh
(Collectively called romance languages)

Germanic

Hellenic
Ancient Greek
Greek

Balto-Slavic
Lithuanian Lettish †Prussian
Russian Ukranian Polish Czech Slovak Bulgarian Serbo-Croat

Albanian

Armenian

Indo-Iranian
Persian Pashto or (Afghan)
Sanskrit
Romany (Gypsy)
Hindustani
Hindi Urdu

†Tocharian

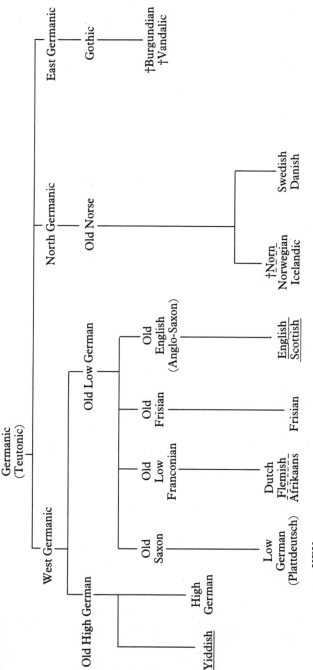

Germanic
(Teutonic)

West Germanic

Old High German
- Yiddish
- High German

Old Low German
- Old Saxon
  - Low German (Plattdeutsch)
- Old Low Franconian
  - Dutch
  - Flemish
  - Afrikaans
- Old Frisian
  - Frisian
- Old English (Anglo-Saxon)
  - English
  - Scottish

North Germanic

Old Norse
- †Norn
- Norwegian
- Icelandic
- Swedish
- Danish

East Germanic

Gothic
- †Burgundian
- †Vandalic

KEY

Continuous underlining (e.g. ENGLISH) indicates that the language is well established in the British Isles having been used for hundreds of years.

Broken underlining (e.g. FRENCH) indicates that the language has been well established in the British Isles at some time, but is now extinct in Great Britain.

An obelus (e.g. †PRUSSIAN) indicates that the language is dead. (Even if, like Latin, it is still artificially preserved.)

The tribal migrations started thousands of years ago, somewhere in Asia, and they continued for many hundreds of years. They spread basic language wherever they went, reaching the extremities of what is now Europe in the west and India in the east. The languages which share this single ancient ancestor are, therefore, said to belong to the Indo-European family; amongst them are the Celtic, Germanic and Romance languages as well as Russian, Persian, Greek and Sanskrit. In fact most of the languages in Europe and Western and Central Asia are derived from the same prehistoric verbal ancestor. A few islands of apparently unrelated speech still exist: for example, Turkish is not an Indo-European language, Hungarian and Finnish are related to each other but not to other major European languages, while Basque, as far as is currently known, does not have a single living relative. By contrast English is closely related to many members of the Indo-European family, either by relatively recent common descent or by incestuous marriage. Anglo-Saxon, like modern German, Dutch and Flemish, belonged to the West Germanic sub-family but modern English has adopted many words from other relations: mainly from Greek and Latin, either directly or indirectly, and often through the medium of French.

Notice that ROMANIAN and ROMANSH are ROMANCE languages and are so called because they are of '*Roman*' origin. ROMANY, however, is named after the Romany word *romani* itself related to the word *rom*, man, and applied specifically to the Romanies themselves. They and their language originated in Northern India although the myth that they came from Egypt has provided their alternative name, GYPSY.

Other peoples who have given their names to the English language include the Vandals who used to rule, among many other places, 'Vandalusia' which we now know as ANDALUSIA, and the Slavs who, being frequently conquered and reduced to servility, became popular as SLAVES.

Scots Gaelic is a Celtic language spoken mainly in the Highlands and Islands of Scotland. Scottish, on the other hand, is spoken mainly in the Scottish lowlands. English and Scottish are sometimes regarded as dialects of the same language but a brief inspection of Robbie Burns' Scottish poetry will usually convince Englishmen that the two are distinct languages.

The Indo-European group of languages is only one of many family groups. At one time there were thought to be only three basic languages, and these were identified with the three sons of Noah: Japhet, Ham and Shem. We no longer call the Indo-European languages JAPHETIC but we do still call certain North African languages HAMITIC after Ham and Middle Eastern ones SEMITIC after Shem.

——— Appendix B ———

Invading Britain by numbers

600 BC	
500 BC	CELTS ARRIVE IN BRITAIN
400 BC	
300 BC	
200 BC	
100 BC	
0	ROMANS ARRIVE IN BRITAIN
100 AD	
200 AD	
300 AD	ROMANS LEAVE BRITAIN
400 AD	GERMANIC INVASIONS OF BRITAIN
500 AD	
600 AD	
700 AD	OLD ENGLISH
800 AD	SCANDINAVIAN INVASIONS OF BRITAIN (ANGLO-SAXON)
900 AD	PERIOD
1000 AD	NORMAN INVASION OF BRITAIN
1100 AD	
1200 AD	
1300 AD	MIDDLE ENGLISH
1400 AD	PERIOD
1500 AD	INTRODUCTION OF PRINTING
1500 AD	REVIVAL OF LEARNING
1600 AD	
1700 AD	
1800 AD	MODERN ENGLISH
1900 AD	PERIOD
2000 AD	

—— Appendix C ——

Invading Britain, an illustrated guide

Before the Indo-Europeans arrived in the British Isles sometime around 500 BC the native inhabitants were a Neolithic people who were shorter and darker than later invaders; folk memories of these people probably account for legends about the 'little people' or faeries. The Picts were of this stock and their language, Pictish, survived until around 1000 AD. Until then their territory had gradually been encroached upon by various Indo-European invaders. First there were the British Celts from the South, then the Irish Celts from the West and the Germanic tribes from the East, and finally the Scandinavian tribes from the North.

The Celts in Britain spoke a language called British. When the Anglo-Saxons pushed the Celts westward the British language became restricted to three distinct areas: Cornwall, Wales and Cumbria. The Anglo-Saxons referred to native Celts as *wealh*, i.e. foreign. As the Celts were driven westward they concentrated in 'foreign' areas now known as WALES and WEST WALES (also called CORNWALL since it is 'corn' or horn-shaped). The Celts referred to themselves, as the Welsh still do, as *Cymri*. Since Celts were also pushed into an area north of Wales, this region became known as the land of the *Cymri*, hence the names of CUMBRIA and CUMBERLAND.

The Irish Celts are generally known as Scots and their language, transferred to and developed in what we now know as Scotland, has come to be known as Scots Gaelic.

For a period in the eighth and ninth centuries various alliances were forged between the seven English kingdoms shown on map 4. ESSEX is the place of the 'East Saxons'; SUSSEX the place of the 'South Saxons'; and WESSEX, the place of the 'West Saxons' (and incidentally, MID-

DLESEX was the area inhabited by the 'Middle Saxons'). EAST ANGLIA was an *eastern* area where *Anglian* invaders settled. MERCIA was named after its borders or 'marches' and NORTHUMBRIA was simply an area *north* of the river *Humber*. Also during the eighth and ninth centuries the British Isles were subject to repeated attack by Scandinavian tribes. The Danish Vikings established Danelaw in the North of England but, their North Germanic speech being so similar to Anglo-Saxon, their language was absorbed into English leaving only a few distinctive words. The Norwegian Vikings, however, established themselves along the Scottish Coast where their North Germanic language, known as Old Norse and later as Norn, survived until the seventeenth century.

The Norsemen also invaded part of France which therefore came to be known as NORMANDY. It is some consolation that the so-called Norman–French who conquered England a few generations later in 1066 were almost proper Vikings and not effete Frenchmen after all. Having already conquered more than half of England the Norsemen left a large number of placenames like NORMANBY and NORMANTON which are still common in the Danelaw.

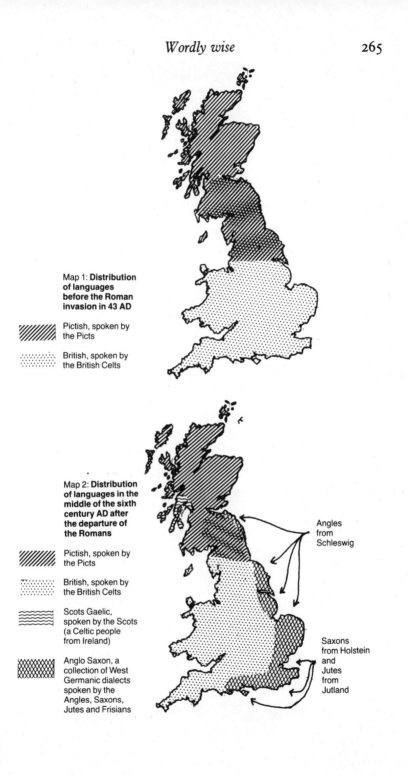

Map 1: **Distribution of languages before the Roman invasion in 43 AD**

Pictish, spoken by the Picts

British, spoken by the British Celts

Map 2: **Distribution of languages in the middle of the sixth century AD after the departure of the Romans**

Pictish, spoken by the Picts

British, spoken by the British Celts

Scots Gaelic, spoken by the Scots (a Celtic people from Ireland)

Anglo Saxon, a collection of West Germanic dialects spoken by the Angles, Saxons, Jutes and Frisians

Angles from Schleswig

Saxons from Holstein and Jutes from Jutland

Map 3: **Distribution of languages around 600 AD**

 Pictish, spoken by the Picts

British, spoken by the British Celts

Scots Gaelic, spoken by the Scots

Anglo-Saxon, a collection of West Germanic dialects spoken by the Angles, Saxons, Jutes and Frisians

Map 4: **Distribution of languages before the settlement of the Vikings towards the end of the eighth century**

Pictish, spoken by the Picts

British, spoken by the British Celts

Scots Gaelic, spoken by the Scots

Anglo-Saxon

CUMBRIA

NORTHUMBRIA

MERCIA

EAST ANGLIA

WALES

ESSEX

KENT

WESSEX

WEST WALES

SUSSEX

Map 5: **Distribution of languages after the settlement of the Vikings towards the end of the ninth century**

 Pictish, spoken by the Picts

British, spoken by the British Celts

 Scots Gaelic, spoken by the Scots

Anglo-Saxon

Old Norse, spoken by the Norwegian Vikings (who attacked from the North and West) and the Danish Vikings (who attacked from the East)

Danelaw

Map 6: **Distribution of languages in the twentieth century**

English and Scottish, successors of Anglo-Saxon

Welsh, the last remnants of British (coloured where spoken by more than 70% of the local population)

 Scots Gaelic (coloured where spoken by more than 70% of the local population)

Appendix D

Boring details

In the interests of clarity some technical details have been simplified in the presentation of this book. For the interested reader who may be tempted to sample more conventional texts on the same subject, as well as for those who are simply interested to know what has been left out, the following notes may be of help.

Phonetic symbols and length marks have been avoided and diacritics kept to an absolute minimum. In general diacritics have been used only where they are customarily employed in the language to which the word in question belongs; for example, French *bât* and Spanish *cañon*. Unfamiliar letters have been used only where they are explained, as ð which is mentioned in Chapter 12 and subsequently used in Icelandic words; some letters have been used without explanation but only where they are sufficiently similar to an English form: for example, Danish *søn* is easily identified with the English word 'son', even though the Danish ø and o are distinct. Otherwise words from languages which have their own alphabets (Sanskrit, Russian, Greek, Arabic and Hebrew, for example) have been transliterated.

The descriptions 'Anglo-Saxon' and 'Old English' are often used in other books interchangeably, the choice generally being a matter of personal preference, but occasionally they are used in specific, well-defined ways. Both terms have been used here, partly to avoid undue repetition of either one, partly to differentiate between true-blooded Saxon words (Anglo-Saxon) and others used by the Saxons but borrowed from elsewhere (Old English). The Anglo-Saxon or original English language was actually made up of a number of West Germanic dialects introduced to England by continental invaders: notably the Angles, Saxons, Jutes and Frisians. The term Anglo-Saxon means 'English Saxon' and is used to contrast the language spoken in England with its continental parent usually known as Old Saxon. The Anglo-Saxon letters þ (thorn) and ð (etha) have both been replaced by the more familiar combination 'th' in this book although the Anglo-Saxon vowel æ, representing the sound of 'a' as in the word 'hat', has been retained. The Anglo-Saxon letter Ƿ (wen) has been transliterated as 'w' and the use of the Middle English letter ȝ (yogh) has been avoided wherever possible. No attempt has been made to distinguish between the 'k' and 'ch' sounds of the Anglo-Saxon letter 'c', both being represented by the modern 'c'; in some books the letters are distinguished by the use of a diacritical mark so that, for example, the Anglo-Saxon equivalent of the modern CHURCH might be rendered *čirče*, *ćirće* or *ćirće*, while the Anglo-Saxon counterpart of CROCK would be simply *croc*.

Words described as Greek or of Greek origin in the book may be assumed to be ancient Greek or of ancient Greek origin unless otherwise stated. Most Greek letters have reasonably exact and accepted counterparts in English but it is worth noting that *upsilon* υ and *chi* χ have here been represented by the letters 'y' and 'ch' respectively, in preference to the alternatives 'u' and 'kh'.

Words described simply as 'Latin' may be assumed to have been in use before the year 200 AD. Words not used before then but found before about 600 AD are described as 'late Latin'. Medieval and modern Latin words which have been coined since then have generally been avoided, or at least have been split into their original Latin components if they are manufactured compounds. Vulgar Latin was an illiterate dialect of Latin spoken throughout the Roman Empire, notably by the uneducated Roman soldiers who spread it far and wide.

Rather than go into specifications of case, tense, mood, number and such like esoteric matters, the infinitive form of foreign verbs is usually given, even though the link between the English word and its foreign progenitor is not always as obvious as it might be if more detail were to be provided. Thus, for example, we might say that the word PATENT is derived from the Latin verb *patere*, to lie open. In truth the

English word is taken from an Old French one which is formed from *patent-*, the stem of the present participle of the Latin verb *patere*.

French substantives are generally formed from the Latin accusative case, so that providing only the Latin nominative is of little help anyway. This is a fact with which we have to live. The French language is a form of bastardised Vulgar Latin and is best regarded as a debased peasants' vernacular.

It sometimes happens that an ancient word is not recorded but may reasonably be assumed to have existed. Accepted practice is to identify such words with an asterisk. Thus, for example, the existence of an Indo-European word something like **medhu* is inferred from the evidence of a number of widely spread European languages (see Chapter 1), yet this presumed progenitor has never been, nor is likely to be, found in any ancient text. Some words, like **medhu*, are unrecorded because they existed before the introduction of writing: some because it so happens that no appropriate text has survived. Apart from the foregoing example unrecorded forms have not been explicitly noted in this book, and this example is given only to illustrate the widely accepted convention.

Words with the same spelling but different etymology are not always explicitly distinguished, especially when some members of the groups are not well-known. Thus, for example, the word 'char' meaning 'tea' is unrelated to the word 'char' meaning 'turn', as in charcoal, charlady, etc. These two categories of the word are mentioned in different chapters but there seems little point in contrasting either of them with another unrelated char, a type of fish. Again, in Chapter 22 the word harrier is cited as the name of a type of bird which harries its prey; but no mention is made of the dogs, also named harriers, which are so-called because they were used as hare-hounds.

Etymologists often disagree amongst themselves and it is not always a simple matter to determine who has put forward the best argument. It is always tempting to go for the best story. The most reliable authorities have been taken as the Oxford English Dictionary, the two Oxford etymological dictionaries and *Origins, a Short Etymological Dictionary of Modern English*.

Details of these and other books consulted are given in the Bibliography.

Bibliography

Baugh, A. C. and Cable, T., *A History Of The English Language*, Routledge & Kegan Paul (1978)

Black, M. & Rowley, H. H. (eds), *Peake's Commentary On The Bible*, Thomas Nelson & Sons Ltd (1967)

Brewer, E. C., *Dictionary Of Phrase And Fable*, Cassell Ltd (1981)

Ekwall, E., *The Concise Oxford Dictionary Of Place Names*, Oxford University Press (1981)

Frazer, Sir James, *The Golden Bough*, Macmillan & Co Ltd (1954)

Leith, R., *A Social History Of English*, Routledge & Kegan Paul (1983)

Lockwood, W. B., *Languages Of The British Isles Past And Present*, André Deutsch (1975)

Onions, C. T.* (ed.) *The Oxford Dictionary Of English Etymology*, Oxford University Press (1982)

The Oxford English Dictionary, Oxford University Press (1971)

Partridge, E., *Origins, A Short Etymological Dictionary Of Modern English*, Routledge & Kegan Paul (1982)

—— *The Routledge Dictionary Of Historical Slang*, Routledge & Kegan Paul (1973)

* This is the *Onions* whose encyclopaedic knowledge of English gave us the phrase TO KNOW ONE'S ONIONS.

—— *Shakespeare's Bawdy*, Percy Lund, Humphries & Co Ltd (1956)

Pei, M., *The Story Of Language*, George Allen & Unwin Ltd (1968)

Potter, S., *Our Language*, Penguin Books (1950)

Potter, S. and Sargent, L., *Pedigree: The Origins Of Words From Nature*, Taplinger Publishing Co (1974)

Reaney, P. H., *A Dictionary Of British Surnames*, Routledge & Kegan Paul (1976)

—— *The Origin Of English Place Names*, Routledge & Kegan Paul (1980)

Reaney, P. H., *The Origin Of English Surnames*, Routledge & Kegan Paul (1980)

—— and Smith, C., *The Place Names Of Roman Britain*, Batsford Ltd (1981)

Robertson, S. and Cassidy, F. G., *The Development Of Modern English*, Prentice-Hall (1954)

Shipley, J. T., *Dictionary Of Word Origins*, Littlefield, Adams & Co (1979)

Skeat, W. W., *An Etymological Dictionary Of The English Language*, Oxford University Press (1983)

Stam, J. H., *Inquiries Into The Origin Of Language*, Harper & Row (1976)

Stratman, F. H., *A Middle English Dictionary*, Oxford University Press (1971)

Strong, B. M. H., *A History Of English*, Methuen & Co Ltd (1979)

Weekley, E., *Words Ancient And Modern*, John Murray (1958)

Withycombe, E. G. *The Oxford Dictionary Of English Christian Names*, Oxford University Press (1945)

Index

fairies, 48
fall, 112, 113
fall guy, 169
familiar, 239
family, 239
fan, 22
fanatic, 22
fancy, 23
fang, 9
fantastic, 23
fantasy, 23
farce, 233
fart, 80
fatal, 37
fate, 37
father, 236
fathom, 196
Faulkner, 223
Faulks, 223
February, 117
fee, 121
fellow, 121
fetish, 48
feudal, 121
fiancé, 245
fiasco, 7
fiddle de dee, 74
fidel, 71
fidelity, 245
Fido, 245
fight, 22
fillecunt, 79
finance, 125
finger, 9
finis, 125
finished, 125–6
fishmonger, 220
fishwife, 240
fit, 22
fitz-, 224
Fitzhugh, 224
flagon, 7
flash in the pan, 191
flask, 7
flatulence, 77
Flecker, 223–4
fledge, 224
fleet, 242–3
Fletcher, 223–4
floating, 199
floral, 123
Florence, 123
florin, 123
flotsam, 200
fluctuate, 199
fluids, 199
fo'c's'le, 208
folly, 159
fool, 159
foolscap, 160

forebode, 39
foreshadow, 39
foresight, 39
forge, 137
forgery, 137
Forster, 223
fortnight, 117
fortune, 38
Frankenstein, 50
Franks, 194
frantic, 21
frater, 64
fratricide, 253
Frau Bertha Krupp, 191
Freefolk, 226
freelance, 182
freeze the balls off a brass monkey, 200
Fremlin's, 49
frenzy, 21
friar, 64
Friday, 119
fuck, 79, 84
Fuller, 221
fuller's earth, 221
fundament, 79
funeral, 254
fusil, 191
fusiliers, 191

gad, 74
gadswoons, 74
gadzooks, 74
gaffer, 238
gage, 244
Galantine, 57
gall, 11–12
gallant, 57
galleon, 206
galley, 206
gambling, 169
game, 169
gamma, 95
gammon, 169
garçon, 103
garnish, 125
garret, 184
gauche, 156
gauze, 221
gazette, 124
geewhiz, 74
gehenna, 57
general, 189
Geneva, 3
genie, 49
genius, 49
genocide, 253
ghastly, 23
ghost, 23
ghoul, 23
GI, 189